INSPIRED

INSPIRED

*The Holy Spirit
and the Mind of Faith*

Jack Levison

WILLIAM B. EERDMANS PUBLISHING COMPANY

GRAND RAPIDS, MICHIGAN / CAMBRIDGE, U.K.

Published 2013 by
Wm. B. Eerdmans Publishing Co.
2140 Oak Industrial Drive N.E., Grand Rapids, Michigan 49505 /
P.O. Box 163, Cambridge CB3 9PU U.K.

Printed in the United States of America

18 17 16 15 14 13   7 6 5 4 3 2 1

Library of Congress Cataloging-in-Publication Data

Levison, John R.
Inspired: the Holy Spirit and the mind of faith / Jack Levison.
pages   cm
Includes bibliographical references and index.
ISBN 978-0-8028-6788-9 (pbk.: alk. paper)
1. Holy Spirit.   2. Bible — Inspiration.
3. Bible — Criticism, interpretation, etc.
4. Gunkel, Hermann, 1862-1932. Influence of the Holy Spirit.
I. Title.

BT123.L48   2013
231'.3 — dc23

2013025783

www.eerdmans.com

"A line will take us hours maybe" — Yeats

• •

To David Laskin

my dear friend
in whose company I while away the hours

Contents

CONTENTS

CONTENTS

Acknowledgments

During two decades of research and writing on pneumatology, I have been the fortunate beneficiary of generous institutions and individuals. The Alexander von Humboldt Foundation supported my first leave in Germany in 1993-94, during which time I completed *The Spirit in First Century Judaism* under the sponsorship of Professor Martin Hengel, of Eberhard-Karls-Universität Tübingen. In 2005-06, a renewal of that initial grant, combined with a sabbatical leave from Seattle Pacific University, gave me time to revise *Filled with the Spirit*, as well as easy access to the ample resources of Ludwig-Maximilians-Universität München and an apartment in the heart of Munich's university district in the Internationales Begegnungszentrum. The Louisville Institute, in 2008, granted me a summer stipend that allowed me to work on *Fresh Air: The Holy Spirit for an Inspired Life*. Finally, Seattle Pacific University funded a sabbatical last year. I read theologies I would not otherwise have had time to read in the normal course of life, as I scratched and clawed away at what I hoped would be a provocative and programmatic agenda for the future of pneumatology—almost a small book in itself.

During my stay in Munich, Professor Jörg Frey and I developed the idea for an interdisciplinary, international research project, *The Historical Roots of the Holy Spirit*. Matching grants for this research from the TransCoop Program of the Alexander von Humboldt Foundation and the Shohet Scholars Program of the International Catacomb Society made month-long visits to Munich possible in 2010 and 2012. My family and I again stayed in the Internationales Begegnungszentrum. During those stays I had an office in the Protestant Faculty, with entrée to library resources and the opportunity to have meaningful conversations, typically over coffee and pastries, with Professor Frey and, during the second stay, Professor Loren Stuckenbruck as well, even though his office was still packed head-height with boxes of books.

Three other colleagues have left their imprint on this book. Ron Herms read the entire manuscript, offered insightful comments, and raised important questions. Daniel Castelo, my colleague at Seattle Pacific University, taught me about sin over meatball heroes. Let me rephrase that. Daniel read the conclusion and challenged me to incorporate more on the reality of sin in the pneumatological agenda I have proposed. From across the continent, John R. Sachs navigated me through the pneumatology of Karl Rahner.

I am indebted as well to the good people at Eerdmans. Before the ink was dry on *Filled with the Spirit,* Michael Thomson encouraged me to write a second book for Eerdmans on the subject of the holy spirit. *Filled with the Spirit* exceeded five-hundred pages, and in it I was reluctant to draw conclusions for the church. *Inspired: The Holy Spirit and the Mind of Faith* contains a far more straightforward message for the church, going so far as to offer an agenda for the future of pneumatology — in less than half the length of *Filled with the Spirit.* Vicky Fanning, of Eerdmans, is a terrific point person, while Jenny Hoffman, and my capable copy-editor David Cottingham, worked hard to minimize literary infelicities. Eerdmans's creative director, Willem Mineur, enlisted Kevin van der Leek to design a cover. I am delighted by the design. Eerdmans got the cover just right.

When it came time to prepare the indexes, I knew exactly whom to consult. Shannon Smythe, who recently completed her doctorate in theology at Princeton Theological Seminary, had compiled indexes for *Filled with the Spirit,* thanks to a research grant from Seattle Pacific University. Without hesitation I turned to Shannon for this book. She has, once again, done a remarkable job.

During the last few years, I have had countless conversations with my dear friend and accomplished author, David Laskin, about all things literary. David writes books people *want* to read, and he has coached me, time and again, on the art of writing to be read.

My children, Chloe and Jeremy, happily came along for the ride, even when trips to Munich were less than convenient. Last summer, for instance, Chloe and Jeremy met in New York and flew together to Munich, where we met them, Bavarian pretzels in hand. That night, exhausted, they made a long trek on foot — without complaint — to a beer garden outside of Munich to celebrate my birthday.

Acknowledgments

Finally, my muse: Priscilla Pope-Levison, an extraordinary blend of wife, colleague, friend, critic, and editor. I trust Priscilla's judgments implicitly. While writing her own book, *Building the Old Time Religion,* for NYU Press, Priscilla engaged mine at every level. Yet to portray Priscilla as editor or author is too clinical. She is more than my colleague, more than my critic, more than my editor. I cherish Priscilla — and have now for over thirty years — from our chats over morning tea to the moment she lays her head on my shoulder at day's end.

Introduction

Somewhere between writing *Filled with the Spirit* for a scholarly reader-ship and *Fresh Air: The Holy Spirit for an Inspired Life* for a popular one, I became aware of this conviction in the early church: *the holy spirit becomes particularly present in the inspired interpretation of scripture.*[1] With this realization I departed from Hermann Gunkel, a scholar whose study of the spirit had a unique influence over twentieth-century pneumatol-ogy. Gunkel identified the spontaneity of speaking in tongues, *glossolalia,* as the clearest sign of the holy spirit in the early church.[2]

BY DRAWING A LINE in the sand between speaking in tongues and the inspired interpretation of scripture, I may have misled you. It took me only a short paragraph to do so — an indication of how intractable di-chotomies can be. So let me offer this corrective. I do not mean to drive a wedge between *glossolalia* and the inspired interpretation of scripture. I mean instead to posit that the early church — Jewish and many Israelite authors too — discovered a rich symbiosis between various experiences akin to ecstasy and inspired intellectual acuity. In this synergy of intellect and inspiration, we discover the genius of early Jewish and Christian con-ceptions of the spirit. Discovering that genius and unearthing enough ex-amples to convince you of this symbiosis is the heart and soul of this book.

The lion's share of this book consists of *exegesis.* I will lay out, with as much clarity and concision as I can muster, data from the literary corpora

---

1. *Filled with the Spirit* (Grand Rapids: Eerdmans, 2009), pp. 185-99, 347-61, 399-404.
2. Hermann Gunkel, *The Influence of the Holy Spirit: The Popular View of the Apostolic Age and the Teaching of the Apostle Paul,* 3rd ed. (Philadelphia: Fortress, 1979; paperback edition, 2008).

of Israel (i.e., the Jewish Bible or Old Testament), early Judaism (roughly 200 BCE through 100 CE), and the early church (i.e., the New Testament).

I also intend to create a bold *agenda* that will determine how the spiritualities of contemporary Christians can flourish when informed by a rich array of enduring — and overlooked — insights from Israelite, Jewish, and Christian antiquity. Readers keen to develop and sustain vibrant contemporary spiritualities will discover ample resources in this book.

This book is a combination of historical description and contemporary prescription, of rigorous exegesis and an unapologetic effort to provide a vital basis for contemporary spiritualities, particularly Christian ones, with which I am best acquainted. It represents the belief that scholarship and the church benefit from a taut relationship. On the practical level of how this book is laid out, historians and biblical scholars receive their due in the central section of each chapter, while pastors and theologians, both seasoned and budding, receive their due at the beginning and end of each chapter. Let me emphasize, however, that exegesis and contemporary relevance are indispensable to one another. I would urge you, therefore, whatever your particular interest in this book — historical or contemporary — to keep an eye open for the dimension that interests you least. You may be surprised by what you inadvertently encounter.

The Spirit, Virtue, and Learning

The themes of this book crescendo chapter by chapter to create, by the book's end, a coherent whole and a consistent agenda. Let me lay out, therefore, the development and contours of this book.

THE THRUST OF THE FIRST chapter is simple: *the spirit inspires virtue and learning.* This element of the agenda I propose arises from a neglected strand in the Jewish scriptures, in which the spirit that people receive from birth is no less divine or holy than the spirit they receive through charismatic endowments. To unearth this strand, we must look first, not to the New Testament, with its emphasis upon new creation, but to the Jewish scriptures. This strand, in which God gives the spirit to human beings at birth, is a foundational — and biblical — model of inspiration.

In this model, some of Israel's luminescent figures are people who have cultivated the spirit within them since birth. Daniel is the epitome of the cultivation of a life of virtue; his first experience of revelations took place while he was avoiding lavish food, studying ancient languages and literature, and living as a young and faithful Israelite in an alien environment. Daniel's virtue, his wisdom, and the spirit in him were recognizable for quite some time — the reigns of three successive foreign rulers (Daniel 4–6). The spirit, then, was a lifelong presence that Daniel had cultivated. Another Israelite luminary, Bezalel, chief architect of the tent of meeting in the book of Exodus, offers a slightly different twist on this model of inspiration. Like Daniel, Bezalel had cultivated skill. He was *already* equipped with wisdom of heart, with knowledge, with spirit. For his role as leader in the construction of the tabernacle, God filled Bezalel, not with a fresh endowment of the spirit but with a supersaturation of spirit, a filling to the brim with the spirit that he had already cultivated. Filling here is not an initial endowment but a topping up — this is what the Hebrew verb often connotes — the way a promise is fulfilled or a house or a bowl are filled completely with flies or food. According to this model of inspiration, Bezalel already possessed spirit and wisdom of heart, which now, in short measure, overflowed in a moment that provided Israel with one of its most magnificent memories of communal largesse (Exod. 36:2-7). Utter fullness of spirit, skill, and generosity went hand in hand in the wilderness.[3]

The Jewish Bible,[4] of course, contains other conceptions of inspira-

---

3. Let me state from the start that I will work with Israelite, early Jewish, and early Christian texts on their own terms. In other words, I do not interpret them as windows to history, the way the gospels, for example, have been used (quite appropriately so, in my opinion), as a window to the historical Jesus. There will be no quest of the historical Daniel or Bezalel or Amasai or Anna, nor will I evaluate such texts as the book of Acts on the basis of how historically reliable Luke's stories are deemed to be. Such evaluations would lead us down too many paths — paths I usually find enjoyable, even profitable on many occasions, but distracting and time-consuming — rather than allow us to focus exclusively on spirit in antiquity. I also do not expend energy to determine the authorship and date of ancient texts. I do assume that Isaiah 40–66 was written during the period of Babylonian Exile or later, that the book of Daniel was composed sometime after 175 BCE, and that the Pastoral Epistles adequately reflect Pauline theology vis-à-vis pneumatology, whether or not they were composed by the apostle Paul. Such decisions do not appreciably affect how I interpret these texts in this book.

4. As a Christian scholar who collaborates with Jewish scholars, I find it difficult to know how to refer to what Christians call the Old Testament. Therefore, I refer to this corpus of literature variously as scripture, Jewish scripture, Hebrew Bible, and Old Testament. I am also aware that "scripture" is a debated term, not least because we do not know with certainty when, and by whom, Israelite literature came to be considered authoritative scripture. Add to this one further difficulty of nomenclature — the identification of the

tion. Onrushing. Resting. Outpouring. Renewing. In each of these models, the spirit comes afresh to inspired individuals and communities from the outside. During the Greco-Roman era, all of these models coalesced with one another and with Greco-Roman models of inspiration, to create a flurry of conceptions of inspiration. In the flux of this cultural alchemy, Jewish authors managed to preserve the belief they found in their scriptures — the spirit is the source of virtue, a reservoir of learning. Whether the spirit inspired the faithful from birth, whether the spirit from birth expanded in inspired moments, whether the spirit-breath roared down as an external impulse, or perhaps in an admixture of all of these, in any case the spirit was believed to inspire virtue and learning.

The early church embraced this symbiosis between inspiration, virtue, and learning, sometimes adopting the view that the spirit-breath from birth is the source of wisdom but more typically focusing on the gift of the spirit afresh, the new creation, a new Adam. In whatever guise, in whichever circumstance, virtue and learning infuse inspiration in the New Testament.[5]

This element in an agenda for the future of pneumatology has significant implications for several dimensions of Christian belief and practice. Chapter one, therefore, concludes with a discussion of:

- how Christians acknowledge the holy spirit in those who are not Christians;
- how Christians pray;
- how Christians learn;
- how Christians cultivate the spirit on a daily basis.

THE SECOND CHAPTER showcases *the symbiosis between ecstasy and comprehension that pervades Jewish and Christian scripture.* Ecstasy, or experiences akin to it, rarely stands alone. In Israelite literature, ecstasy is present only in trace amounts. Similarly, in the New Testament, only a few visions offer entrée to ecstasy, and these are accompanied by serious re-

---

earliest church with early Christianity. This too may be anachronistic because we do not know how early on Jesus' followers were considered a branch of faith separate from Judaism. Even the early moniker, Christians, which Luke says arose first in Antioch (Acts 11:26), does not suggest a complete separation from Judaism.

5. I am indebted to Frank Macchia for pressing me to discern continuity between Israelite and early Christian literature. See his "The Spirit of Life and the Spirit of Immortality: An Appreciative Review of Levison's *Filled with the Spirit*," *Pneuma* 33 (2011): 69-78.

flection. Peter puzzles over his noonday vision of clean foods, for example, and he even modifies its meaning as he enters into new experiences (Acts 10–15). The experience of speaking in tongues, in the letters of Paul and the book of Acts, is of value principally when accompanied by — or when it consists of — comprehensible speech. Ecstasy on its own was simply not considered a clear sign of the holy spirit.

If we were to trace unambiguous occurrences of ecstasy in Jewish and Christian antiquity, our diagram would look like a fairly flat line in Israelite literature and a fairly flat line in Christian literature, interrupted by a jagged and prominent bump in the Greco-Roman world, including Judaism, many corners of which succumbed to the seduction of Greco-Roman ecstasy.

To underline the value early Christians placed on the close relationship between ecstasy and comprehension, chapter two looks at key moments from the book of Acts where the paired experiences of inspiration and rigorous reflection come together: the tandem visions of Paul and Ananias; the tandem visions of Peter and Cornelius; the word of the spirit spoken in Antioch; and the Jerusalem Council. In all of these episodes, the holy spirit inspires something of comprehensible consequence.

The realization that ecstasy is tied at the hip to comprehensible thought and speech has significant implications for several dimensions of Christian belief and practice. Chapter two, therefore, concludes with a discussion of:

- how cultural borders are crossed;
- how believers prepare to experience a work of the holy spirit;
- how believers respond to the work of the holy spirit;
- how churches can make inspired compromises.

THE THIRD ELEMENT in this agenda emerges genetically from the second: *the quintessential expression of the presence of the holy spirit in Israelite, Jewish, and Christian literature is the inspired interpretation of scripture.* If ecstasy and comprehension complement one another, they do so supremely when the holy spirit inspires the interpretation of scripture. In Israelite literature, relatively unknown figures, such as Amasai and Jahaziel, receive the spirit in a way that leads a reader to expect a military confrontation, as in the book of Judges. Yet instead, these men bundle up elements of Israel's literary heritage and connect them persuasively to defuse potentially dangerous situations.

The inspired interpretation of scripture burgeons among Jewish authors of the Greco-Roman era, for whom Israel's literature is now part of the sacred and inspired past. Ben Sira, the head of an academy in Jerusalem early in the second century, claims that a scribe can "be filled by (a) spirit of understanding" and pour out wisdom, counsel, and knowledge, as he reflects upon hidden matters — presumably the obscure details of scripture (Sir. 39:6-8). Philo Judaeus claims several fascinating forms of inspiration to explain his peculiar ability to interpret Torah allegorically. The author of the Qumran Hymns believes that the holy spirit reveals mysteries to him. Even Josephus attributes his decision to turn traitor to the inspired interpretation of prophetic texts.

The New Testament is rife with the inspired interpretation of scripture — Simeon's song at the dedication of Jesus, the role of the Paraclete in the Fourth Gospel, inspired sermons in the book of Acts, the letter to the Hebrews, and Paul's multivalent take on Moses' veil. From nearly every corner of the New Testament — the gospels, Acts, letters — the locus of inspiration is the interpretation of scripture.

Like chapters one and two, the findings of chapter three have significant implications for Christian belief and practice. This chapter, therefore, concludes with a discussion of:

- how Christians assess the value of the Old Testament;
- how Christians can appreciate the role of the community for inspired interpretation;
- how assiduous preparation paves the way for inspiration.

A Suggested Agenda

The substantial conclusion to this book should not be mistaken for a summary, a précis, or a reiteration of the first three chapters. I intend it to be read, rather, as a contribution in its own right. This fourfold conclusion spells out the significance of pneumatology, as I have developed it, along four trajectories: theological, hermeneutical, cultural, and ecclesiological.

Theology. The conclusion leads, first, to a theology — or more accurately, a pneumatology — of creation, according to which the holy spirit is the divine presence in all human beings. This statement, of course, cracks the door to another: the presence of the divine spirit outside the community of Christian faith. To explore this idea, we will spend a bit of time with the theologies of Karl Barth, Wolfhart Pannenberg, Jürgen Moltmann, Karl Rahner, and Frank Macchia. Their effort to connect (or disconnect, in the case of Barth) the spirit of creation with the spirit of salvation, *spiritus sanctificans* with *spiritus vivificans,* the spirit in all people with the spirit in Christians, is essential to understand one of the impulses of this book, particularly its first chapter, in which virtuous people are those who cultivate the spirit-breath that is given to them at birth.

Hermeneutics. The second section of the conclusion demonstrates the significance of starting-points for interpreting the Bible. Readers of this book will notice that my starting-point is not traditional. I do not begin with the judges, as does Michael Welker, or with Luke-Acts, as do many Pentecostal scholars and theologians.[6] I begin with the spirit-breath in all people — a conception spread throughout Jewish scripture: Psalm 51, the sayings of Elihu in the book of Job, and the stories of Joseph, Bezalel, and Daniel. The borders between this starting-point and others are porous, so this portion of the conclusion explores possible connections with other pneumatological points of departure: the outpouring of the spirit; the anointed leadership envisaged in Isaiah 11; the judges and Saul. Starting-points are not discrete dots on a hermeneutical horizon but a web of connections, not without the beauty, engineering, and mystery of a spider's web. We would be remiss to conclude without noting, even in passing, those points of connection and the potential they possess to develop a full-orbed conception — and experience — of the holy spirit.

Culture. The conclusion continues by delving into the crucible of Christianity. Long ago, Hermann Gunkel, the twenty-six-year-old (at the time he wrote his pioneering first book) father of modern pneumatology, chastised biblical theologians for leapfrogging from the Old Testament to the New.[7] Judaism, he contended, provides what the Old Testament cannot. Although he construed Judaism far too negatively, he was absolutely right to press for the significance of Judaism — a point that would become indisputable following the discovery of the Dead Sea Scrolls in 1947. In this, the third part of the conclusion, I demonstrate that ancient Jewish corpora are indispensable for understanding the rise of early Christian pneumatology. We simply cannot revert to a model of historical reconstruction that reigned supreme prior to the publication of Gunkel's *Büchlein.* We cannot be satisfied with a Christian pneumatology that

---

6. See Martin William Mittelstadt, *Reading Luke-Acts in the Pentecostal Tradition* (Cleveland, TN: CPT Press, 2010).

7. See Gunkel, *Influence,* pp. 3, 12-13, 76.

misrepresents or ignores altogether the spiritual vitality of early Judaism. Jews and Christians deserve better, both in terms of historical accuracy and the anti-Semitic atrocities of the twentieth century.

Church. In the fourth and final section of the conclusion, I develop a model of inspiration that has the potential to provide a unified future for the church. Claims to the holy spirit, rather than promising unity, tend to provoke schism and factions. We see this in a local church in Hinton, North Carolina, split by the charismatic movement.[8] We see this in the divide that has separated Roman Catholics from Pentecostals in Latin America. We see this in a growing gulf between a more staid Global North and a more ecstatic Global South — countries such as Nigeria. The final section of this conclusion, and the book as a whole, is my modest attempt to offer common ground to an increasingly divided church by connecting scripture and the spirit, ecstasy and edification, inspiration and investigation.

A Discernible Trajectory

Originally this book was to function as an abbreviated version of my scholarly study, *Filled with the Spirit.*[9] As I began to write, however, I found myself writing a different sort of book — a book full of biblical study, personal stories, and practical application. What emerged was a book written for a wide readership, titled *Fresh Air: The Holy Spirit for an Inspired Life.*[10]

This book lies midway between *Filled with the Spirit* and *Fresh Air.* It contains pivotal exegesis and ideas from *Filled with the Spirit;* diligent devotees of that book will discover some of its ideas condensed in this book.[11] Yet this book is organized according to key topics rather than, like

8. Nancy L. Eiesland, "Irreconcilable Differences: Conflict, Schism, and Religious Re-structuring in a United Methodist Church," in *Pentecostal Currents in American Protestant-ism,* ed. Edith L. Blumhofer, Russell P. Spittler, and Grant A. Wacker (Urbana and Chicago: University of Illinois Press, 1999), pp. 168-87.

9. Eerdmans asked me to write a book along the lines of Larry Hurtado's *How on Earth Did Jesus Become a God? Historical Questions about Earliest Devotion to Jesus* (Grand Rapids: Eerdmans, 2005), which provides in a shorter form the key ideas of *Lord Jesus Christ: Devotion to Jesus in Earliest Christianity* (Grand Rapids: Eerdmans, 2003).

10. Brewster, MA: Paraclete, 2012.

11. If your primary interest lies in the study of early Jewish literature, such as Philo and the Dead Sea Scrolls, you may want to read *The Spirit in First-Century Judaism,* Arbeiten

Filled with the Spirit, canonically or chronologically. Further, this book is more topical; many of the ideas scattered throughout *Filled with the Spirit,* such as the inspired interpretation of scripture, are presented as coherent units in this book. Finally, I have done substantially more research since the appearance of *Filled with the Spirit.* Consequently, readers familiar with *Filled with the Spirit* will discover in this book a cache of new insights, which percolated after I wrote *Filled with the Spirit.*[12]

This book also shares the perspective of *Fresh Air: The Holy Spirit for an Inspired Life,* particularly the agenda I propose for the future of pneumatology. *Fresh Air,* written for a popular readership, is replete with personal stories, which provide the glue for its exegesis. In this book, by way of contrast, exegesis dominates, and the agenda I have drawn for the future of pneumatology arises directly from that exegesis. Written for students, theologians, scholars, and intellectually engaged pastors, this book contains dense thickets of exegesis, accompanied by a clear agenda.

After reading this book, if you crave more in-depth exegesis of a broader range of ancient texts, you may want to turn to *Filled with the Spirit.* If you yearn for a deeper spirituality, with more textured experiences of the holy spirit, you will want to read *Fresh Air: The Holy Spirit for an Inspired Life.*

Key Definitions

A brief word is in order, before we press on, about three key terms: ecstasy, virtue, and learning.

Ecstasy. No single definition can encompass ancient conceptions of ecstasy. A brief glance at two entries in leading dictionaries of the Bible will make this point crystal clear. John Pilch's entry on ecstasy in *The New Interpreter's Dictionary of the Bible* begins with various altered states of consciousness, which are "subjectively felt departures from ordinary waking consciousness characterized by nonsequential thought and uncontrolled perception." Pilch continues, "Ecstacy often, though not necessarily always, includes rapture, frenzy, euphoria, extremely strong emotion, and some-

---

zur Geschichte des antiken Judentums und des Urchristentums 29 (Leiden: Brill, 1997; paperback edition 2002).

12. In general, I am indebted to my Pentecostal colleagues, whose critiques and my responses to them can be found in *Pneuma* 33 (2011): 1-4, 25-93, and *Journal of Pentecostal Theology* 20 (2011): 193-231.

times appears to imply the loss of 'rational' control and self-control."[13] The caveat, *not necessarily always,* coupled with a lengthy list of characteristics rather than a precise definition, reveals how difficult it is to define ecstasy. Yet even such a wide-ranging definition — a description, really — does not even include trance, which "on the other hand, suggests a hypnotic or dazed state." In the end, Pilch throws in the towel rather than offering a tidy definition; he writes, "While the proposed characteristics are present in some experiences of ecstacy and trance, respectively, they are not always present. Thus each case needs to be examined on its own merits."

Compare Pilch's definition with the one offered by Helmer Ringgren in the *Anchor Bible Dictionary,* in which ecstasy is "an abnormal state of consciousness, in which the reaction of the mind to external stimuli is either inhibited or altered in character. In its more restricted sense, as used in mystical theology, it is almost equivalent to trance."[14] While Pilch's definition of ecstasy excludes trance, Ringgren narrows ecstasy to trance.

Where, then, to begin a definition of ecstasy? Should one begin with ancient definitions, such as Plato's classic definition of *mania* in *Phaedrus* 265B? Socrates discusses "four divisions of divine madness, ascribing them to four gods, saying that prophecy was inspired by Apollo, the mystic madness by Dionysus, the poetic by the Muses, and the madness of love, inspired by Aphrodite and Eros," the last of which Socrates claims is best.[15] Or should we begin with Jesus' contemporary, Philo Judaeus, and his definition of *ekstasis* in (LXX = Septuagint) Genesis 15:12? "Now 'ecstasy' or 'standing out' takes different forms. Sometimes it is a mad fury producing mental delusion due to old age or melancholy or other similar cause. Sometimes it is extreme amazement at the events which so often happen suddenly and unexpectedly. Sometimes it is passivity of mind, if indeed the mind can ever be at rest; and the best form of all is the divine possession or frenzy to which the prophets as a class are subject."[16] Neither Plato nor Philo arrives at a single definition of ecstasy; ancient authors, it seems, are in the same boat as John Pilch in their effort to pinpoint the characteristics of ecstasy.

13. *The New Interpreter's Dictionary of the Bible,* ed. Katharine Doob Sakenfeld, 5 vols. (Nashville: Abingdon, 2007), 2:185-86.

14. Helmer Ringgren, "Ecstasy," in *Anchor Bible Dictionary,* 6 vols., ed. David Noel Freedman (Garden City, NY: Doubleday, 1992), 2:80.

15. All classical references and translations, including those of Philo Judaeus and Flavius Josephus, are from the Loeb Classical Library.

16. Philo Judaeus, *Who Is the Heir?* 249.

In light of such trenchant difficulties, I will not proffer an overarching definition of ecstasy. The varieties of religious experience are too variegated and, as we will see in the second chapter, too difficult to characterize. Nevertheless, I do utilize two dichotomies to clarify the nature of ecstasy — one ancient, the other modern. First, the ancient one. Greco-Roman authors distinguished between artificial — omens and the like — and natural divination, which includes dreams and visions. Authors as distinct from one another as Ben Sira, who led an academy in Jerusalem during the second century BCE, and Philo of Alexandria, who wrote commentaries on Torah in first-century Egypt, were aware of this dichotomy. Both distinguished between the activities of artificial divination and the dreams and visions of natural divination.[17]

The second, modern dichotomy I derive from social anthropologist I. M. Lewis, who offers a concise and well-illustrated discussion of ecstasy in his classic work, *Ecstatic Religion: A Study of Shamanism and Spirit Possession*.[18] Lewis distinguishes central from peripheral contexts of ecstasy. Ecstasy in what Lewis identifies as central contexts — where clear social hierarchies dominate — lends divine support to the status quo. Ecstasy in peripheral contexts, which may look like an illness at first, ultimately enhances the marginal status of the ecstatic. Female ecstatic mediums, for example, tend to function in peripheral social contexts because they can speak directly as a conduit of the divine, free of the constraints of the status quo. Men typically speak within a central social context that is already supported by the status quo. As I read Lewis's perceptive analysis of women in contemporary cultures, my mind turned invariably to female Corinthian prophets and Paul's puzzling notion of head coverings. Did the coverings allow women to speak as conduits of God's glory rather than, in the confines of the status quo, as mouthpieces for the glory of their husbands (1 Cor. 11:2-16)?[19]

These distinctions — central versus peripheral contexts of inspiration and artificial versus natural forms of divination — do not allow us to pinpoint with complete accuracy the nature of ecstasy in antiquity. They do help us to plot various experiences on a spectrum of ecstatic alternatives.[20]

17. See *Filled with the Spirit*, pp. 121-22, and my "The Prophetic Spirit as an Angel according to Philo," *Harvard Theological Review* 88 (1995): 191-92.

18. I. M. Lewis, *Ecstatic Religion: A Study of Shamanism and Spirit Possession*, 2nd ed. (London/New York: Routledge, 1989).

19. Lewis, *Ecstatic Religion*, pp. 59-113, 170-71, especially 62-64, 90-113.

20. See further John Ashton, *The Religion of Paul the Apostle* (New Haven: Yale Uni-

Virtue. The notion of virtue in this book is not fixed by Aristotelian categories or virtue theory, as Alasdair MacIntyre and his interlocutors frame it.[21] Virtue is, in this book, a more malleable term that can encompass a range of activities, such as dietary simplicity (Daniel), courageous honesty (Daniel in the book of Susannah), avoidance of greed (wisdom admonitions in the Dead Sea Scrolls), living according to reason (Seneca), sexual purity (Paul's admonition in 1 Thessalonians 4), communal generosity (the church in Antioch in Acts 13), and countless other actions and attitudes that embody a holy, just, and devout life. The word *virtue* does not function in this book as a technical term for a particular way of life; its meaning is more fluid and should be construed in the contexts of disparate literary corpora as a cipher for what is deemed to be holy, true, and right, understood according to an author's point of view, when this is discernible from a literary corpus.

Learning. Conceptions of ecstasy and virtue cannot be squeezed into a single ideological straitjacket, ancient or modern. Nor can learning be defined in singular terms. There are occasions when a particular type of learning can be identified — Ben Sira's strict scribal training, for instance — but typically we can only piece together snatches of formal education. Learning, like ecstasy and virtue, is a malleable concept that ranges from Bezalel's extraordinary technical skill (Exodus 31–36) to Simeon's deep knowledge of Isaiah 40–55 (Luke 2) — though whether Simeon learned this formally in the synagogue or informally no one can say. Paul and Barnabas's yearlong teaching stint at Antioch (Acts 13) represents a form of learning that remains inaccessible to us, as does Paul's clear awareness of how the story of Moses was read in the synagogue (2 Corinthians 3). In short, no single model of education dominates Israelite, Jewish, and early Christian perspectives, but a passion for learning, for knowledge, for wisdom emerges from page after page. This passion for knowledge, and the discipline that hones it, is what best represents learning.

In the worlds of Israel, early Judaism, and the early church, learning was not a dispassionate exercise, what we might call "book learning"

---

versity Press, 2000); Oskar Holtzmann, *War Jesus Ekstatiker? eine Untersuchung zum Leben Jesu* (Tübingen, 1903); John Pilch, *Visions and Healing in the Acts of the Apostles: How the Early Believers Experienced God* (Collegeville, MN: Liturgical Press, 2004); and Colleen Shantz, *Paul in Ecstasy: The Neurobiology of the Apostle's Life and Thought* (Cambridge: Cambridge University Press, 2009).

21. Alasdair C. MacIntyre, *After Virtue: A Study in Moral Theology,* 2nd ed. (Notre Dame: Notre Dame University Press, 1984).

as opposed to tangible and practical knowledge. Learning, from the perspective of antiquity, is intense, driven by dissatisfaction, prompted by curiosity. Learning is wide-ranging, expansive, eye-opening. Learning is life-changing, transformative, re-creative. Learning is an all-absorbing process, a synergy between competence, passion, and persistence.

Examples of this sort of knowing abound in antiquity, but one text illustrates this point with a particular salience. The conclusion of the book of Ecclesiastes, in an epilogue that may have been an appendage, describes the Teacher — the supposed writer of Ecclesiastes — in this way: "Besides being wise, the Teacher also taught the people knowledge, weighing and studying and arranging many proverbs" (Eccles. 12:9).

Three verbs describe the task of the knowledgeable teacher: *weigh, study,* and *arrange.*

The verb *weigh* is related to balances or scales used to weigh money (Lev. 19:36). When the biblical prophet Jeremiah bought a field, he paid, signed a deed, sealed it, got witnesses, and weighed shekels on scales (Jer. 32:10). What does a teacher do? He or she weighs proverbs — testing them, checking them to make sure they are true. Evaluative engagement is essential to learning — and teaching.

The verb *study* has more to do with exploration, searching to the absolute limit of knowledge, than with rote memorization or the piling up of facts. For instance, "[Miners] put an end to darkness, and *search out* to the farthest bound the ore in gloom and deep darkness" (Job 28:3). The verb occurs in Psalm 139:1, where God *searches* our deepest selves. It is used of cross-examining witnesses in court cases — and showing that the initial examination was superficial: "The one who first states a case seems right, until the other comes and *cross-examines*" (Prov. 18:17). The depth of this exploration can even unmask smugness and self-deception: "The rich person is wise in self-esteem, but an intelligent poor person *sees through* the pose" (Prov. 28:11). What then is required of student and teacher alike? Pressing the limits of what we know, even undermining what we believe, is essential to learning — and teaching.

What, then, of the verb *arrange*? This verb makes me think of my grandmother's tea table, with its china pot, dainty cups and saucers, and her milk and sugar set neatly displayed on the lace doilies she brought over from Italy. Everything arranged neat and tidy. *Arranging* makes learning sound like tidying up proverbs and setting them on delicate mental doilies. This impression, however, is misleading. The same verb in Ecclesiastes 1:15 reads, "What is crooked *cannot be made straight,* and what is lacking cannot be counted." Or Ecclesiastes 7:13: "Consider the work of God; who can *make straight* what God has made crooked?" This verb in the epilogue to Ecclesiastes is about fixing, repairing, straightening out inscrutable literature. A teacher does not arrange proverbs on a mental doily, but wrestles texts and wrests meaning out of them. Wrestling with texts is essential to learning — and teaching.

Weighing texts in the balance to see if they are true. *Exploring* the limits of knowledge, beyond the edge of darkness. *Wrestling* texts into place. This is the essence of learning. This is the essence of teaching. This is the core of knowledge, wisdom, and learning. This is the heart of *Inspired: The Holy Spirit and the Mind of Faith.*

Ecstasy, learning, and virtue. One of the most important contributions of this book is to provide readers with a conceptual framework rooted in a trustworthy interpretation of ancient texts. This framework captures the intimate, occasionally seamless union of apparent antagonists — ecstasy, virtue, and learning — which comprise a life inspired by the holy spirit. Christian songwriter Nichole Nordeman's words, which she wrote about *Fresh Air,* may be an equally suitable description of the book you are about to read, so I close this introduction with her words: "There are few elements of our faith that are as passionately debated or largely ignored as the Holy Spirit, a topic that can easily induce both fiery discourse and faint shrugs. Mystery has always made for an awkward bedfellow." How vital it is, she continues, "to dig deep into the soil of Biblical study on the topic, unearth and examine its complex root system, and then marvel at the beauty that blooms above. Wild and growing in imperfect rows. Let it be so with my own knowledge of the Holy Spirit. Careful examination all tangled up with a wide wonder."

CHAPTER ONE

The Spirit and the Cultivation of Virtue

Priscilla and I bought our first house in a sketchy corner of Kansas City, about a mile or two from the seminary where I taught at the time. It was a big old house with a grandiose stone front porch, rich wooden beams, and small crystal chandeliers. We had failed to notice that the electricity was outmoded, the basement walls porous, the roof leaking, a ceiling sagging, and the neighborhood questionable, with a past shrouded in memories of Kansas City mafia. Still, it was a great house for a young couple with lots of energy, and on Wednesday nights we gathered a couple dozen students together, covered the dining room table with chips and dip and pies and brownies, stoked up the fire, sang hymns, and discussed John Wesley's sermons.

The house had those wonderful old cast-iron hot water radiators, the kind that clinked and belched, the kind you can dry underwear and socks on. One weekday winter morning, I sat on the living room floor and leaned against one of the radiators. I was reading my Bible and praying, and something happened. I felt myself, not quite mumbling and not quite speaking, but falling into some wordless moments. Not speechless exactly. There was speech. But wordless. When I told a friend who had experiences with such things, he was pretty sure I had spoken in tongues. I am still not so sure. I think maybe I just experienced the wordless speech of ecstasy in the presence of God.[1] In the twenty-five years since that morning, I have never had another experience like this (I was like the elders of

---

1. See the accessible discussion of primal speech in Harvey Cox, *Fire from Heaven: The Rise of Pentecostal Spirituality and the Reshaping of Religion in the Twenty-first Century* (Reading, MA: Addison-Wesley, 1995), pp. 81-97.

Israel who prophesied — but only once), so to this day I don't know what happened that winter morning.[2]

I do know this experience emblematizes much of my Christian life. I've spent much of my life *wanting more.* Not just more — but *new* experiences, *fresh* experiences of the holy spirit. And naturally the experiences for which I have hankered include what most Christians either want or despise: speaking in tongues, prophesying, miraculous healing — what Paul calls, in one of his letters to the Corinthians, gifts of the spirit.

Paul's letters are not the only books in the Bible that fed my desire for new and fresh experiences of the spirit, especially spectacular ones. The Bible is full of them. Start with the way the spirit rushed upon the judges. The spirit clothed Gideon, who outwitted the Midianites.[3] Samson, when the spirit rushed upon him, tore a lion apart, killed thirty enemies and gave their party clothes away, then broke out of ropes and killed a thousand opponents with the jawbone of an ass.[4] King Saul picked up where the judges left off. The spirit of the LORD rushed upon him in power.[5] He "prophesied" with a group of wandering prophets and was transformed into a different person.[6]

I would have been satisfied with a less spectacular experience. Some inspired knowledge would do. A modicum of revealed wisdom would suffice. There is plenty of this, too, in the Bible. Take Jesus, for example. He needed an influx of the spirit to accomplish his life's work. When he rises in the arms of his cousin straight from the Jordan River, he hears words, "This is my son, the beloved," which resonate with the description of the inspired teacher of Isaiah 42:1-4. When he sits to read scripture in his hometown synagogue, he knows that the words of Isaiah — he will proclaim good news to the poor — are his words, his vocation, his purpose. To accomplish this task, to rescue the sinners, the prostitutes, the poor, he needs to be anointed by the spirit. If Jesus needed this spirit to rest upon him, then certainly I did — *we do.* And so I wanted a fresh influx of the spirit, an anointing, whether to lead or teach or be quiet or bring good news to the poor or speak in tongues or prophesy or heal someone.

2. The story of the elders is found in Numbers 11:16-30.
3. See Judges 6–8, especially 6:34.
4. See Judges 13–16, especially 13:25, 14:6, 19; and 15:14.
5. See 1 Samuel 11:6.
6. 1 Samuel 10:5-13; 19:18-24. For further analysis, see Lee Roy Martin, *The Unheard Voice of God: A Pentecostal Hearing of the Book of Judges,* Journal of Pentecostal Theology Supplement Series 32 (Blandford Forum, UK: Deo, 2008).

This sense of yearning — or is it inadequacy? — for something new, something spectacular, is fueled by passage after passage in the Bible. So, braced by my Bible, which lay splayed on the wood floor as I leaned against the radiator and held my head in my hands, I thought for sure I needed more — some novel experience of the spirit. Yet I received only an ambiguous little trickle on a living room floor in a tattered corner of Kansas City.

Still, that inauspicious moment would blossom over the years, if not into a green tamarisk on a desert horizon, as in Isaiah's vision of the spirit outpoured (Isa. 44:3), at least into an idea, a possibility no less rooted in scripture than that tamarisk. The idea was this: *we do not need to hanker after the spirit, to call our spirituality into question, to beat ourselves up for not experiencing the spectacular gifts of tongues or healing or prophecy, for not delivering inspired speeches, for leaving the sick sometimes still bedridden.*

We do not need to bemoan the absence of an outpouring or a resting or a rush of the spirit because all people — every last one of us — has the spirit-breath of God within us from birth. This too is a tradition, a belief, a conviction in the Bible. It has gone largely unnoticed, overshadowed by spectacular gifts, but it is a strand of scripture nonetheless.

Let me put it this way: it is time to embrace the belief that the power of God's spirit pulses in every breath we take. This may not be the whole experience of the spirit. There are judges and kings and prophets and apostles and Jesus himself, all of whom received fresh doses of the spirit to accomplish their grand tasks. Yet the place to start lies elsewhere, with the scream and gulps of a newborn baby that let us know she is alive and kicking, or, better yet, with the old and infirm, whose final breaths, when full of integrity, are a testimony to the spirit of God. This realization, too, finds a home in the Bible.

The Benign Betrayal of Translations

This theme is not readily apparent in English versions of the Bible, however, which translate the Hebrew, *ruach,* either as spirit or breath, even though the Hebrew word can mean both. The single Hebrew word, *ruach,* in fact, ranges widely in meaning, from breath to breeze to wind to angel to demon to spirit. Unfortunately, English requires different words for each domain of meaning.

The difference between Hebrew and English is apparent in Ezekiel's vision of the valley of dry bones. In English translations of this vision, three words — breath, winds, and Spirit — occur.[7] Ezekiel is told, "Prophesy to the *breath* . . . 'Come, *breath,* from the four *winds* . . .'"[8] As a result, "*breath* entered them," and the bones "came to life and stood up on their feet — a vast army." The vision ends with the luscious promise, "I will put my *Spirit* in you and you will live, and I will settle you in your own land. Then you will know that I the LORD have spoken, and I have done it, declares the LORD." In English translations such as this one (New Revised Standard Version), a reader is led to believe that the *breath* which is inbreathed into the bones is somehow different from both the four *winds* that gather and the *Spirit* that will be put into the nation of Israel. Translations miss out on the drama of the original Hebrew, where all three of these English words are only one: *ruach.* Ezekiel repeats the word, *ruach,* in order to emphasize that the one and only *ruach* of God inspires the resurrection of Israel — a resurrection that is at once a personal creation like Adam's *(ruach = breath),* a cosmic rush of vitality *(ruach = winds),* and a promise of national integrity *(ruach = Spirit).* Ezekiel piles up the connotations of *ruach* to bring Israel's deadened psyche back to life. His hearers, after all, are mired in the sands of exile — like the bones in his vision, which fill a desert valley, and Ezekiel needs to breathe new life into their deadened hopes, their moribund imaginations.[9] If English translations lose the dramatic recurrence of the word *ruach,* it is not their fault. This is simply a difference in languages. The English words cannot shoulder the breadth of meaning that the original languages can. To make up for the gap between Hebrew and English, I will often refer to *ruach* as "spirit-breath" rather than spirit or breath.[10]

7. See Ezekiel 37:1-14.

8. In general, I cite the New Revised Standard Version of the Bible, though I tweak it amply.

9. This notion comes from Walter Brueggemann, *The Prophetic Imagination,* 2nd ed. (Minneapolis: Fortress, 2001).

10. Apropos of this, see Wolfhart Pannenberg's discussion of Genesis 1:2 in *Systematic Theology,* 3 vols. (Grand Rapids: Eerdmans, 1994), 2:77-79, in which Pannenberg takes into consideration all three nuances of *ruach:* wind, breath, and spirit. Pannenberg notes that the spirit of God in Genesis 1:2 must relate to the words that God will soon speak throughout Genesis 1; in short, God's spirit is also breath. Further, he asks (78), "But why do we have to regard 'Spirit' and 'wind' as alternatives?" Pannenberg refers, therefore, to "Spirit-wind."

Another challenge faces English translators. When they encounter the words *ruach* and *pneuma,* translators need to decide whether to capitalize the word, and they typically do so based upon whether these words are thought to refer to the human spirit or the divine spirit. If they think the biblical authors are referring to physical life, translators tend to render *ruach* or *pneuma* as "breath" or "spirit." If they think the biblical authors understand *ruach* or *pneuma* as a charismatic gift of God, they use capitalization, translating *ruach or pneuma* as "Spirit." Sometimes translators cannot decide. For instance, in a description of Joshua in Deuteronomy 34:9, the New International Version contains the words, "[Joshua] was filled with the spirit," though a footnote reads, "or, Spirit." Obviously the translators could not decide whether Joshua was filled with a life-force ("spirit") or a divine gift of the Spirit. The problem — and the reason for their footnote — is the absence in English of a word that can simultaneously mean human spirit or breath and divine Spirit or breath. In Israel and the early church, however, this distinction simply did not come into play. One word, *ruach* or *pneuma,* could communicate *both* the spirit or breath of God within all human beings *and* the divine spirit or breath that God gives as a special endowment. It is not the fault of Hebrew or Greek, but the limits of the English language, that forces the unfortunate choice between spirit and Spirit.

This quandary is accompanied by a third. The English language requires articles even when the original languages lack them. It is awkward in English to say, "She was filled with holy spirit," and natural to say, "She was filled with *the* holy spirit." Yet the second translation adds a definite article and, more important, the trove of associations that accompany the idea of the Holy Spirit — capitalized. This quandary is illustrated by 2 Corinthians 6:6, where Paul includes "holy spirit" in a list of virtues that describe the manner in which he accomplishes his life's work: "in patience, in kindness, in holy spirit, in genuine love," and so on (2 Cor. 6:6). The translators of the New Revised Standard Version think Paul is referring to his own integrity and translate the words as "holiness of spirit." In contrast, the translators of the New International Version think Paul is referring to a distinct gift of the Spirit and translate the words with "in the Holy Spirit." These translations are poles apart. Both are possible in this context, where Paul may be describing either his integrity (holiness of spirit) or his inspiration (in the Holy Spirit). Yet both translations betray the original, which allows for ambiguity. It might have been better to use notes to explain that this Greek phrase could be translated as "(a/the) holy spirit," which could mean any of these: holy spirit; a holy spirit; *the* Holy Spirit.[11]

These three challenges, then, confront English translators. First, they must choose from a range of English words — breath, wind, spirit — to translate a single Hebrew or Greek word. Second, translators must decide whether to capitalize the word *spirit*. And third, they must decide, in the absence of a definite article in the Hebrew or Greek original, whether to include a definite article. These translations raise an intractable problem: they introduce a dichotomy between the human spirit or breath and the divine Spirit.

It is time to put this dichotomy behind us if we are to understand *ruach* or *pneuma* for what it is — both breath and Spirit.[12] I will do this in part by refusing, in every case, to capitalize the word *spirit,* and by being careful to represent the absence and presence of definite articles in original languages. I will also frequently refer to *ruach* and *pneuma* as spirit-breath. In these ways, I will circumvent the distinction between the breath of life and the Spirit of God — or other variations of this dichotomy.

I have written this chapter to do more than discuss translations and lexical issues. I hope rather to expand our sense of the holy spirit in antiquity by identifying a neglected strand in the Jewish scriptures, in which the spirit that people receive from birth is no less divine or holy than the spirit they receive through charismatic endowments. We cannot reach this goal merely by recognizing the challenges I have identified. The real work lies in serious exegesis, which is our focus in the following pages.

Spirit-Breath in Israelite Literature

A Steady Spirit

The poignant penitence of Psalm 51 allows us to close the gap between the breath of life and the spirit of God. The psalmist (traditionally David after succumbing to sexual sin with Bathsheba) cries out:

11. For a more detailed analysis of the dilemma of translation, accompanied by several examples, see my *Filled with the Spirit* (Grand Rapids: Eerdmans, 2009), pp. 36-41.

12. See also Wolfhart Pannenberg's interpretation of Psalm 104 in "The Working of the Spirit in the Creation and in the People of God," in Carl E. Braaten, Avery Dulles, and Wolfhart Pannenberg, *Spirit, Faith, and Church* (Philadelphia: Westminster, 1970), pp. 16-17.

Have mercy on me, O God,
    according to your steadfast love;
according to your abundant mercy
    blot out my transgressions.
Wash me thoroughly from my iniquity,
    and cleanse me from my sin.
For I know my transgressions,
    and my sin is ever before me.
Against you, you alone, have I sinned,
    and done what is evil in your sight,
so that you are justified in your sentence
    and blameless when you pass judgment.
Indeed, I was born guilty,
    A sinner when my mother conceived me. (Ps. 51:1-5)

Such trenchant self-awareness does not lead the psalmist to damaging self-denial but to hope that lies beyond his bruised psyche. The psalmist expresses this hope in a series of pleas that have one element in common — *ruach:*

Create in me a clean heart, O God,
    and *renew (a)* right *spirit* within me.
Do not cast me away from your presence,
    and do not take your holy *spirit* from me.
Restore to me the joy of your salvation,
    and sustain (in) me [with] a generous *spirit.*
                 (Ps. 51:10-12; Hebrew 51:12-14)

This prayer for purification begins not with the more usual language of public temple worship or private devotion but with the language of creation: "Create in me a clean heart, O God, and put a new and right spirit within me." The verb *create* recalls vividly the second word in the Hebrew Bible, "In the beginning *created* God . . ." (Gen. 1:1).[13] Despite its resemblance to the creation of the cosmos, Psalm 51 addresses a different arena of existence: not the deep disarray of the cosmic abyss but the disordered depths of the human heart.

    The psalmist says later:

---

13. This command resembles as well Ezekiel's grand vision of re-creation, where a new spirit enters a shattered Israel, where a new *adam* emerges, inspired, from the dust and bones of death (Ezek. 37:1-14).

> For you have no delight in sacrifice;
>> if I were to give a burnt offering, you would not be pleased.
> The sacrifice acceptable to God is a broken *spirit;*
>> a broken and contrite heart, O God, you will not despise.
>>>>>> (Ps. 51:16-17; Hebrew 51:18-19)

The lean words "your holy spirit" (v. 11) — one of two references to "holy spirit" in the entirety of Israelite literature[14] — do not refer to the holy spirit as some sort of charismatic endowment, as in early Christianity; such an understanding would seethe with anachronism. In this poem, rather, the adjective, "holy," takes its place alongside other adjectives, such as "steadfast" and "generous." These adjectives are an indication that the spirit is a lifelong presence within the psalmist. The psalmist wants a steadfast spirit. The psalmist wants a generous spirit. The psalmist wants a *holy* spirit.

The spirit also lies in an indispensable relationship with the "heart," a permanent reality at the core of the psalmist's life. Together, heart and spirit represent the essence of the psalmist — what must be cleansed, instructed, and redirected. The relationship between these two core realities, heart and spirit, is evident in the taut parallel between a "broken spirit" and "broken . . . heart" (Ps. 51:17), where the same word *broken* describes in close succession both spirit and heart.[15] The psalmist is not praying, therefore, in this unprecedented reference, about *the* holy spirit which he or she received in an act of faith or a moment of inspiration. The holy spirit is yoked to the steadfast heart; both must be broken; both can be cleansed.

When therefore the psalmist pleads, "Do not cast me away from your presence, and do not take your holy spirit from me," he is praying not to die, as in Psalm 104:29, where the loss of spirit signals death: "When you hide your face [presence], they [the animals] are dismayed; when you

---

14. The other is Isaiah 63:10-11.

15. This intimate association of heart and spirit is evident as well in the description of the spirit as "right" or "steadfast" and "generous" — words elsewhere associated with the heart: "My heart is steadfast [right], O God, my heart is steadfast. I will sing and make melody" (Ps. 57:7); "Their heart was not steadfast [right] toward him; they were not true to his covenant" (Ps. 78:37); "My heart is steadfast [right], O God, my heart is steadfast; I will sing and make melody. Awake, my soul!" (Ps. 108:1); "They are not afraid of evil tidings; their hearts are firm [right], secure in the Lord" (Ps. 112:7). The word *generous* repeatedly depicts the generous hearts of those who gave offerings voluntarily for the construction of the tent of presence (e.g., Exod. 35:5, 22).

take away their spirit, they die and return to their dust." This understanding of the spirit explains the plea, "Deliver me from bloodshed" (51:14; Hebrew 51:16).[16] Quite simply, the psalmist does not want to die, and the presence of God's spirit, the psalmist believes, keeps him from doing so.[17]

Yet God's *presence* is also a holy place, a mysterious face, and the psalmist's spirit is not mere spirit, nor mere breath, but a *holy* spirit. This holy spirit is the locus of God's presence. In order to maintain the security of God's presence, the psalmist's spirit must break, so that it can become right, holy, and generous — what it was always intended to be. There is, in short, something that holds death at bay, something that can keep the psalmist from being a castaway from God's presence. This is the psalmist's broken spirit, which the psalmist offers in lieu of sacrifice in the hopes of a new and right spirit, a generous spirit, God's holy spirit. The spirit is not merely a human spirit, a breath, a gulp of air that dwindles at death. The spirit is also the locus of virtue and God's presence, the core of what is stable and steadfast, generous and willing, even holy.

Spirit-Breath as Siege Works

This, too, is what Elihu thinks as he towers over Job, who has parked himself, broken and breathless, on the ash heap, where he scratches his sores with rubble. Though Elihu is dead wrong about his own insight, this errant young man gives us perhaps the clearest glimpse of the way in which breath and wisdom join in the ancient conception of *ruach*. Elihu is about to burst because he has listened *ad nauseam* to the endless doggerel of older men. So he launches his ill-advised soliloquy.

> I am young in years, and you are aged;
> therefore I was timid and afraid
> To declare my opinion to you.

16. This interpretation is supported by the observation that, in nearly every request for deliverance of this sort, the one who prays is the victim or potential victim, not the perpetrator. This means that the potential victim pleads to God to have his or her life spared. E.g., Genesis 32:11; Psalm 31:15; 69:15; see Isaiah 44:17. Bloodshed refers to the psalmist rather than to someone whose blood he may shed.

17. For further analysis of Psalm 51, see *Filled with the Spirit,* pp. 28-31. On the Septuagint version, which seems to follow the Hebrew original with an interpretation of the holy spirit as the permanent spirit-breath that sustains life, see my *The Spirit in First-Century Judaism* (Leiden: Brill, 1997; paperback edition, 2002), pp. 65-66.

> I said, "Let days speak, and many years teach wisdom."
> But truly it is the spirit in a mortal,
> the breath of the Almighty, that makes for understanding.
> It is not the old that are wise,
> Nor the aged that understand what is right. (Job 32:6-9)

The spirit of God, the breath of the Almighty — not age or years or experience — is the well of virtue. The elders have proven that with their endless prattle. Now it is young Elihu's turn to demonstrate the wisdom that God's spirit-breath within him has imparted.

Elihu bursts with spirit-breath, or so he thinks. "And am I to wait, because they do not speak, because they stand there, and answer no more?" he asks. Then he takes the offensive against their specious solutions to Job's plight. "I also will give my answer," he bellows. "I also will declare my opinion."

> For I am full of words; the spirit within me lays siege works
>   against me.
> My heart is indeed like wine that has no vent;
> Like new wineskins, it is ready to burst.
> I must speak, so that I may find relief;
> I must open my lips and answer. (Job 32:16-20)

The spirit-breath in Elihu lays siege works against him. The verb he chooses to describe the spirit's impact is used elsewhere of enemies' *bringing on* a siege, which results in such desperate straits that the Israelites will eat the flesh of their sons and daughters (Deut. 28:53, 55, 57).[18] The verb even expresses the relentless *nagging* of Delilah that finally drives Samson to divulge the solution to a riddle (Judg. 14:17) and the mystery of his hair (16:16). The impact of the spirit-breath of God is visceral. Elihu cannot stop the spirit-breath from traveling up his throat, over his tongue, and out of his mouth. The words will come because he has a surfeit of spirit-breath.

Elihu is wrong about the wisdom of his words, of course. He manages only to take the fruitless dialogue of the old men to a sadder level still. Just after claiming, "The spirit of God has made me, and the breath of the Al-

---

18. Jeremiah describes a siege that will *afflict* Jerusalem (Jer. 19:9), and Isaiah claims that God will *distress*-besiege-Jerusalem, as David had besieged it, and that "there shall be moaning and lamentation . . . siege works against you" (Isa. 29:2-3). Yet the nations who fight against Jerusalem, "who *distress* her," will vanish (Isa. 29:7).

mighty gives me life" (Job 33:4), he claims as well to be just like Job: "See, before God I am as you are; I too was formed from a piece of clay" (33:6). How could Elihu possibly think that he, with the robust spirit-breath of youth, could be anything like Job, who sits beleaguered and breathless at his feet? At best, he can show only shallow empathy. Petty compassion. Not wisdom. Certainly not inspiration.

Still, Elihu seals the case that, in Israelite antiquity, breath and spirit are one and the same; words and wisdom arise from the same place in a body. A distinction between mere breath and divine spirit must go by the wayside. What shudders in Elihu is not just the breath that will roll over his tongue and create words; what gurgles in Elihu is also the spirit that will — or so he thinks — suffuse those words with wisdom. Spirit and breath are one — a physical and spiritual concoction, to which Elihu has no right to lay claim.

Spirit in the Courts of Pharaoh

Elihu is outspoken to a fault and wedded to a dodgy dichotomy: *not age but spirit-breath.* This, at base, is the root of his errant effort to solve the problem of Job's plight. This ill-advised dichotomy between age and inspiration, to which Elihu clings, has no toehold in the world of Israel's luminaries. In a slew of stories, prophecies, and wisdom texts, there is a keen relationship between the quality of the spirit within, the possession of wisdom, and practice. Joseph, whose shadow extends for centuries in Israel's memory, offers a quick read in this department.

Impressed by Joseph's proposal about how to handle seven years of plenty followed by seven of famine, Pharaoh asks, "Can we find anyone else like this — one in whom is (the) spirit of God?" (Gen. 41:38). He is Pharaoh and quite capable of answering his own question: "Since God is making known all of this to you, there is no one discerning and wise like you" (41:39). There is a clear connection between question and answer. Pharaoh asks if anyone can be found "*like this* one — one in whom is (the) spirit of God," and answers that "there is no one discerning and wise *like you.*" Spirit of God in Joseph is the font of his discernment and wisdom.

This spirit is not the product of an endowment, as in early Christian charismatic gifts.[19] Pharaoh attributes Joseph's ability to interpret dreams

---

19. George Montague, *Holy Spirit: Growth of a Biblical Tradition* (Peabody, MA:

to the divine character of the spirit within him — not the divine spirit that has come upon him. Other references to the spirit of God in the book of Genesis support this reading: "My spirit shall not remain *in adam* for ever, because he is flesh, but the days shall be a hundred and twenty years" (Gen. 6:3). At issue in Genesis 6:3 is the length of an entire life span. Though the language is different, the scenario is much the same in the following flood story, in which God destroys nearly all of those who have "spirit of life" (6:17; 7:15) or "the breath of the spirit of life" (7:22).

Pharaoh recognizes in Joseph a spirit of supremely divine character that will equip Joseph in the long run to function as second-in-command. How does Joseph's spirit attain such a distinctive character? Not, it would seem, through an instantaneous influx of spirit that reveals the meaning of Pharaoh's dream. Joseph's success arises from long years of practice. His own dream (Gen. 37:5-11) is followed later by the dreams of the cupbearer and baker (40:1-23), which he correctly interprets, and then by Pharaoh's dream about the seven fat and lean cows (41:1-36). In other words, Joseph has hands-on practice in dream interpretation, prompting Pharaoh to recognize that Joseph has (the) spirit of God within him.

Joseph's ability to scheme for the salvation of Egypt is also the product of hard-won wisdom. Pharaoh commends Joseph, not just for his interpretative skill, but for his practical advice about what to do during periods of feast and famine. Joseph's pointed advice goes well beyond dream interpretation: Pharaoh should set aside a fifth of the grain during the good years, etcetera. This sort of wisdom is the product of experience. By the time Pharaoh identifies Joseph as one in whom is (the) spirit of God, Joseph has shown himself to be a capable administrator. Joseph served so well over both Potiphar's house and the prison, in fact, that neither Potiphar nor the chief jailer worried about what lay under his care (Gen. 39:6; 39:23). Joseph brings to this moment in time, when Pharaoh identifies (the) spirit of God in him, a track record of administrative excellence.

This triangle — spirit of God, practice in dream interpretation, and the exercise of administrative foresight — comprises the essential ingre-

---

Hendrickson, 1994), p. 13, assumes that this refers to a special, secondary endowment. To counter this interpretation, at least in part, we might also take into consideration other references in Genesis, such as Isaac and Rebekah's bitterness of spirit, which is brought about by Esau and his wives (26:34-35), or the revival of Jacob's spirit when he recognizes the telltale signs of Joseph's hand in his family's survival of famine (45:27). While these are common enough idioms in the Hebrew Bible, neither is merely physical, purely life-breath; both texts reflect a belief that the spirit is also the home of emotions and qualities.

dients that equip Joseph to interpret dreams, to plot and plan and, consequently, to rise to power. His is a life lived well, with skills well learned and wisdom gotten hold of throughout a lifetime of pain and disappointment. When Pharaoh asks, "Can we find anyone else like this — one in whom is (the) spirit of God?" (Gen. 41:38), and then answers his own question, "Since God is making known all of this to you, there is no one discerning and wise like you" (41:39), he recognizes that the spirit-breath of God in Joseph is the lifelong locus of learned wisdom.[20]

Spirit in the Wilderness

Joseph's mercurial rise to power in Egypt was a blip in a series of events that led Israel to ruthless slavery. Long after his death, the story picks up with courageous midwives who defied Pharaoh, a mother whose cunning led her to send her boy into the Nile in a waterproof basket, and a daughter whose courage brought mother and son together as wet nurse and child.[21] These women paved the way for the exodus from Egypt, when the basket-borne son, Moses, led a rabble of escaped slaves, who spurned his leadership by shaping a golden calf from the jewelry they had extracted from the Egyptians (Exodus 32). Nonetheless, stories of grace cradle this tale of calf-crafting: bracketing this story of Israelite impatience are meticulous instructions on how the tent of presence, the tabernacle, should be prepared (Exod. 25:1–31:11 and 35:4-33). The tent of presence offered stability in the midst of transition, steadiness for an impatient people, and the story of its construction offers instances of unsurpassed generosity. The people who built it did so not by divine compulsion but through sheer desire: "The LORD said to Moses: Tell the Israelites to take for me an offering; from all whose hearts prompt them to give you shall receive the offering for me" (25:1-2).

If this magisterial endeavor begins with God's request for an offering from those with willing hearts, it ends with an astonishing divine decree. Moses is forced by an outpouring of generosity to offer this command: "No man or woman is to make anything else as an offering for the sanctuary" (Exod. 36:6). There is no begging and pleading for more; there

---

20. For a more detailed analysis of the story of Joseph, see *Filled with the Spirit,* pp. 48-51.

21. See Exodus 1–2.

is — if this is imaginable — *too much generosity.* All of what was made, constructed, woven, sewn, and overlaid came from the freewill offering of those whose own hearts prompted them. This was a moment when the coffers were full; this was a protracted pause in Israel's recalcitrance. It is not surprising that the lavish language of filling with spirit should occur, for the first time in the Bible, in this story of lavish giving.

WHEN IT COMES TIME to sew the vestments for Aaron and the priesthood, the spirit arrives on the scene, though not spontaneously, as at Pentecost or upon Israel's judges. God tells Moses, "And you shall speak to all the *wise of heart* whom *I have filled with spirit of wisdom,* and they will make Aaron's vestments . . ." (Exod. 28:3). God selects these skilled laborers, not to receive an influx of skill but because *already* they have demonstrated their skill.[22]

How, if they are filled with wisdom already, can God "fill" the artisans with spirit of wisdom? The first clue to the answer lies in the lavishness of this scene. The ingredients of priestly garments — breastplate, ephod, tunics, and sashes — are listed lavishly and in extensive detail. The scene is splashed with hues of gold, blue, purple, and crimson — vivid colors that would make a New England fall blush. In such a lavish scene, the artisans who produce such splendid garments are depicted in lavish terms as "the wise of heart whom I have filled with spirit of wisdom." They are *filled* with (a) spirit of wisdom; they are wholehearted, brimful of wisdom.

This leads to the second clue: the meaning of the word *fill* (Hebrew *ml'*). At first glance, the verb *fill* appears to point to an initial filling: a skin is filled with water (Gen. 21:19), a horn with oil (1 Sam. 16:1), and a bag with grain (Gen. 42:25). This impression is misleading. A charismatic endowment could have been communicated by any number of other verbs. Elsewhere the spirit is *put upon* people (Num. 11:29), *comes upon* them (e.g., Num. 24:2; Judg. 3:10; 1 Sam. 10:6; 16:13), *clothes* them (Judg. 6:34), *rushes upon* them (Judg. 14:6), and *rests upon* them (Isa. 11:2). All of these verbs vibrate with the pulse of charisma.

The verb *fill,* in contrast, takes us in another direction, away from initial filling and toward fullness or completeness or topping up, as in this remarkable story in the wilderness, when Israel gives too much to

---

22. Throughout this story, in fact, the phrase "wise of heart" refers to skilled laborers in contrast to unskilled laborers. See, for example, Exodus 36:8: "All the 'wise of heart' [skilled laborers] among the workers [unskilled laborers] made the tabernacle. . . ." For a detailed analysis of these texts, see *Filled with the Spirit,* pp. 51-65.

God rather than too little, when Israel's leaders and artisans are capable of bringing the project to fruition, of fulfilling — *filling full* — their vocation. This verb's sense of full-filling is apparent when periods of time must be completed. Jacob's wait for Rachel was over — *filled* (Gen. 29:21). A pregnancy could come to term — *be filled* (Gen. 25:24). A period of purification could be completed — *filled* (Lev. 12:4, 6). A vow could be *fulfilled* (Num. 6:5). Banquets could come to an end — *be filled* (Esther 1:5). Babylonian exile would eventually be over — *be filled* (Jer. 25:12).[23] The same sense of completion also characterizes the verb *fill* when words are at stake: God's own hand or power fills — brings to fruition — what is promised (e.g., 1 Kings 8:15; 2 Chron. 6:4); people, too, are capable of full-filling promises (Jer. 44:25).[24]

God's presence, too, fills sacred spaces. God is able to fill the tent of meeting (Exod. 40:34), the earthly temple (1 Kings 8:10), and the heavenly temple (Isa. 6:1). These mysterious depictions of God's presence do not fixate upon the moment at which God filled these places for the first time but upon the reality that God's presence is *fully* in them. When Jeremiah contends that the glory of God fills the earth (23:24), he emphasizes the inescapability of the divine everywhere in creation, just as Habakkuk contends that the knowledge of the glory of the Lord fills the earth (2:14). When Ezekiel remembers, "I looked, and lo! the glory of the LORD filled the temple of the LORD; and I fell upon my face" (44:4), he is not describing the entry of God's glory into the temple but the reality that God's glory filled every nook and cranny of the temple.[25] The tent of presence, too, is full to the brim with God's glory: "Moses was not able to enter the tent of meeting because the cloud settled upon it, and the glory of the LORD filled the tabernacle" (Exod. 40:35). The glory is here so dense — it has *filled* the tabernacle — that Moses cannot even enter the tent of presence.

By the same token, the simple phrase, "whom I have filled with spirit of wisdom," suggests something other than an initial endowment, a rushing or resting or clothing or coming of the spirit. Filling means comple-

---

23. The verb *fill* functions synonymously with the Hebrew verb *tmm* to indicate completeness, fullness, or an end (e.g., Lev. 25:29-30).

24. The verb *to fill* appears as well in spatial contexts. When Jeremiah recounts how a cistern was filled with the slain, he makes it a point to emphasize that the cistern was a large one. In other words, it took very many corpses finally to fill it *completely* (Jer. 41:9). The emphasis here lies upon the large quantity rather than upon the act of initial filling.

25. This is the case with respect to the glory of God, or the cloud, which fills the temple (e.g., 1 Kings 8:11; Ezek. 43:5).

tion, fulfilling, fruition, wholeness, fullness. When Egyptian houses are filled with swarms of flies, more than a few flies beginning to buzz about can be expected (Hebrew Exod. 8:17). When the hem of God's robe fills the temple, in Isaiah's grand vision, more than a tip of the garment occupies the inner sanctum (Isa. 6:1). When Jeremiah protests that the land is filled with idols, it is not because he is troubled by the occasional idol that dots Judah's hillsides (16:18). When the Jordan is said to fill all its banks during the time of harvest, the river overflows those banks, filling them — flooding them — beyond the brink (Josh. 3:15).

This simple verb, *fill,* communicates that there is now more than enough spirit within these gifted laborers to accomplish the task, to complete it perfectly. They are not moderately well equipped. They are full to the brim with a wise spirit. Their hearts, in short, are full of wisdom.[26]

BECAUSE THEY ARE FULL to the brim, the responsibility for overseeing this unprecedented labor falls to Bezalel and Oholiab, about whom God says to Moses:

> See, I have called by name Bezalel son of Uri son of Hur, of the tribe of Judah: and I have filled him with spirit of God, with wisdom, intelligence, and knowledge in every kind of craft, to devise artistic designs, to work in gold, silver, and bronze, in cutting stones for setting, and in carving wood, in every kind of craft. Moreover, I have appointed with him Oholiab son of Ahisamach, of the tribe of Dan; and I have given wisdom in the heart of all the wise of heart, so that they may make all that I have commanded you. . . . (Exod. 31:1-6)

Bezalel resurfaces in a reprisal of this story that occurs in the context of Israel's extraordinary generosity:

> Then Moses said to the Israelites: See, the LORD has called by name Bezalel son of Uri son of Hur, of the tribe of Judah; he has filled him with spirit of God, with wisdom, intelligence, and knowledge in every kind of craft, to devise artistic designs, to work in gold, silver, and bronze, in cutting stones for setting, and in carving wood, in every kind of craft. And he put into his heart to teach, both him and Oholiab son of Ahisamach, of the tribe of Dan. He has filled them with wisdom of heart

---

26. For slightly more analysis, including the adjective *full* and the noun *fullness,* see *Filled with the Spirit,* pp. 52-58.

to do every kind of work done by an artisan or by a designer or by an embroiderer in blue, purple, and crimson yarns, and in fine linen, or by a weaver — by any sort of artisan or skilled designer. (Exod. 35:30-35)

The correspondence between spirit and heart that characterizes Psalm 51 and the description of artisans in Exodus 28:3 occurs in Exodus 31 and 35 with increasing precision and unavoidable clarity.[27]

> 28:3: speak to all the *wise of heart* whom *I have filled with spirit of wisdom*
>
> 31:1: and *I have filled him* [Bezalel] *with spirit of God,* with wisdom, intelligence, and knowledge in every kind of craft
>
> 31:6: and *I have given wisdom in the heart of all the wise of heart* so that they may make all that I have commanded you
>
> 35:31: [God] *has filled him* [Bezalel] *with spirit of God, with wisdom . . . for every craft*
>
> 35:35: [God] *filled them* [Bezalel and Oholiab] *with wisdom of heart . . . to do every craft*

In each of these instances, the narrator clearly understands that the locus of wisdom is the heart. Taken alongside the corresponding image of wisdom-of-heart, God's filling Bezalel with "spirit of God, wisdom," does not mean that he received an entirely fresh influx of spirit, a rush of the spirit, or a new spirit altogether. The mirror images of heart and spirit suggest that the filling with (the) spirit ought to be understood as a full-filling with spirit. This is not so much an endowment of the spirit as an enhancement of spirit.

Like the other artisans, Bezalel and Oholiab's hearts were already skilled, their spirits already knowledgeable, in which case this gift of wisdom came to hearts and spirits that were already wise through acquired learning. Although there is no new heart or spirit in this narrative, there is

---

27. In Exodus 28:3 and 31:6, artisans/skilled laborers are "wise of heart." In Exodus 31:3, Bezalel is filled with spirit of God, with wisdom, intelligence. Exodus 35:31 and 35:35, which describe Bezalel and Oholiab, fold both images; filling with the spirit and "wisdom of heart" communicate that Bezalel and Oholiab, while leaders of the whole enterprise, are still themselves included among the artisans, as they are later in Exodus 36:1: "Bezalel and Oholiab and every one wise of heart to whom the LORD has given wisdom and understanding to know how to do every craft in the construction of the sanctuary shall work in accordance with all that the LORD has commanded."

something new here: at this point in Israel's history, spirits are, in an unparalleled way, full to the brim with skill, overflowing with competence. *The spirit of God with which God had filled Bezalel and the artisans from the start, the spirit in them that was already the source of skill, was ever more richly enhanced with wisdom, insight, and intelligence at this salutary moment in Israel's history.*

ONE UNREMARKABLE LINE toward the end of this story tells us what Bezalel and Oholiab actually did with their acquired knowledge, with (the) spirit of God, with the wisdom, knowledge, and understanding that filled them: "And [God] gave in his heart to teach, both him and Oholiab son of Ahisamach, of the tribe of Dan" (Exod. 35:34).[28] Their role was not to take over and dominate the monumental project that lay before them. Nor did they spend all of their time in the trenches. Their vocation was to teach others the skills that they had mastered. For all of the lavish language that coalesces around them in this story, what Bezalel and Oholiab did, quite simply, was to teach.

This inconspicuous line suggests a good deal about how the artisans were "filled with spirit of wisdom," how God could claim, "I have given wisdom in the heart of all the wise of heart." The language of filling with spirit and giving of wisdom evokes images of direct, divine intervention, but this simple mention of teaching suggests otherwise. Whom did Bezalel and Oholiab teach? The artisans, of course. The artisans were filled with spirit of wisdom and given wisdom in the heart because they learned from capable teachers who had mastered the skills of every craft.

Spirit in the Corridors of Power

The story of Daniel unfolds during a horrific era that etched itself on Israel's memory, an era when Israel was shattered by Babylon, its princes deported, its temple crushed, its king blinded. Babylon's imperial policy was to privilege the cream of their captives' crop by training them to become leaders of their people. Set in this historical context, the story of

---

28. The translation of the NRSV, with the verb *inspire,* is too evocative of a special endowment: "And he has inspired him to teach, both him and Oholiab son of Ahisamach, of the tribe of Dan." It is better to translate the Hebrew root *ntn* as "gave," following the lead of the LXX. God *gave* into his heart to teach.

Daniel — and the presence of the spirit in him — lasts for three generations. This is a substantial length of time:

- *Generation 1:* King Nebuchadnezzar of Babylon claims three times
  that Daniel has *"a spirit of the holy God in him"* (Dan. 4:8, 9, 18 in English; 4:5, 6, 15 in the Aramaic version).
- *Generation 2:* Nebuchadnezzar's daughter-in-law, after hearing about
  the baffling writing that appears during Belshazzar's party, recalls,
  "There is a man in your kingdom in whom is *the spirit of a/the holy
  God.* In the days of your father he was found to have enlightenment,
  understanding, and wisdom like the wisdom of the gods." Later, she
  recalls that "an *'excellent' spirit,* knowledge, and understanding to
  interpret dreams, explain riddles, and solve problems were found in
  this Daniel . . ." (Dan. 5:11-12). Her husband, Nebuchadnezzar's son,
  Belshazzar, also knows about Daniel's *"excellent spirit"* (5:14).
- *Generation 3:* by the time a whole new empire is on the scene, Darius
  of Media plans to appoint Daniel to the heights of the empire because
  "an 'excellent' spirit is in him" (Dan. 6:3; 6:4 in the Aramaic).

This is ample spirit language: over half a dozen references to the spirit in
only three chapters. And it fits precisely the pattern we discovered in the
stories of Joseph and the artisans who engineered the tent of presence.

What we discover in the story of Daniel is this: the spirit is in Daniel
for the long haul. The spirit is not, from where Daniel or any of the empire
builders around him stand, a momentary divine ambush. Throughout
three generations — Nebuchadnezzar, Belshazzar, and Darius — Daniel
exhibits such wisdom that a succession of foreign rulers recognize a spirit
in him that can only have come from God. If Daniel possesses wisdom
throughout three generations, it is not because occasionally he receives a
special endowment of the spirit of God but because the spirit within him
is the perennial source of enlightenment, wisdom, and prescience.

We discover as well quite a lot of excellence, though not "excellence" in
the sense of the English word. Daniel has *yattirah* spirit in him. This word
is too tamely translated by the English word *excellent.* It tends to communicate degree or extraordinary measure, so it should be translated, *to the nth
degree.* Nebuchadnezzar's statue was huge, and its brilliance was "exces-
sive" *(yattirah)* or, in this context, "blinding" (Dan. 2:31). The fiery furnace
was "excessively" *(yattirah)* overheated, so that "the raging flames killed the
men who lifted Shadrach, Meshach, and Abednego" into the furnace (Dan.

33

3:22). In a vision, a fourth beast is described as "exceptionally [*yattirah*] terrifying" (7:19). The choice of this word to describe Daniel's spirit indicates more than mere excellence. The statue was brilliant to the nth degree, the furnace hot to the nth degree, and the beast terrifying to the nth degree. This word communicates, on the one hand, lavishness and fullness: there is so much brilliance, so much heat, so much terror — *and so much spirit.*[29] It communicates, on the other hand, quality. There is sheer brilliance, sheer heat, sheer terror — *and sheer spirit,* spirit as spirit is intended to be, spirit so perfectly spirit that it is clearly a spirit from God. This is spirit to the nth degree. This is *yattirah* spirit.

We discover something else in this sequence: what rendered Daniel's spirit so distinctive was the wisdom that characterized it to no less a degree. In Daniel 5 there is a striking parallel between spirit and wisdom. Daniel has:

"*yattirah* spirit . . . in him" (5:12);
"*yattirah* wisdom in him" (5:14).

How does Daniel come to be characterized as a person who possesses spirit and wisdom to the nth degree over the long haul? The answer to this question lies in the very first story of the book that bears his name. After the exile, there arrives in Babylon a group of young, noble, Israelite men who already are "without physical defect and handsome, versed in every branch of wisdom, endowed with knowledge and insight, and competent to serve in the king's palace; they were to be taught the literature and language of the Chaldeans" (1:4). Daniel is a rare specimen who has it all: intellectual brilliance, physical strength, and good looks.

Yet Daniel uses none of this to climb the ladder of imperial power. Unlike nearly all of the other royal refugees, who for three years were treated to lavish food and wine from the king's own table, to prepare them for a lifetime in the king's court, Daniel "resolved that he would not defile himself with the royal rations of food and wine; so he asked the palace master to allow him not to defile himself" (Dan. 1:8). Daniel was joined by three companions of fiery furnace fame. Together they ate vegetables rather than rich food and wine. It is here, in the crucible of Daniel's re-

---

29. On degrees of filling, with an understanding of spirit in terms of quantity, see excursus four in Cor Bennema, *The Power of Saving Wisdom: An Investigation of Spirit and Wisdom in Relation to the Soteriology of the Fourth Gospel,* Wissenschaftliche Untersuchungen zum Neuen Testament 2.148 (Tübingen: Mohr Siebeck, 2002), pp. 253-55.

sistance to royal rations, in his repudiation of ambition, in his rejection of power, in his penchant for simplicity, in his refusal to seek status, that Daniel is first recognized as an interpreter of visions and dreams. The storyteller tells us, "to these four young men God gave knowledge and skill in every aspect of literature and wisdom; Daniel also had insight into all visions and dreams" (1:17). This first story offers a clear signal that wisdom, the wisdom that will radiate from Daniel's spirit for generations to come, arises from dogged faithfulness, from a rejection of luxury and a rare simplicity. When their years of refusing royal rations are over, Daniel and his friends appear before Nebuchadnezzar, where, "in every matter of wisdom and understanding concerning which the king inquired of them, he found them ten times better than all the magicians and enchanters in his whole kingdom" (1:20).

DANIEL COMBINES THIS PENCHANT for fidelity with a passion for wisdom. He undertakes a three-year education in the literature and language of the Chaldeans (Dan. 1:4-6), learns to read the language of his captors, Aramaic (5:17, 24-25), records dreams in writing (7:1), and incorporates Torah in his prayers (9:11-14). His spirit is divine, wise, and extraordinary in large measure because Daniel has a passion for education.

Fast-forward to the last story about Daniel's exceptional spirit, where the identical theme emerges.

> Soon Daniel distinguished himself above all the other presidents and satraps because excellent spirit was in him, and the king planned to appoint him over the whole kingdom. So the presidents and the satraps tried to find grounds for complaint against Daniel in connection with the kingdom. But they could find no grounds for complaint or any corruption, because he was faithful, and no negligence or corruption could be found in him. (Dan. 6:3-4)

The theme of faithfulness, which punctuates this final story, is nothing new. The gist of the first story is that the faithfulness of Daniel and his friends prompts them to refuse royal rations. And the consequences? They emerge hale, hearty, and wise, with Daniel even able to interpret dreams and visions. There is no shortcut to spirituality, we learn — no frequent, fleeting influx of the spirit that transforms Daniel into a sage. In a quick succession of stories, rather, we learn that the spirit-breath within him — a lifelong source of wisdom — is rooted in three essential qualities:

- resistance to ambition, to the aspiration for a well-placed position in the corridors of power;
- wholehearted faithfulness to food laws rooted in Torah that seem, at first blush, to have precious little to do with the grandeur of God's spirit;
- a penchant for education, even education in languages and literature that lie outside the purview of sacred Jewish texts.

These stories surrounding Daniel are among the latest in the Jewish Bible, and they provide an apt resumption of earlier themes. In the book of Daniel, these themes become inescapable, as characteristics of the spirit that were apparent in earlier narratives now reverberate through the corridors of Babylonian and Median power.

Spirit-Breath of God in the World of Israel: Summary

The world of the spirit is lavish. Elihu understands that the spirit does not trickle down to the wise; the spirit exists in such measure, with such force, that it holds a sage hostage, laying siege works against him. His heart is like a wineskin about to burst. Elihu's sensation of compulsion goes a long way toward explaining why select Israelites are depicted as full of (the) spirit. This is lavish language because these are not individuals who follow God halfheartedly.

Pharaoh's question, for example, implies a rich draft that rises from within Joseph: "Can we find anyone else like this — one in whom is (the) spirit of God [gods]?" The sages and magicians of Egypt are captive to their ignorance. Joseph alone solves the conundrum of Pharaoh's dream and then, without external prompting, takes the initiative to devise a strategy for survival intended to serve the common good. Joseph alone, of all the leaders in Egypt, mirrors the divine world with a full measure of discernment and wisdom — hard-earned wisdom, long-awaited discernment.

This lavishness of spirit continues in the midst of Sinai's desolation, where Israelites *en masse* offer much more than is needed, where hearts are prompted, spirits lifted to offer goods and services with unprecedented munificence. There are others as well — artisans, the wise of heart — who are filled with (the) spirit of wisdom. The materials from which they spin and hammer are depicted with vivid hues and delectable detail.

Small wonder that their leaders, Bezalel and Oholiab, are described as being *filled* with (the) spirit of God and wisdom of heart and with an additional cumbersome parataxis that drips with lavish praise: Bezalel was filled with spirit of God, wisdom, intelligence, and knowledge. Here in the unyielding wilderness of Sinai, there is excess, imposing generosity, a stunning collection of skills, a fullness marked by adept artisans who exhibit extraordinary craftsmanship and, no less salient, hearts at the ready to teach.

The stories of Daniel in foreign courts galvanize these strands. Three successive stories about three successive reigns call attention to his extraordinary wisdom and knowledge. Throughout these stories Daniel garners enormous praise, for he, like Joseph, is both an unparalleled interpreter of the inscrutable and an administrator par excellence. And why? Because in him is God-given spirit to the nth degree — an extraordinary measure of the divine vitality that, when cultivated through simplicity and skill, becomes the source of knowledge and wisdom.

Spirit within in the World of Early Judaism

This strand of pneumatology, which emerges from the stories of Joseph and Bezalel, to name a couple of Israelite luminaries, had a vibrant afterlife in the world of Judaism. Rather than shrivel, the Israelite belief — that some people were full of the spirit and wisdom — blossomed in the era that gave birth to Christianity. In fact, this belief detonated during the Maccabean era — the 160s BCE — when the book of Daniel may have been written. (Though it is included in the canonical scriptures, the book of Daniel may have been written later than other Jewish literature, such as the collection of Ben Sira's sayings in the book of Sirach, or Ecclesiasticus.) Daniel, far more even than Joseph, had a spirit within him to the nth degree that gave him wisdom to the nth degree. Daniel, far more even than Joseph, cultivated this spirit through self-imposed discipline, through rejecting the exquisite dainties of royal feasts and the niceties of an existence among the elite-in-training. And far more even than Joseph, foreign dignitaries, both enemies and allies, recognized the quality of Daniel's spirit over a length of time that spanned three successive administrations.

A Holy Spirit within as the Heart of Virtue

Daniel features also in the picturesque tale of Susanna, a young woman of inordinate beauty and impeccable virtue. One day, having sent her servants to fetch what she needed, she bathed in a garden. Two elders, who had longed for her sexually, hid themselves in the garden. While Susanna's servants were away, the elders approached her and demanded that she have sexual relations with them or else they would accuse her of adultery with a young man. She refused. When Susanna was put on trial, the word of the two elders was naturally taken as truth, despite her protests. God, however, "raised up the holy spirit of a young man," Daniel, who began to shout, "I am innocent of this woman's death!" He devised a plan to discern the truth: he interrogated each separately and asked under which tree each saw her committing adultery. Each elder identified a different tree, so they were put to death — the same penalty they had sought for Susanna.

This quaint yet disturbing tale is a lightning rod, around which several of the themes of biblical literature coalesce. Daniel's spirit exhibits wisdom that is typically characteristic of elders, so the other elders follow his strategy for discerning the truth of the matter. This is one of the main points of the story, which is made with an exclamation point when the elders say to him, "Come, sit among us and inform us, for God has given you the standing of an elder" (Susanna 50).

This story also places the accent upon the raising up or prompting of Daniel's spirit. His spirit is already holy, and the movement of this exact moment demands that it be prompted into action. God raises Daniel's holy spirit, therefore, to devise a plan to exonerate Susanna. This prompting is reminiscent of the magnificent outpouring of possessions and skills that accompanied the construction of the tent of meeting, when God prompted the spirits and lifted the hearts of the Israelites (Exod. 35:5, 21; 36:2).

The single line, "God raised up the holy spirit of a young man," in this simple tale gathers elements that emerged first in Israel's earlier literary tapestry — though now with something new: the spirit that Daniel has within him is, in no uncertain terms, the holy spirit. He is characterized as having a holy spirit within that unmasks sexual harassment and exhibits wisdom well beyond his years. Rather than accepting a false verdict, the young man with a holy spirit screams, "I want no part in shedding this woman's blood!" (46). How different — yet similar — Daniel is from the more self-absorbed and self-defeated psalmist, who begs God, "Do not take your holy spirit from *me,*" and "Deliver *me* from bloodshed" (Ps. 51:11, 14).

What the tale of Susanna offers in story form, the Dead Sea Scrolls offer in the language of the academy. In the Damascus Document, which prescribes a way of life for communities scattered throughout Palestine, the human spirit is a "holy spirit."[30] Members of the community are told ". . . to keep apart from every uncleanness according to their regulations, without anyone *defiling his holy spirit*" (CD 7.3-4).[31] What this means is clear when we set this statement alongside one slightly later: "No one should *defile his soul* with any living being or one which creeps, by eating them, from the larvae of bees to every living being . . . which creeps in water" (CD 12.11-13). The form and vocabulary of CD 7.4 and 12.11 communicate a shared conception with different words; the Hebrew word *nephesh* (soul) in one reappears as *ruach* (holy *spirit*) in the other.[32]

The terms *ruach hakodesh* and *nephesh* are used synonymously elsewhere in the Dead Sea Scrolls in several early wisdom-oriented fragments that together have been titled *4QInstruction.* In a portion concerned with financial wherewithal, there occurs an admonition against dishonesty, possibly some shady strategy that is intended to delay the repayment of a debt.[33] This admonition cautions against exchanging a holy spirit for money:

> [Do not in your affairs demean] your spirit; do not for any money exchange your holy spirit, for no price is adequate. . . . (4Q416 fr. 2 II.7)

30. For an overview of the word *ruach* in the Dead Sea Scrolls, see the appendix in A. E. Sekki, *The Meaning of Ruah at Qumran,* Society of Biblical Literature Dissertation Series 110 (Atlanta: Scholars, 1989), pp. 225-39.

31. It is not possible to be completely certain that the possessive "his" in the words "his holy spirit" refers to a member of the community rather than to God, even though the antecedent of this possessive pronoun is a member of the community rather than God.

32. A further signal that soul and holy spirit are synonymous here is that the word *ruach* functions in the Scrolls in place of *nephesh* in Leviticus 11:43 and 20:25. The way in which the Damascus Document (CD) 7.4 draws upon the phraseology of Leviticus 11:43 and 20:25 is an indication that the words *holy spirit* in the Damascus Document were considered an apt replacement for the word *nephesh* in Leviticus. For background and bibliography, see Sekki, *Meaning,* pp. 112-14. For a more detailed layout of the relevant Hebrew, see my *Spirit in First-Century Judaism,* pp. 74-75.

33. See further Matthew J. Goff, *The Worldly and Heavenly Wisdom of 4QInstruction,* Studies on the Texts of the Desert of Judah 50 (Leiden: Brill, 2003), pp. 80-167; on the repayment of debt and a holy spirit, see p. 226.

These instructions recur slightly later.

> [Do not se]ll your soul for money. It is better that you are a servant in
> the spirit, and that you serve your overseers for nothing. (4Q416 fr. 2
> II.17)[34]

Adherents of the covenant must not demean their spirits or exchange their
holy spirits for money; they must not sell their *souls* for money. Holiness
is more important than financial gain; integrity must always take priority
over economic ambition.[35]

Merely three brief snippets from the Dead Sea Scrolls, read alongside
the tale of Susanna, provide a lucid perspective on an early Jewish belief
that human beings have God's holy spirit in them from birth. No less significant, this holy spirit is the locus of holiness and integrity. The human
spirit is not neutral territory, not mere breath. It is a holy region. This holy
spirit can be sold off, bartered for paltry currency, so the wisdom teacher
of *4QInstruction* urges his readers not to demean the spirit in daily affairs,
not to exchange one's holy spirit, not to sell a soul for measly money.

THE TALE OF SUSANNA and the Dead Sea Scrolls were probably composed in Palestine, a distant outpost of the Greek East — none more re-
mote than Qumran, along the northwest corner of the Dead Sea. Yet Jews
cherished the sanctity of the spirit within in Greek urban centers as well.
Particularly in Alexandria, authors struck the inbreathing of Genesis on
the anvil of Greco-Roman conceptions, both medical and philosophical.
In this way, they reshaped the notion of spirit, though not without re-
taining their belief that the spirit is the locus of virtue. This was not, we
should note, an especially difficult task, since Stoicism, the most popular
of Greco-Roman philosophies, championed this point of view.

Spirit and the Pursuit of Virtue

Stoics tended to believe that *pneuma* pervades a living and rational cosmos. Alexander of Aphrodisias summarized the view of Chrysippus (ca.

---

34. See parallel fragments 4Q417 frag. 1 II.8, 21; 4Q418 frag. 8.3-4, 14.

35. In the second instance, one should serve "with the spirit" for no pay at all if this
is the way to preserve one's integrity. In this command, the words *soul* and *spirit* are once
again synonymous.

280-207 BCE), one of Stoicism's most renowned thinkers: "he assumes that the whole material world is unified by a *pneuma* which wholly pervades it and by which the universe is made coherent and kept together . . ." (*On Mixture* 216, lines 14-17). Lucilius Balbus, a competent and careful summarizer of Stoicism in Cicero's *On the Nature of the Gods,* which was composed during the years 46-44 BCE, claims that the world order is "maintained in unison by a single divine and all-pervading spirit" (*On the Nature of the Gods* 2.19).

If *pneuma* was the unifying element that permeates the cosmos, the human soul was a fragment of the cosmic soul: "the world . . . is a living thing in the sense of an animate substance. . . . And it is endowed with soul, as is clear from our several souls being each a fragment of it."[36] The human soul is, in brief, a fragment of the divine. *Pneuma* unifies both cosmos and soul, which is a portion of it, by maintaining each in a living, unifying tension.

No ancient author, Jew or Roman, male or female, expresses the character of the human spirit more poignantly than the Stoic statesman Seneca (ca. 4 BCE-41 CE), who counseled the recipient of the forty-first of his moral letters, Lucilius, to look to himself rather than to gods and idols. Seneca focuses in this letter upon a "holy spirit" that indwells human beings:

> We do not need to uplift our hands towards heaven, or to beg the keeper of a temple to let us approach this idol's ear, as if in this way our prayers were more likely to be heard. God is near you, he is with you, he is within you. This is what I mean, Lucilius: a holy spirit indwells within

36. Diogenes Laertius 7.143. As a fragment of the divine, the human soul was believed by Stoics to carry divine characteristics. Like the purest aether, the ruling portion of the cosmos, the mind as *pneuma* was regarded as the ruling (hegemonic) part of the soul. Sextus Empiricus, in *Against the Mathematicians* 8.400, lucidly defines the Stoic position: "since therefore the soul and the ruling spirit is purer than any spirit. . . ." See also H. von Arnim, *Stoicorum Veterum Fragmenta,* 4 vols. (Leipzig: Teubner, 1903-24), 4:65. Diogenes Laertius quintessentially expresses the Stoic conception of the human soul: "Nature in their view is an artistically working fire, going on its way to create; which is equivalent to a fiery, creative, or fashioning breath. And the soul is a nature capable of perception. And they regard it as the breath of life, congenital with us; from which they infer first that it is a body and secondly that it survives death. . . . Zeno of Citium and Antipater, in their treatises *De anima,* and Posidonius define the soul as a warm breath; for by this we become animate and this enables us to move" (7.156-57). More generally, see Samuel Sambursky, *Physics of the Stoics* (Princeton: Princeton University Press, 1987).

us [sacer intra nos spiritus sedet], one who marks our good and bad deeds, and is our guardian. As we treat this spirit, so are we treated.[37]

The person who fulfills the Stoic ideal of being unterrified in the face of dangers, untouched by desires, does so by virtue of a spirit that, while abiding within, remains allied with its heavenly origin:

> When a soul rises superior to other souls, when it passes through every experience as if it were of small account, when it smiles at our fears and at our prayers, it is stirred by a force from heaven. . . . Therefore, a great part of it abides in that place from whence it came down to earth . . . the great and hallowed soul, which has come down in order that we may have a nearer knowledge of divinity, does indeed associate with us, but still cleaves to its origin. . . . (41.5)

The concept of the soul as that which "has come down in order that we may have a nearer knowledge of divinity" suggests quite clearly Seneca's adherence to the Stoic notion that the human soul is a fragment of the cosmic soul. What marks this perfect soul is not external accoutrements that can be passed on to someone else, but a life lived according to reason, a life lived according to one's nature:

> Praise the quality in him which cannot be given or snatched away, that which is the peculiar property of the person. Do you ask what this is? It is soul, and reason brought to perfection in the soul. For a human is a reasoning animal. Therefore, a person's highest good is attained, if he has fulfilled the good for which nature designed him at birth. And what is it which this reason demands of him? The easiest thing in the world, — to live in accordance with his own nature. (41.8-9)

In this eloquent essay, the task and character of the holy spirit, understood in Stoic terms, are explained with exceptional clarity: living according to reason (the Stoic ideal) and living according to one's own nature are synonymous because one's own nature consists in part of a holy spirit, the god within, which has descended from the divine, rational world and continues, within humans, to seek association with the divine world.

It is no leap at all from Seneca's pen to the parchment of the Wisdom of Solomon, from the mind of Chrysippus to the musings of Philo Judaeus. The impact of Stoicism was immense, not least in the development

---

37. Seneca, *Moral Epistles* 41.2.

of Jewish perceptions of the *pneuma,* particularly in the Egyptian city of Alexandria, a hotbed of Greco-Roman philosophical dialogue.

IN A FRONTAL INDICTMENT of idol-builders, the Alexandrian author of the Wisdom of Solomon takes the inbreathing of Genesis 2:7 to a whole new level, with nuance so rich as to be nearly untranslatable: "the one who [God] breathed into him an energizing soul and implanted a living spirit."[38] The author (the Sage) believes that the spirit is borrowed from God for a time and destined to return to God; because idol-crafters fail to recognize this spirit, and the God who implanted it, "their heart is ashes, their hope is cheaper than dirt, and their lives are of less worth than clay" (Wisd. 15:10).[39]

The failure of such idol-builders lies in the blatant inability to recognize, not mere breath, but a profoundly holy spirit within human beings. This conception is so important to the Sage that it occurs in the opening lines of the Wisdom of Solomon:

> For a holy spirit of discipline will flee from deceit, and will leave foolish thoughts behind, and will be ashamed at the approach of injustice. . . . For wisdom is a humane spirit, but will not free blasphemers from the guilt of their words; because God is witness of their inmost feelings, and a true observer of their hearts, and a hearer of their tongues. Because the spirit of the Lord has filled the world, and that which holds all things together knows what is said, therefore those who utter unjust things will not escape notice, and justice, when it punishes, will not pass them by. (Wisd. 1:5-8)

From the start, the Sage champions a Stoic view of the spirit as that which fills the world and holds all things together.[40] He also describes, right from

---

38. This description of inbreathing goes far beyond Genesis 2:7 by introducing the vocabulary of the Alexandrian medical tradition. The prolific medical historian, Galen, for instance, could attribute to Erasistratus, the Alexandrian physician, the belief that the body contained not only "a *living* power" but also a *psychic* one; these dimensions are reflected in the words *soul* or *psyche* and *living spirit (pneuma zōtikon).*

39. See my *Portraits of Adam in Early Judaism: From Sirach to 2 Baruch,* Journal for the Study of the Pseudepigrapha: Supplement Series 1 (Sheffield, UK: Sheffield Academic, 1988), pp. 53-54.

40. He refers as well to a "holy spirit" as one leg of the triangle of human existence, alongside the body and the soul: ". . . wisdom will not enter a deceitful *soul,* or dwell in a *body* enslaved to sin. For a holy *spirit* of discipline will flee from deceit" (1:4-5a). This triad

the start, the *pneuma* as a spirit "of discipline," or "of teaching." With such a striking addition, the Sage affirms that this holy spirit can be taught, educated, corrected so as to flee deceit, leave foolish thoughts behind, and be ashamed at the onslaught of injustice. We have learned this about the spirit already. Daniel might well have been identified, in the book that bears his name, as a hero with a "holy spirit of discipline" in him, for he had studied, prayed, and fasted along the hard-fought journey to wisdom.

Nowhere in these opening lines does the Sage offer safe haven to a single soul. *All people,* not only those with exclusive claims to inspiration, can be guided by a disciplined holy spirit; the idolaters whom the author subsequently condemns fail precisely because they refuse to recognize this aspect of God's creativity, not because they lack this spirit. Theirs is not just a failure of biology but a failure of theology.

IF THE WISDOM OF SOLOMON provides glimpses of the spirit as the reservoir of virtue, these glimpses are relatively slender and fleeting. Philo repeatedly champions a conception of the spirit as the locus of virtue. This conception, at once scriptural and Stoic, comes to the fore especially when Philo interprets Genesis 2:7 to mean that God "breathed into him [humankind] from above of God's own Deity."[41]

Like Seneca, Philo identifies the inbreathing of Genesis 2:7 with the gift of purest mind, a fragment of God's cosmic spirit, "for that which God breathed in was nothing else than a divine breath that migrated hither from that blissful and happy existence for the benefit of our race. . . ."[42]

---

of body, soul, and spirit, like the interpretation of Genesis 2:7 in Wisdom of Solomon 15, provides yet another instance in which the human spirit — what characterizes human beings from birth — is a *holy spirit.*

41. Philo Judaeus, *The Worse Attacks the Better* 86. This is no mere life-giving moment, but a gift of divinity itself. The human being was "judged worthy to receive his soul not from any other thing already created, but through the breath of God imparting of His own power in such measure as mortal nature could receive" (*On the Virtues* 203). In *On the Special Laws* 4.123, he writes that the "essence or substance of that other soul is divine spirit" because, as Moses "in his story of the creation says. . . . God breathed a breath of life into the first human, the founder of our race. . . . And clearly what was then thus breathed was *aether*-spirit, or something if such there be better than *aether-spirit,* even an effulgence of the blessed, thrice blessed nature of the God."

42. *On the Creation* 135. Similarly, he writes only slightly later of the human soul and body, "Every person, in respect of the mind, is allied to the divine Reason, having come into being as a copy or fragment or ray of that blessed nature, but in the structure of his body is allied to all the world . . ." (*On the Creation* 146). On the relationship between the effulgence of *pneuma* and fragments of it, see T. Tobin, *The Creation of Man: Philo and the*

While Philo's anthropology is complex, one aspect is incontrovertible: only the purer soul, the mind, is divine breath: "and the divine breath or spirit [is] its most dominant part . . . he [Moses] did not make the substance of the mind depend on anything created, but represented it as breathed upon by God. For the Maker of all, he *says,* 'blew into his face the breath of life, and the human became a living soul . . .'" (*Who Is the Heir?* 55-57). Only the higher part of the soul, particularly the mind, is capable of virtue. The lower part of the soul gets dragged into the muck of physical existence.

In this interpretation, as in all of his interpretations of Genesis 2:7, Philo leaves no doubt that inspiration is the gift of God's spirit at birth (though he also sees it as a gift to prophets and the interpreters of scripture, as we will see in chapter three of this book). This is no mere inbreathing of breath but a full infusion of deity, of mind, of purest soul. This sounds like Seneca — "the great and hallowed soul, which has come down in order that we may have a nearer knowledge of divinity" — or what Seneca might have written to Lucilius had he been raised in a Jewish home.

Genesis 2:7 is also a gateway to Philo's belief in the centrality of virtue. As in the Wisdom of Solomon, where a soul can be deceitful, a body enslaved to sin, and a holy spirit subject to teaching or discipline, so also for Philo can the spirit God inbreathes provide the basis for virtue. As in Seneca's letter to Lucilius, where the purpose of the holy spirit within is to attain the highest human good, so for Philo does life lived in accordance with the mind lead to the highest good of being lifted in a rapturous vision of God. This spirit within, according to Philo, exists principally to provide the foundation for virtue and the culpability for vice. This spirit draws a human being from his or her tether to the passions of the body and provides release to fly in the heavens toward the divine.

This association of the spirit emerges when Philo grapples with the difficulties raised by the notion of a physical inbreathing in Genesis 2:7. Philo asks, first of all, why God breathed into "the earthly and body-loving mind" of Genesis 2 rather than the Platonic ideal of the mind in

---

History of Interpretation, Catholic Biblical Quarterly Monograph Series 14 (Washington, DC: Catholic Biblical Association of America, 1983), p. 78. When he interprets the curse of Genesis 3:14, "earth you shall eat all the days of your life," Philo presses the Stoic interpretation of Genesis 2:7 even more vigorously: "The body, then, has been formed out of earth, but the soul is of the *aether,* a particle detached from the Deity: 'for God breathed into his face breath of life, and the human became a living soul'" (*Allegorical Interpretation* 3.161). See also *On Dreams* 1.34 and *Who Is the Heir?* 283.

Genesis 1, which he understood as the image of God (Gen. 1:26-27).[43] Philo responds that God loves to give, *even to the imperfect,* in order to encourage in them a "zeal for virtue." The inbreathing, then, is the means by which God "created no soul barren of virtue, even if the exercise of it be to some impossible" (*Allegorical Interpretation* 1.34).

Philo continues on the theme of virtue by pressing the point that those "into whom real life" has been breathed now bear responsibility for the exercise of virtue. Had God not inbreathed this authentic life into those "without experience of virtue," they might have claimed injustice in God's punishment. It was God's fault that they sinned, they might have argued, because they failed through ignorance and inexperience. Now, they have no right to blame God for having "failed to breathe into him [or her] any conception of" virtue.[44]

The second question Philo raises is simply what the verb *breathed into* means.[45] In the context of a complex answer, Philo associates the inbreathing with the ability to conceive of God: "For how could the soul have conceived of God, had God not breathed into it and mightily laid hold of it?"[46] Simply put, inbreathing allows humans to conceive of God.

In the third question — why God breathed into the *face* — virtue retains its prominent role. By incorporating Stoic physiology, Philo is prepared to contend that God breathes only into the mind, which in turn inspires that portion of the soul which is devoid of reason:

> As the face is the dominant element in the body, so is the mind the dominant element of the soul: into this only does God breathe. . . . For the mind imparts to the portion of the soul that is devoid of reason a share of that which it has received from God. . . . For the mind is, so to speak, God of the unreasoning part.[47]

The inbreathing of Genesis 2:7, therefore, is much more than a mere making alive of a body. It is the impartation of the capacity for virtue, the possibility of knowing God, the vitalization of the mind, the purest portion of a human being, which shares its substance with the cosmos. Little wonder, according to Philo, that the first man lived in unalloyed bliss, in

43. Philo Judaeus, *Allegorical Interpretation* 1.33.
44. Philo Judaeus, *Allegorical Interpretation* 1.35.
45. Philo Judaeus, *Allegorical Interpretation* 1.33.
46. Philo Judaeus, *Allegorical Interpretation* 1.38.
47. Philo Judaeus, *Allegorical Interpretation* 1.39-40.

concert with the stars, "since the divine *spirit* had flowed into him in full current." Because of this current, the first man "earnestly endeavoured in all his words and actions to please the Father and King, following God step by step in the highways cut out by virtues. . . ."[48]

Spirit-Breath in Early Judaism: Summary

When the curtain rises on the human drama, revealing an unspoiled garden, the human being, who is merely dust from the earth, rises when the creator God meets him face-to-face in order to breathe life into him. This is a simple scene, an intimate scene.

Compare this simplicity with the complexity of Philo's take on the action. This is no intimate contact between a creator and the creation. Philo understands this moment of inspiration in anything but such simple terms. This may be the impartation of the human mind — but it is no wind within. It may be the gift of deity — but it is no simple puff of enlivening breath. It may be the infusion of a capacity for virtue — but it is certainly no mere inbreathing of clay. Despite the complexity of his commentaries, Philo never forfeits his fascination with the divine inbreathing. On the contrary, he is riveted by this first moment of inspiration to the extent that he cites it, word for word, dozens and dozens of times in his effort to explain the generosity of God, the incomparable gift of "real life," the unparalleled capacity for virtue, the inestimable opportunity for an intimate knowledge of God that this first breath gives to human beings.

Other Jewish authors are no less aware of the inspiration that renders all human beings capable of virtue. The author of the Wisdom of Solomon, who understands Genesis 2:7 as the temporary loan of a soul, opens his book of wisdom with a fleeting reference to the "holy spirit of discipline" that flees from deceit. Though this reference to a holy spirit is terse, it is enough to provide the basis for the Sage's teaching on the pursuit of virtue and wisdom.

This appreciation for a holy spirit within was not the exclusive intellectual property of the Alexandrian Jewish philosophical tradition. The quaint tale of the book of Susanna also expresses the conviction that the

48. Philo Judaeus, *On the Creation* 144. For further discussion and bibliography, see my *Portraits of Adam,* pp. 81-82, 84-85. More recently, see Jonathan Worthington, *Creation in Paul and Philo: The Beginning and Before,* Wissenschaftliche Untersuchungen zum Neuen Testament 2.317 (Tübingen: Mohr Siebeck, 2011).

spirit within is the locus of virtue. There are no surprises here, as Daniel, in the book named for him, is characterized time and again by an extraordinary spirit within, by a robust degree of spirit, even by a holy spirit, according to various Greek translations. Nor is there any surprise in the metamorphosis of a scriptural expression, "God prompted the spirit," by the addition of the word *holy:* "God prompted the *holy* spirit of a young man . . ." The book of Daniel depicts a young man of extraordinary integrity who faithfully hones his skills through fasting and study. To introduce him now without the necessity of explanation, as the author of the tale of Susanna does, as a young man whose holy spirit compels him to uncover injustice, is entirely in character with the stories that circulated around his rise to power in the courts of the Babylonians and Medians.

All of these ancient texts share the conviction that the locus of virtue in human beings is a holy spirit that God prompts (Daniel and Susanna), a holy spirit that can be defiled *(Damascus Document)* and exchanged for financial security *(4QInstruction),* and a "holy spirit of discipline" that flees deceit *(Wisdom of Solomon).* Philo alone does not adopt the actual words *holy spirit.* Yet Philo, despite the intricacy of his interpretation and his preference for the words *divine spirit,* offers us the richest glimpse of a world bursting with the holy spirit. In this world, other authors, though with less flamboyance than Philo, referred readily, unequivocally, unambiguously to the locus of virtue and wisdom within as the holy spirit.[49]

Spirit-Breath within in Early Christianity

Return with me for a moment to the warm radiator on the living room floor in that worn corner of Kansas City, where I may — or may not — have spoken in tongues. Follow my thinking from there to the likelihood that my quest for the ecstatic, the uncontrollable, the unknowable was ill-advised. What you've read so far suggests instead that I needed to experience the spirit in me already, the spirit-breath as a locus of virtue and learning.

Is this interpretation of the spirit just sour grapes? Did I begin to believe this because I hadn't spoken in tongues in a definitive way? Or was

49. The Septuagint translation of Psalm 51:12-14 (LXX Psalm 50) is less ambiguous than the Hebrew original because it contains several translational pointers to an understanding of the holy spirit as the spirit-breath within human beings. For a detailed discussion, see my *Spirit in First-Century Judaism,* pp. 67-68.

I, deep down, afraid of the experience to which I thought I was attracted? The church I first learned my faith in was afraid. When I was a young boy, one man would speak gibberish during our worship service. He was Hispanic, so I figured he was speaking Spanish. I learned later that the elders ordered him to leave because he spoke in tongues. A decade or so later, when I was fifteen, a visiting minister came to our house and pronounced, with unnerving confidence, that the words in 1 Corinthians 13:10, "when the perfect comes, the imperfect will pass away," mean that the gift of speaking in tongues is no longer viable. The "perfect" was the Bible; once the Bible arrived, there was no more need for "imperfect" spiritual gifts. A few years later still, once I had decided to head to Wheaton College in Illinois rather than to one of our Bible colleges, a church leader pulled me aside and whispered, "You don't want to go to Wheaton. I hear they speak in tongues out there."

Perhaps my whole interpretative agenda is misdirected. Am I championing an arcane strand of an obsolete portion of scripture — the so-called Old Testament — which the New Testament has surpassed and superseded? Does my proposal — that the Hebrew Bible and early Jewish literature preserve a tradition in which the spirit-breath from birth is the locus of virtue and learning — create an irreparable rift between the testaments and privilege the first over the second? Is there nothing in the New Testament about the holy spirit in human beings for the long haul that tethers it to the Jewish Bible and the Jewish people?

There is. Though slight, there are pinpricks of this tradition in the New Testament, where the locus of virtue and learning is the lifelong spirit within. In the next few pages, we will probe some of these New Testament texts.

Yet another point of connection binds the testaments via early Judaism. Many passages about the holy spirit in the New Testament, despite its strong conviction that the spirit is given in an endowment long after birth, reflect the impulses of the Old Testament, with their deep appreciation for the life of the mind, with their embrace of inspired learning, with their accent on the practice of virtue. The holy spirit may not be understood as a gift from birth, but the qualities of the spirit, when the spirit is given, coalesce around virtue and learning.

As we continue our study of the holy spirit in antiquity, therefore, I will draw your attention first to those places in the New Testament — admittedly just a few — where the spirit from birth is the locus of virtue and wisdom. I will then identify those places where the holy spirit, although a charismatic endowment in the new creation rather than a gift from birth, is the handmaid of virtue and wisdom.

The Lifelong Spirit within as the Locus of Virtue and Learning

The conviction that virtue resides in a holy spirit, whether it is expressed in the simple language of the tale of Susanna, in which Daniel's holy spirit is prompted, or the flamboyant language of Philo's commentaries, in which God inbreathes into every human being the capacity for virtue, offers a slender segue to the convictions of early Christian authors. Their letters and stories and apocalypse contain vestiges of this conception of the holy spirit, a holy spirit given to all human beings by dint of creation, a spirit that can be cultivated through study and discipline, a spirit that is the locus of virtue. This sort of holy spirit nearly evaporates in early Christian writings, where the good gifts of God arrive with a subsequent filling by the holy spirit. Still, vestiges of Israel's conception of the spirit within remain.

SUCH REMNANTS SURFACE occasionally in Paul's letters, as in 2 Corinthians 6:6-7, where the expression "holy spirit" is included in a list of virtues: "by purity, by knowledge, by patience, by kindness, by (a) holy spirit, by genuine love, by truthful speech, and by the power of God. . . ."[50] This may be a reference to *the* Holy Spirit as the driving force of Paul's ministry rather than a holy human spirit. In light of the early Jewish identification

---

50. Paul is aware of the distinction between the divine spirit and the human spirit, for he refers in Romans 8:16 to "that very spirit bearing witness with our spirit that we are children of God." This distinction is evident in 1 Corinthians 2:11, where Paul attempts to explain the divine spirit through a comparison with the human spirit: "For what human being knows what is truly human except the human spirit that is within? So also no one comprehends what is truly God's except the Spirit of God." It is this spirit within that can pray and sing without the mind or, as Paul prefers, in tandem with the mind (14:14-16). A similar conception applies to prophesying in 1 Corinthians 14:32, where the prophets have responsibility over their own spirits. For a recent discussion of this issue, see Desta Heliso, "Divine Spirit and Human Spirit in Paul in the Light of Stoic and Biblical-Jewish Perspectives," in *The Spirit and Christ in the New Testament and Christian Theology,* ed. I. Howard Marshall, Volker Rabens, and Cornelis Bennema (Grand Rapids: Eerdmans, 2012), pp. 156-76. More generally, see the fine study of Volker Rabens, *The Holy Spirit and Ethics in Paul: Transformation and Empowering for Religious-Ethical Life,* Wissenschaftliche Untersuchungen zum Neuen Testament 2.283 (Tübingen: Mohr Siebeck, 2010).

of the spirit within as a holy spirit, however, and this particular context, with its catalogue of virtues, these words fit the Israelite and early Jewish conviction that the holy spirit with which God has endowed human beings is the locus of virtue.[51]

Paul also expresses his conviction that the human spirit, the locus of holiness and virtue, can be tainted, as in the *Damascus Document,* or even exchanged, in a loose sense, as in *4QInstruction,* when he advises the Corinthian church to exclude a man who commits the egregious sin of living with his father's wife. Paul hopes with this decision that "his spirit may be saved in the day of the Lord" (1 Cor. 5:5). When Paul turns his attention, slightly later in the letter, to sexual relations within marriage, he writes that an unmarried woman is free from worry about human affairs, such as pleasing a husband; she can instead "be holy in body and spirit" (1 Cor. 7:34).[52] Then, in support of his view that believers should not be too intimately associated with unbelievers, Paul urges the Corinthians to cleanse themselves "from every defilement of body and of spirit, making holiness perfect in the fear of God" (2 Cor. 7:1). Each of these brief bits of Paul's Corinthian correspondence provides a sliver of his conviction that the spirit within, though not to the exclusion of the body, can become holy by the practice of virtue, by single-minded devotion (1 Cor. 7:34), by a process of self-cleansing (2 Cor. 7:1).

It is tempting perhaps to see this spirit as the *human* spirit rather than *the Holy Spirit.* Without any knowledge of Judaism, in which the apostle was reared and educated, we might succumb to this temptation. Yet Philo's commentaries on Genesis 2:7 put the lie to this exegetical judgment. For Philo or the author of the Wisdom of Solomon, even for the authors who composed the stories of Daniel and Susanna, and certainly for the writers of the Dead Sea Scrolls, the human spirit *is* a divinely given holy spirit — even *the* holy spirit. The distinction between a human and holy spirit becomes moot for a skilled interpreter such as Philo, for whom the inbreathing of breath in Genesis 2:7 is the impartation of the capacity for virtue, the gift of deity, a fragment of the divine. We need to resist interpretations that draw an unnecessary wedge between these spirits,

---

51. The last four items in the list contain a noun and an adjective or a noun with a genitive noun; in other words, literary consistency demands that we acknowledge the adjectival character of the word *holy;* it is not merely an identity marker, or a technical term, to indicate that this is "the holy spirit."

52. See also the triad of spirit, soul, and body, which are to be kept sound and blameless, according to 1 Thessalonians 5:23.

INSPIRED

because Paul was not a nineteenth-, twentieth-, or twenty-first-century Christian. Paul was a first-century Jew raised in a Greco-Roman world in which Stoicism was the regnant popular philosophy. For such Jews, the spirit within *was* a holy spirit.

Paul's clearest reference to the spirit from birth occurs in a flurry of references to the spirit in his letter to the Romans. After urging his readers to live by the spirit rather than the flesh because they have received a "spirit of adoption" rather than a "spirit of slavery," Paul draws a connection between the spirit given at birth and the spirit given with faith: "When we cry, 'Abba! Father!' it is that very spirit bearing witness with our spirit that we are children of God, and if children, then heirs . . ." (Rom. 8:15-16). Of forty-seven words in this section, six — about thirteen percent — are the word *pneuma*. In this cluster of references, Paul is clear about one thing: the spirit of God cooperates with our spirit(s)[53] in a prayer that expresses an intimate relationship between human beings and God. The cry "Abba! Father!" is a pure and direct expression of living as God's children rather than as slaves to fear. In a backhanded sort of way, this text testifies to the powerful place of the spirit given at birth. *Our* spirit is the primary mover in prayer, the locus of the relationship between God and the believer, the place from which humans cry "Abba! Father!" The spirit of God may confirm this prayer, but it does not prompt or inspire this prayer. This prompting, that inspiration, comes from within.

Despite Paul's unshakable belief that Christians live in a new creation, empowered by a magnificent spirit, then, he continues to believe that within human beings lies an inner person, a spirit within, where one finds a locus of prayer and a landscape of renewal.[54] Paul may believe that the

53. Literally, "with our spirit," though the noun should perhaps be interpreted as a reference to "our spirits."

54. If Paul's undisputed letters offer at least a few unambiguous glimpses of a spirit that can be holy, the Pastoral letters contain one of the most puzzling references to the spirit in early Christian literature. Timothy is urged "to rekindle the gift of God that is within you through the laying on of my hands; for God did not give us a spirit of cowardice, but rather a spirit of power and of love and of self-discipline" (2 Tim. 1:6-7). Is this spirit what filled Timothy from birth or what filled him subsequently in tandem with the laying on of hands? On the one hand, this spirit is described by means of a list of virtues — power, love, and self-control. This, of course, fits neatly the conception of a holy spirit as the locus of virtue. The contrast of this spirit with cowardice, moreover, mirrors the Wisdom of Solomon, in which the spirit is portrayed as strong and courageous, "for a holy spirit of discipline will flee from deceit . . . and be ashamed at the approach of injustice . . ." (Wisd. 1:5). Nor does the portrayal of Daniel's holy spirit, which is prompted courageously to decry injustice, lie

spirit is a divine endowment given in relation to faith, but he does not forfeit altogether his conviction that the spirit within is also a locus of virtue.

THE SPIRIT WITHIN from birth appears as well in the opening of Luke's Gospel. John the Baptist, Luke writes, "grew and became strong in spirit, and he was in the wilderness until the day he appeared publicly to Israel" (Luke 1:80). This statement precisely parallels the progressive maturing of the child Jesus, who "grew and became strong, filled with wisdom" (2:40a):

> The child grew and became strong *in spirit* . . . (1:80)
> The child grew and became strong, *filled with wisdom* . . . (2:40)

In these depictions of John and Jesus, "in spirit" and "filled with wisdom" occupy parallel positions, following the verbs *grew* and *became strong*. Luke does not supplant the Israelite and early Jewish conception of the spirit as the lifelong locus of virtue with belief in a subsequent infilling, which will become familiar territory in the inspired sermons that pepper the gospels and the book of Acts. Here, long before the descent of the dove, the spirit's guidance in the wilderness and powerful preaching impelled by the spirit, there is still the spirit from birth that can become strong and full of wisdom.

This Israelite and early Jewish association of the spirit with wisdom reemerges in the book of Acts when the fledgling church, early in its life together, faces the need for racial reconciliation. Greek-speaking widows from the far-flung Jewish Dispersion are neglected in the distribution of food; Hebrew- or Aramaic-speaking widows, who are at home in their

---

far afield of the contrast that is drawn between Timothy's spirit and a spirit of cowardice (Susanna 44–45). This piece of advice, against this background and in this context, would be a reminder to Timothy that the core God has given him, the essential strength, the vitality that he possesses by virtue of being human, must continually be kindled. Timothy is urged to dig deep into that resource, to delve into that reservoir of power, love, self-discipline, to rekindle the fire that is in his spirit because Paul laid his hands upon him. On the other hand, this could be a simple reference to the gift of the spirit that Timothy received subsequently. The verb *give* occurs frequently in the New Testament to describe a subsequent gift of the spirit. (See *Filled with the Spirit,* pp. 253-67.) The gift of God within may be nothing other than the spirit that was given to Timothy when he became a believer. Ultimately it may not be possible to determine whether the author of the Pastoral letters understands the spirit as the vitality that all human beings possess — vitality that Timothy is urged to rekindle into a life of power, love, and discipline rather than cowardice — or as a gift that was given to Timothy by the laying on of hands.

native Jerusalem, are not. The church's resolve results in an amicable solution that avoids an early apartheid. The leaders of the church, its apostles, understand their vocation with unwavering clarity. "It is not right," they announce, "that we should neglect the word of God . . ." (Acts 6:2). They know what they have to do, and this is not to serve food to hungry widows. Yet the apostles also recognize that even mundane matters are essential to church life. So along with this announcement, they make a recommendation. "Select from among yourselves seven men of good standing, full of spirit and of wisdom, whom we may appoint to this task, while we, for our part, will devote ourselves to prayer and to serving the word" (6:3).

For all of its practicality, this is a startling recommendation because the character of the people they select seems disproportionate to the task at hand; they are people of integrity, full of (the) spirit, and wise. Stephen, one of them, is "full of faith and holy spirit" (Acts 6:5). This is a stupendous group, whose purpose is relatively pedestrian: "to wait on tables" in the daily distribution of food to widows. Why they should require integrity, inspiration, faith, and wisdom is not clear — until we realize that the words *waiting on tables* could also entail tabulating tables or, in modern parlance, creating spreadsheets or keeping financial tables. They ensure that everyone is fed, that communal provisions are distributed equitably.

By pulling back the curtain of a dispute in the early church, we are able to glimpse again the lavishness of a wise spirit within, the supersaturated measure of a holy spirit, of wisdom, of faith. These men, in short, are the heirs of Joseph, who excelled in practical administration, of Bezalel, whom God filled with spirit of God, wisdom, intelligence, and knowledge of every craft to construct a tent in the desert, and of Daniel, who had spirit to the nth degree and, like Joseph long before him, a keen eye for administration.[55]

IF TRACES OF THIS TRADITION remain in the Fourth Gospel, they are virtually undetectable. Even the characterization of Jesus is barely recognizable from the standpoint of the belief that human beings receive at birth the gift of a holy or divine spirit. The closest the Fourth Gospel brushes against this perspective lies in a possible oblique association between the laying down of his life (John 10:17; 15:13)[56] and Jesus' handing over of spirit or breath on the cross (19:30). This is only a distant cousin

55. On the ambiguity of "spirit" in Acts 6–7, see *Filled with the Spirit,* pp. 243-45.
56. See also John 13:37.

to the conception of the holy spirit of Daniel or the holy spirit that can be forfeited and defiled in the Dead Sea Scrolls or the divine *pneuma* that flowed into the first human "in full current," so that he "earnestly endeavoured in all his words and actions to please the Father and King, following God step by step in the highways cut out by virtues. . . ."[57] John lays no emphasis upon the potential for virtue or learning that resides in the spirit within. If John is saying that "Jesus possibly handed over the divine Spirit that had sustained his physical life as well as empowered his mission," he does so with stunning subtlety.[58]

Another possible brush with this tradition lies earlier in the Gospel, toward the conclusion of Jesus' soliloquy about the life-giving bread: "It is the spirit that gives life; the flesh is useless. The words that I have spoken to you are spirit and life" (John 6:63). The contrast of flesh and spirit, alongside the association of words and spirit, may suggest that the spirit about which Jesus is speaking in this context is "the life-giving spirit . . . Jesus' breath, the breath from his mouth on which his spoken words are carried."[59] The clarity of this spirit-breath, however, is muddied by Jesus' earlier reception of the spirit at his baptism (1:32-33). Jesus *already,* in the Fourth Gospel, has received an endowment of the spirit. If, therefore, John preserves the traditional association of words and spirit-breath, he does not make it clear that this is the spirit Jesus received at birth. In the narrative context of the Fourth Gospel, on the contrary, the inspiration of Jesus must be traced primarily, if not exclusively, to his reception of the spirit at his baptism.

THIS CONCEPTION OF THE SPIRIT, however, may underlie one of early Christianity's most enigmatic references to the spirit:

> For if the blood of goats and bulls, with the sprinkling of the ashes of a heifer, sanctifies those who have been defiled so that their flesh is purified, how much more will the blood of Christ, who through the eternal spirit offered himself without blemish to God, purify our conscience from dead works to worship the living God! (Heb. 9:13-14)

57. Philo Judaeus, *On the Creation* 144.
58. Bennema, *Saving Wisdom*, p. 253.
59. Delbert Burkett, *The Son of Man in the Gospel of John,* Journal for the Study of the New Testament Supplement Series 56 (Sheffield, UK: Sheffield Academic, 1991), pp. 139-40.

First things first: in the Greek, the words *eternal spirit* do not have a definite article, as in English translations, so we cannot assume that these words refer to "*the* Holy Spirit" understood as a charismatic endowment, as in so many other New Testament texts. The words can be translated in different ways:

"through the eternal spirit," with a definite article added
"through an eternal spirit," with an indefinite article added
"through eternal spirit," with nothing added

The absence of the definite article in the original text makes it difficult to know how to understand this eternal spirit.

Perhaps this eternal spirit is *the* holy spirit, just as, slightly later, the "spirit of grace" is another way of referring to the holy spirit (Heb. 10:18). The author's preference for the word *eternal* rather than *holy* in this context may be due to the force of rhetoric. He or she adopts the word *eternal* three times: of redemption (9:12); of spirit (9:14); of inheritance (9:15). The question, then, is whether the holy spirit, from the author's perspective, came to Jesus to aid him as he underwent death. We might point, as a parallel, to Romans 1:4, where Jesus was raised from the dead by the spirit of holiness. According to this interpretation, the eternal spirit is the means by which Jesus offered himself in death (and not, as in Romans, the means by which he was raised from the dead). Although there is no hint of this interpretation in the gospels, the author of this letter may be communicating that the eternal spirit came to Jesus to strengthen him to face death, perhaps by giving him a vision of the eternal salvation he was about to inaugurate and a glimpse of the eternal covenant he was about to initiate.

Another alternative is possible: a lifelong spirit — the spirit-breath Jesus cultivated over the course of a lifetime — gave him the fortitude to undergo death en route to the eternal covenant, the eternal salvation of the resurrection. Understood from this perspective as the eternal spirit within Jesus for the long haul, the logic becomes clear: because he had within him an eternal spirit, a spirit with eternal qualities, like Daniel's spirit to the nth degree, Jesus was able to offer himself without blemish. Recall Psalm 51, where the psalmist begs for a clean heart, a right spirit, and a willing spirit (51:10-12), or Daniel's holy spirit in the story of Susanna, or the holy spirit in the Dead Sea Scrolls that must not be forfeited for money, or the spirit of John the Baptist that grew strong, according to the

Gospel of Luke. Similarly, Jesus is said to have within him an eternal spirit that makes it possible for him to endure the horror of his death because it accomplishes nothing less than eternal redemption (Heb. 9:12) and yields nothing less than an eternal inheritance (Heb. 9:15). Such a spirit within Jesus matches — and makes possible — the salvation that the author of this letter depicts in magnificent terms as "eternal salvation" (5:9), "eternal judgment" (6:2), and the blood of the "eternal covenant" (13:20).

The New Creation, Learning, and Virtue

The small number of New Testament texts that sustain a view of the spirit given at birth as the locus of learning and virtue is an indication of how little confidence early Christian authors placed in the old creation rather than the new. There is no Joseph, whose clairvoyance and practical advice are so stunning that the Pharaoh knows of no one else in whom there is a spirit of God. There is no Daniel in the early church, who for three generations is full to the nth degree with spirit, a strapping figure who would shape the destiny of empires, whose holy spirit God would prompt to rise in outcry against the injustice perpetrated against a wholly innocent Susanna. There is no Bezalel, a learned, skilled craftsman in whom the spirit existed, full to overflowing, because he had mastered a full range of crafts required to build the unlikeliest of tents for God in a godforsaken desert. There is no simple command to avoid at all costs defiling one's holy spirit. Nor is there anything as strongly worded as Philo's belief that the inbreathing of Genesis 2:7 imparted a capacity for virtue.

When we turn to the New Testament, it is hard to ignore the all-encompassing character of an exclamation such as, "if anyone is in Christ, there is a new creation: everything old has passed away; see, everything has become new!" (2 Cor. 5:17). Even the act of faith is depicted by Paul as an act of creation: "For it is the God who said, 'Let light shine out of darkness,' who has shone in our hearts to give the light of the knowledge of the glory of God in the face of Jesus Christ" (4:6). In the letter to the Colossians, the language of Genesis 1:26, of clothing oneself with "the new self, which is being renewed in knowledge according to the image of its creator," is integral to a bold vision of humankind free of distinctions between Greek and Jew or slave and free (Col. 3:10-11). Paul's mirror-image contrast of the first and second Adams, too, reveals thoughtful and thorough reflection upon two nodal points of existence: the entry of sin and its companion, death, at life's beginning (Rom. 5:12-21) and the erasure of sin and its companion, death, at life's end (1 Cor. 15:42-58).

Paul's radical division between old and new creation shares a family resemblance with the book of Acts, in which a tidy line between belief and unbelief shapes community and mission. The baseline from which all variations emerge is a direct plea for repentance: "Peter said to them, 'Repent, and be baptized every one of you in the name of Jesus Christ so that your sins may be forgiven; and you will receive the gift of the holy spirit. For the promise is for you, for your children, and for all who are far away, everyone whom the Lord our God calls to him'" (Acts 2:38-39). Paul's speech in Athens, on the other hand, in which he claims that God "gives to all mortals life and breath and all things," is met with far less success than Peter's (17:25). When Paul blurs the lines between believer and unbeliever by portraying God as the giver of breath to all people, as a God who is near at hand to every person (17:27), there is no overwhelming response, no recounting of thousands upon thousands of baptisms.

The Fourth Gospel, in which the paraclete is prepared to reveal marvelous knowledge, exhibits no less consanguinity with the letters of Paul and the book of Acts. What knowledge the paraclete will reveal is strictly unavailable to a world that is shaped by the values of the old creation, by the darkness of this world. There is no one among the Jews of the Fourth Gospel who is filled to the brim with a spirit that has been cultivated through patient waiting, prayer, and practice. There is no holy spirit within men and women that God can prompt. There is no divine spirit within that guides the characters who populate the Fourth Gospel along an uninterrupted path to virtue.

We might be led by this little survey to conclude that this radical disjuncture precludes the possibility of continuity between the old and new creations. Drawing such a conclusion, however, would be an egregious misjudgment, because there is a good deal of continuity between old and new. What happens in much of the New Testament is this: *the qualities of the spirit given at birth are transferred to the spirit given as an endowment later in life.* The spirit given to believers, received by believers, becomes the locus of virtue and learning. The hues change slightly. Emphases shift a bit. Yet in the end there is a strong resemblance between the qualities of the spirit within from birth and the qualities of the spirit given to believers as a gift. Preeminent among these qualities are virtue, learning, holiness — and the various activities that accompany them.

WE HARDLY HAVE TO EXCAVATE the New Testament to discover the early church's keen commitment to learning and virtue. No sooner do we open its pages than we see Jesus learning something when he receives the spirit at his baptism: he is God's beloved son, with whom God is pleased.[60] Upon closer scrutiny, we see that he has learned more than this through allusions in God's words. "This is my son, the beloved," recall the words spoken to the king in Psalm 2:7: Jesus is royalty. "With whom I am well pleased" recall the words spoken to the servant of Isaiah 42:1, who brings good news to the nations and lives to die in silent suffering on behalf of others (Isa. 52:13–53:12). Jesus learns, in brief, that his vocation is to become a suffering king, a royal servant. The spirit does not simply vanish, however, after descending like a dove upon Jesus at his baptism. It expels Jesus (in Mark's Gospel), leads him into the desert (in Matthew's Gospel), or guides Jesus in the desert (in Luke's Gospel), where Jesus undergoes a period of intense discipline that includes forty days of fasting. In the desert he learns, while forgoing food, that the angels care for him, the animals cooperate with him, and the devil cannot overcome him.

The single promise Jesus makes in the Gospel of Mark also encompasses the realm of discipline:

> As for yourselves, beware; for they will hand you over to councils; and you will be beaten in synagogues; and you will stand before governors and kings because of me, as a testimony to them. And the gospel must first be proclaimed to all nations. When they bring you to trial and hand you over, do not worry beforehand about what you are to say; but say whatever is given you at that time, for it is not you who speak, but the holy spirit. Brother will betray brother to death, and a father his child, and children will rise against parents and have them put to death; and you will be hated by all because of my name. But the one who endures to the end will be saved. (Mark 13:9-13)

In this prediction, Jesus promises the holy spirit exclusively to people in mission who are handed over, against their will, to official councils, people about to be punished through official channels, who are dragged before high government officials. Then, and only then, will the holy spirit speak for them and in them. The word they receive will not consist of a miraculous dénouement; the spirit will speak in testimony, even while

---

60. See Matthew 3:13-17.

the speakers are asked to "endure to the end" in the face of hostility and hatred (Mark 13:13).

The mechanics of inspiration — if inspiration is the right word to describe a word of *martyrion* that leads to martyrdom — Mark leaves vague. Luke, in contrast, preserves parallel versions of this saying, and in the first, he clarifies, as Mark does not, the mode by which Jesus' disciples will receive what they are to say: "When they bring you before the synagogues, the rulers, and the authorities, do not worry about how you are to defend yourselves or what you are to say; for the holy spirit will teach you at that very hour what you ought to say" (Luke 12:11-12). *Teach.* Even when their backs are to the wall, Jesus' disciples will be precisely that — disciples — students whom the holy spirit teaches. In another version of this saying, Luke leaves the mechanics vague but adds the word *wisdom,* with which he is able to indicate that the product of the spirit is not spontaneous exclamations: "So make up your minds not to prepare your defense in advance; for I will give you words [a mouth] and a wisdom that none of your opponents will be able to withstand or contradict" (Luke 21:14-15).

This portrayal of what is in store foreshadows the compelling and comprehensible witness of Stephen in the book of Acts, about whose opponents Luke writes, "But they could not *withstand* the *wisdom* and the spirit with which he spoke" (Acts 6:10). Stephen's speech, which follows, is a model of rhetorical force — well organized, focused, and incendiary — in which Stephen argues to the death that God is not bound to the temple or the land (Acts 7:1–8:1). Luke has made the point crystal clear: the spirit has taught Stephen well how to testify wisely in the throes of hostility.

Elsewhere in the book of Acts, learning and virtue go hand in hand in the building up of strong churches. In Antioch (a church we will explore in detail in the next chapter), the spirit spoke a word that opened the floodgates of mission: "While they were worshiping the Lord and fasting, the holy spirit said, 'Set apart for me Barnabas and Saul for the work to which I have called them'" (Acts 13:2). This word came to a church with a penchant for learning. Earlier, Barnabas had brought Saul to Antioch, where "for an entire year they met with the church and taught a great many people" (11:26). Alongside spiritual disciplines — fasting, prayer, and worship — a thirst to learn characterized life for the believers in Antioch. This combination of communal practice and learning made Antioch the perfect place from which the spirit would launch a mission into Asia Minor.

We will see in chapter three that the relationship between study and the spirit is the quintessential expression of inspiration throughout the book of Acts. Time and again, the spirit equips believers to speak, and they speak, with remarkable consistency, as the interpreters of scripture. This activity of the spirit also characterizes the Fourth Gospel (though a detailed study of this particular dimension of inspiration will have to wait until chapter three). For now, we can observe generally that Jesus' promise of the holy spirit, the paraclete, in the Fourth Gospel is rife with the language of teaching and learning. Twice Jesus refers to the spirit *of truth* (John 14:17; 16:13), a description that recalls what he said earlier to the Samaritan woman, as they spoke next to a well: "But the hour is coming, and is now here, when the true worshipers will worship the Father in spirit and truth, for the Father seeks such as these to worship him. God is spirit, and those who worship him must worship in spirit and truth" (4:23-24). Truth is a spiritual matter; the spirit must bring truth in its train. By the same token, worship must offer a combination of both truth and spirit. Jesus also promises that the paraclete will: teach and remind believers (14:26); prove the world wrong about sin, righteousness, and judgment (16:7-11); and guide believers into (or in) all the truth, speak whatever it hears, declare the things that are to come, take what is Jesus' and declare it to them (16:13-15). In a gospel that is indebted to a vision of listening and learning, one that is rooted in the wisdom tradition, one in which Jesus as the *logos* speaks words that are "spirit and life" (6:63), it comes as no surprise that the spirit of truth, the holy spirit, the paraclete, is nothing if not a teacher and a revealer.

THESE ACTIVITIES MIRROR Paul's description of the spirit as revealer and teacher in his first letter to the Corinthians (1 Cor. 2:10-13). Paul launches the first section of this fascinating and occasionally provocative letter by recalling that he came to Corinth without rhetorical polish, that he approached the Corinthians with weakness, fear, and trembling. "My speech and my proclamation were not with plausible words of wisdom," he reminds them, "but with a demonstration of the spirit and of power, so that your faith might rest not on human wisdom but on the power of God" (1 Cor. 2:4-5).[61] The principal lesson of 1 Corinthians 2 is that the

---

61. Elsewhere in Paul's letters, power produces hope (Rom. 5:5; 15:19; 2 Cor. 2:21-22), signs and wonders, as in Romans 15:19, where Paul describes the obedience of the nations that has been won by word and deed, "by the power of signs and wonders, by the power of the spirit of God" (see Gal. 3:5), and full conviction in hearers, as in the case of the Thes-

content of his message — and not just the demeanor of the messenger or the response of the hearers or attendant miraculous activities — consists of weakness: "For I decided to know nothing among you except Jesus Christ, and him crucified" (2:2).

Trustworthy content is an essential endowment of the holy spirit. So too is virtue. Even miracles are not a substitute for the virtues of the spirit. In his letter to the Galatians, Paul casts an eye toward virtue when he draws a direct contrast between the works of the flesh, such as impurity, quarrels, and envy, and the works of the spirit: "love, joy, peace, patience, kindness, generosity, faithfulness, gentleness, and self-control."[62] Spirit and the cultivation of virtues go hand in hand, even for a community, Paul recalls, that experienced miracles firsthand (Gal. 3:1-5).

One particularly urgent passage in Paul's letters emblematizes the liaison between the *holy* spirit and *holiness.* In 1 Thessalonians 4:8, Paul throws his weight around — what he has to say must be important — and writes, "Therefore whoever rejects this rejects not human authority but God, who also gives his holy spirit into you." The syntax of this reference to the spirit is slightly odd. First, Paul adopts the verb *give,* rather than his preferred verb, *send.* Second, his choice of the preposition is atypical; he says the spirit is given "into you," rather than, as we might expect, "to you," or "in you." The reason for these oddities is Paul's indebtedness to Ezekiel 37. Twice in this vision of the valley of very many, very dry bones, we find the expression, "*give* my spirit *into* you/them . . ." (Ezek. 37:5, 6, 10, 14). Paul preserves nuggets of Ezekiel's grand vision, though he absorbs the language of Ezekiel into a particular concrete concern: *sexual purity.* "For this is the will of God," Paul writes, "your sanctification: that you abstain from fornication" (1 Thess. 4:3). The portion of the letter in which Paul urges the Thessalonians to maintain a life of sexual purity ends with an admonition that is grounded in Ezekiel 37: "Therefore whoever rejects this rejects not human authority but God, who also *gives* his holy spirit *into* you."

Ezekiel's vision of the renewal of Israel, which contains the highest concentration of references to the spirit in the entire Hebrew Bible, communicates two themes that are essential for the interpretation of 1 Thessalonians 4:3-8. One is sanctification and holiness: God's name will be

---

salonians, to whom he writes, "our message of the gospel came to you not in word only, but also in power and in the holy spirit and with full conviction" (1 Thess. 1:5).

62. Galatians 5:19-22.

sanctified when Israel lives in the presence of the nations in holiness. The other is the knowledge of God. These themes coalesce in Ezekiel 36:23:

> I will sanctify my great name, which has been profaned among the nations, and which you have profaned among them; and the nations shall know that I am the LORD, says the Lord GOD, when through you I display my holiness before their eyes.

Both themes, holiness (or making holy — sanctification) and the knowledge of God, reemerge in Paul's letter to the Thessalonians, in a discussion of sexuality that ends with an exclamation point rooted in Ezekiel 37: "who also gives his holy spirit into you." Paul picks up three facets of Ezekiel's vision — the spirit given into Israel, holiness, and knowledge of God — and adapts them to the situation of the Thessalonians.

> For this is the will of God, your sanctification: that you abstain from fornication; that each one of you knows how to control your own body in holiness and honor, not with lustful passion, like the Gentiles who do not know God; that no one wrongs or exploits a brother or sister in this matter, because the Lord is an avenger in all these things, just as we have already told you beforehand and solemnly warned you. For God did not call us to impurity but in holiness. Therefore whoever rejects this rejects not human authority but God, who also gives his holy spirit to you. (1 Thess. 4:3-8)

No longer is the vision one of national resurrection, though on a much smaller scale, the themes remain relevant. The Thessalonians are filled with the *holy* spirit, which God gives into them. Equipped with the holy spirit and a knowledge of God that their pagan neighbors do not possess, they ought to live in holiness and purity (4:3). They must control their own vessel in holiness (4:5), for God called them not in impurity but in holiness (4:7). It is not now the nation but individual believers in a local community whom Paul calls to embody the values of Ezekiel's vision. Filled with a holy spirit, they cannot — they must not — live, like their neighbors, an unholy and impure life characterized by lack of sexual control (4:4, 7).

The struggle for sexual control is not merely a matter of the past, of a moment when the Thessalonians turned toward faith, when they "received the word with joy inspired by the holy spirit" (1 Thess. 1:6) and "turned to God from idols" (1:9). Nor is it a matter alone for the future, when the dead in Christ will rise and the living be caught up in the clouds (4:16-17). Sexual control is a matter for the present circumstances, since the Thessalonians are in danger of falling asleep (5:6), of losing control over their sexual lives, of failing to grasp God's will: their holiness.

It is undoubtedly the urgency of the present, the ease with which marital fidelity can be forfeited, that impels Paul to localize Ezekiel's vision and to tweak his own use of tenses. Where Paul normally describes the sending of the spirit, he refers to a point in time in the past, presumably baptism or an equivalent moment when his readers turned to God; in the Thessalonian case, of course, this would have been the moment when they received the message of the gospel and turned to God from idols (1 Thess. 1:5-9). When he encourages the Thessalonians to maintain a life of sexual control, however, he adopts the present tense. Instead of writing that the Thessalonians ought to be holy because God "*gave* the holy spirit in them," Paul writes that God *is giving* the holy spirit to the Thessalonians.

This is a salutary shift in syntax. The reminder Paul proffers when the issue at hand is sexual control and the exploitation of others for sexual gratification (1 Thess. 4:6) is not, "You have been filled with the holy spirit," as if a single moment in time could suffice for an ongoing life of struggle toward holiness. The reminder consists rather of this: "You are *being filled* with the holy spirit." There may have been a radical conversion in the past, and there may be the hope of resurrection in the future; but at the moment, in the daily grind of believers, the struggle for sexual purity is grounded in the *ongoing* gift of God's holy spirit into the inner being of believers.

The importance of sexual purity for Paul cannot be overestimated. He begins his instruction by identifying nothing less than the will of God with holiness, which he immediately identifies with abstention from illicit sex (1 Thess. 4:3). He tells the Thessalonians in the harshest of terms that "the Lord is an avenger in all these things" and that he had already warned them about this beforehand (4:6). Finally, he makes it clear that the rejection of this life of sexual purity is not a rejection of "human authority but God, who also gives his holy spirit to you" (4:8). God's will, God's vengeance, and God's authority are at stake in the sexual habits of believers. Yet this is not too much to ask, for God continually breathes holy spirit into believers, energizing them toward a life of sexual control.

The inspiration of scripture[63] in the Pastoral letters is intended also

63. Presumably the Greek version of the Jewish scriptures.

for the purpose of learning and the practice of virtue: "All scripture is inspired [*theopneustos*] by God and is useful for teaching, for reproof, for correction, and for training in righteousness [or justice], so that everyone who belongs to God may be proficient, equipped for every good work" (2 Tim. 3:16-17).[64] The words in this description could describe Bezalel or Daniel: well taught; well trained; proficient or skilled; well equipped and ready for every good work.

The Significance of the Spirit-Breath

This conception of the spirit-breath as the reservoir of virtue, of learning, of skill, has serious implications for four aspects of the Christian faith: (1) how Christians acknowledge the holy spirit in those who are not Christians; (2) how Christians pray; (3) how Christians learn; and (4) how Christians cultivate the spirit on a daily basis.

How Christians Acknowledge the Spirit in Others

My dear friend is Jewish, or what he calls Jew-*ish*, an expatriate New Yorker in Seattle who was expelled from a synagogue when he was sixteen for asking too many questions, which the rabbis interpreted as too little respect. David and I talk about spirituality fairly often. When we do, I find it difficult to look my friend in the eye and tell him that God sequesters the spirit only among Christians. Maybe I have lost my steely will or my youthful confidence or the compass of truth, but I have difficulty claiming that Christians are the sole possessors of the holy spirit.

My inability to claim for Christians the exclusive right to the spirit is not, however, due to a loss of will or confidence. My inability is due in no small measure to my acceptance of the whole Bible — including early Jewish literature that makes the borders between old and new testaments porous.

The bottom line in the Jewish Bible is that key figures in Israel possessed the spirit. Because they possessed this spirit, they were wise, capable, full of knowledge, and skilled. Joseph's ability to interpret dreams

---

64. Even if it is not Pauline in authorship, this text functions nevertheless as an apt précis of inspiration in a Pauline key.

and, on a more practical level, to create a strategy for tackling a famine, led Pharaoh to see in him a spirit of God. Bezalel could be so filled with the spirit of God, with knowledge and understanding, that he could teach the artisans exactly what they needed to know in order to build a spectacular tent for God's presence in the middle of the wilderness. Daniel could have within him spirit to the nth degree for so long that three generations of foreign rulers could attribute wisdom to the nth degree in him. And the psalmist could pray to retain God's holy spirit.

None of these was a Christian. None of these received the spirit by confessing Jesus as Lord or believing that God raised him from the dead or participating in a sacrament such as baptism. There may be ways of explaining this reality away, but none of them holds water in my book. This is not, for instance, some sort of breath as opposed to the Holy Spirit. False dichotomy. *Ruach* is *ruach,* and *ruach* here is not just physical breath; *ruach* is also the locus of virtue and wisdom and knowledge and holiness. When the translators of the Septuagint dealt with these texts, they did not shy away from using the word that would feature in the New Testament: *pneuma.* Joseph had "spirit of God." Bezalel received "divine spirit of wisdom and understanding and knowledge of all things." The Greek translations of Daniel are more complicated, yet none of the translators avoided identifying the spirit within Daniel as (the) holy spirit. The Septuagint, in fact, tends to heighten, rather than dispel, this scenario with the reading, "holy spirit in him," rather than *yattirah* spirit, spirit to the nth degree in him.[65]

This is where I begin. The full biblical canon permits its readers — even prompts them — to affirm that people who are other than Christian can experience the spirit of God within them from birth as a source of wisdom, knowledge, skill, and holiness.

Yet this is not a facile acknowledgment that everyone has a *holy* spirit. I stand in this respect with Philo: God breathes the potential or capacity for virtue into everyone. God does not inbreathe actual virtue into everyone. The spirit of God within us must be taught, disciplined, cultivated. For Joseph, cultivation came through patient waiting and the practice of dream interpretation in prison cells. For Bezalel, skill came through the usual channels of apprenticeship and learning, and communication of skill came through the unremarkable practice of teaching. For Daniel, understanding came through simplicity and study. For the devotees

65. Daniel 5:12; 6:4. For further analysis, see my *Spirit in First-Century Judaism,* p. 73.

along the Dead Sea, holiness could be retained by the rejection of greed. For Paul, ministry was a product of the sustained practice of virtues — holiness of spirit, for one — much more than instantaneous revelation. For the church at Antioch, intense learning and devotion to disciplines — worship, prayer, and fasting — paved the way for receiving an unprecedented revelation of the spirit. The spirit of God within, in other words, must be tended by the right practices if it is to remain a *holy* spirit.

How Christians Pray

In years past, I prayed for the holy spirit to come upon students. When I realized that the spirit is already in them, Christian or not, I began to pray differently. I prayed also for the spirit that was already in them to stir, and I prayed for students to discern this stirring, that prompting. I asked God to fill them — in the sense of fill full or top up — in the fray of college life.

Let me take you back a few decades to a college classroom, where my Greek teacher, Jerry Hawthorne, led us through the little letter of 1 John. When he came across the point at which the author asks his people, "How does God's love abide in anyone who has the world's goods and sees a brother or sister in need and yet refuses help?" (1 John 3:17), Jerry pointed out that the bland English verb, *refuses help,* misses the visceral — literally, visceral — quality of the statement, which he translated something like this: *and locks up his or her viscera.* Compassion is visceral. In Seattle, beggars populate the interstate exit ramps and line the alleys of Pike Place Market. When I see someone standing with a sign ahead, hat on the hard cement, dappled with quarters, nickels, and dimes, my gut tightens, especially if I have forgotten to replenish our stash of granola bars and juice boxes. On those occasions, I steel myself to pass. It doesn't matter that we give to the Union Gospel Mission or World Vision. I still clutch my gut.

That, according to this chapter, is where the holy spirit lingers and labors. In a woman's innards. In a man's guts. So when I pray for students now, I pray that the spirit within them will stir, will thicken the gravy of their desire for God, deep down, somewhere in their intestines, below their rationalizations, beyond their resistance, beneath their preoccupations. I am not, of course, sure that God responds to this prayer in any way differently from the ways in which God answers a prayer for the spirit to come upon them. Yet this is how I now pray, with a hope that the holy spirit within them will stir, filling them to the brim with skill, insight, and knowledge — like Joseph, Bezalel, and Daniel.

How Christians Learn

A few years ago, a student asked me to be the advisor for a project. When I asked the student to clarify her plans, she responded, "I don't want to plan too much. I want to leave that to the holy spirit." This student believed that hard work, deliberation, and careful planning destabilize the truest work of the holy spirit. I expect this sort of response from indolent students, but this was a straight A student. She did not want to leave things unplanned because she was lazy but because she honestly believed that too much preparation could undermine the inspiration of the holy spirit. I cannot blame her. For many Christians, the surest sign of the spirit is an irresistible influx of emotion or uncontrollable physical symptoms — and certainly not a lifetime of dogged discipline.

Perhaps better than anyone else, the misguided figure Elihu encapsulates my student's misconception. Elihu fails to recognize that the spirit-breath of the Almighty does not automatically make for understanding; the spirit in a mortal does not inevitably yield wisdom. Because Elihu mistakenly assumes that an excess of energy, an abundance of vitality, a burst of words equals a surfeit of the spirit and surplus wisdom, he chides rather than encourages the defeated man on the ash heap.

The relationship between wisdom and spirit in Israelite literature is far more closely aligned with the cultivation of skill and knowledge than Elihu cares to recognize. The wisdom of the spirit within demands the painstaking mastery of crafts and the persistent pursuit of understanding. Joseph, for example, acquires knowledge through practice and experience in the home of Potiphar and an Egyptian prison, where his leadership is so exceptional that everything is left in his hands. This experience comes to fruition in Joseph's ability to interpret Pharaoh's dream and to offer wholesale advice on how to hedge against the famine ahead. Pharaoh does not respond principally by commending Joseph's finely tuned skills; Pharaoh identifies in this man an unsurpassed spirit and unparalleled wisdom.

Israel's literary legacy also isolates a symphony of skilled laborers, the wise of heart, who contribute to the construction of the tent of presence. Bezalel and Oholiab, leaders in this skilled labor, are first introduced as being filled, not only with (the) divine spirit, but with ability, intelligence, and knowledge in every kind of craft. They are reintroduced later as "filled with spirit of wisdom" and "filled with wisdom of heart" — with wisdom and understanding of every craft (36:1-3a). They are, in other words, chosen because they are highly skilled artisans in Israel. God tops them up with the spirit, not to learn new skills, but to teach the ones they have already mastered through a lifetime of learning and practice.

The association of wisdom and spirit explodes in the stories surrounding Daniel, an alien in foreign courts with an uncompromising commitment to Torah, to a simple life, and to education. The result of his discipline is stunning: a succession of influential foreign rulers recognize spirit and wisdom to the nth degree within him.

How Christians Cultivate the Spirit

I met recently with a group of students to discuss their experiences of the holy spirit. One by one, the students — no exceptions — said they associated the spirit with exceptional events: a retreat, an evening of consecration around a fire, a particularly robust and energetic worship service. None of them — no exceptions — associated the holy spirit with spirit-breath or with the mundane realities of everyday life. None of them, in short, believed that the spirit moves in the long haul, in the crevices of life, in the nooks and crannies of daily details.

There is no need to rehearse my contention that *ruach* is spirit-breath, the energizing reservoir of virtue and learning that lies within every human being from birth to death. There is no need to document the emphasis on education that punctuates the stories of Bezalel and Daniel. There is no need to inventory the daily disciplines of luminaries from Joseph to the men and women of the church in Antioch. There is no need to recollect the tandem descriptions of Jesus and John the Baptist — how a young Jesus "became strong in spirit" and a young John "became strong, filled with wisdom." Nor is there a need to call further to mind that the spirit in the new creation inspires virtue and learning. The promised spirit teaches and reveals, bringing into sharp focus the person of Jesus and the weakness of the cross.

There is a deeply personal dimension as well to the perpetual presence of God's spirit. Recall how carefully Paul writes to reinforce for his Thessalonian brothers and sisters the rich relationship that exists between sexual holiness and the holy spirit. When he speaks of sexual holiness, Paul cannot simply revert to familiar language, such as "God sent the holy spirit to you." Sexual holiness is too elusive, too easily mislaid. So Paul emphasizes that the spirit *is being given into* believers constantly, continually, relentlessly. The gift of the spirit is not a moment's work. The gift of the spirit is not tethered to unusual experiences. The gift of the spirit is steady and continuous — something worth knowing in the struggles that have the potential to shatter life into meaningless shards.

CHAPTER TWO

Putting Ecstasy in Its Place

A few years ago a career missionary couple sat in our living room with us. Decades ago, the husband passed up the prospect of a lucrative career in the United States as a medical doctor. The wife had just completed her masters in intercultural studies. Both have spent well over twenty years in the farthest reaches of South America in order to work among the poorest of the rural poor. They have sent remarkable letters over the years — not the sort that talk about all the grand and glorious things God is doing in their lives but letters about walking for two days through fields to treat a sick old man with two aspirin, or telling us about the old Quechua women, all of them seventy-five years old because no one knows their birth date, who unwrap their shawls to unveil two or three eggs — their payment for an intricate medical procedure, or as intricate as our friend can manage in the small clinic he and his brother built in an isolated rural village. Our friends mentioned that they would probably move to a nearby city, since there are now seven medical staff in the clinic they founded, a clinic where they once labored alone. In the city, they will tender medical care to native Quechuans who have moved to the city to find work. They described the racism in the city perfectly: the native Quechua are small and dark, while the descendants of the Spaniards are tall and white. Enough said. They have thrown in their lot with the small and dark people.

That evening in our living room, our friends told us of an acquaintance who thinks they should speak in tongues. She even gave them the name of her pastor to help them. Their reaction to this woman stunned me: they wondered out loud if they should call him. Here is a man, once a very talented young doctor in the United States, who left potential affluence and prestige for work among the poorest and most destitute of

71

South America's people. Here is a woman who watched surgical procedures on the dining room table, who leads countless Bible studies, who tends hordes of children, and who is an expert in cross-cultural communication. The first thought I voiced was, "NO! Don't call that pastor! You are living in the anointing of the holy spirit. You are living the life of the servant in Isaiah, of whom God said, 'Here is my servant, whom I uphold, my chosen, in whom my soul delights; I have put my spirit upon him; he will bring forth justice to the nations. He will not cry or lift up his voice, or make it heard in the street; a bruised reed he will not break, and a dimly burning wick he will not quench; he will faithfully bring forth justice. He will not grow faint or be crushed until he has established justice in the earth; and the coastlands wait for his teaching.'[1] You are bringing justice to the nations. You are teaching those on the margins. You heal bruised reeds with barely a whisper. You are God's delight! God's spirit already rests upon you!"

After they left, I began to wonder, "What would prompt career missionaries with a strong devotional life, a deep commitment to God, a love of Jesus, a repudiation of wealth, a medical clinic built from the ground up, an exceptional reputation in the field of medicine (our friend was once offered a position in the government and, of course, turned it down to remain in the rural village), a teaching ministry throughout South America, and the anointing of the holy spirit in their twenty-plus-year career among the world's poor to want a further work of the holy spirit?" Such, I suppose, is the allure of ecstasy. We had all agreed, as we sat in front of the fire, that a twinge of ecstasy would be a nice touch in the daily grind, a bit of respite from responsibilities and obligations, a way around our overactive, analytical minds. All of us would welcome the gift of speaking in tongues, we agreed. But we are all adults, seasoned Christians with meaningful vocations and lively callings; we know that an ephemeral experience can hardly stack up against the fullness of a life well lived. So why do we want this particular sign of the spirit? How is it possible that embodying the work of the spirit in practicing medicine among the poor or mentoring college students is inadequate? What is it about speaking in tongues that captivates us?

This itch for ecstasy, which, you may remember, I felt while leaning against my radiator a quarter-century ago, is alive and well. Nearly a billion Pentecostals worldwide (not to mention devotees of other religions) provide ample testimony to the yearning for ecstasy.

1. Isaiah 42:1-4.

This longing for an ecstatic experience, as intense and earnest as it may be, does not rest easily on scripture because ecstasy occupies a surprisingly isolated and slender patch of scripture. Perhaps more surprising still, scripture offers precious little information on exactly what actions and mental states ecstasy entails. We learn much more about the character of ecstasy from Greek, Roman, and Jewish literature than we do from the Bible itself. If we were to track the emergence of ecstasy, in terms of what is available in ancient literature, we would see a virtual flat line with a few bumps in Israelite literature, followed by a huge swell in Greek, Roman, and Jewish literature, followed again by a flat line with a few small bumps representing the New Testament. If ecstasy is present in scripture, it exists in small doses. It might even be possible to talk about a suppression of ecstasy in biblical literature — especially in comparison with other ancient literary corpora, in which writers describe ecstasy in elaborate detail.

The Rise and Demise of Ecstasy

A Sliver of Ecstasy in Israelite Literature

With the sole exception of Ezekiel, Israelite prophets left only fragments of their experience of the spirit; their fragile memoirs must be pieced together carefully and cautiously. Only in the postexilic era, in fact, as Israel rebuilt its little nation, did writers begin to look retrospectively at the sweep of prophetic inspiration and to link the spirit with the whole of prophecy. Nehemiah, an architect of the new Jerusalem during the 400s BCE, prayed, "Many years you were patient with them, and warned them by your spirit through your prophets; yet they would not listen. Therefore you handed them over to the peoples of the lands" (Neh. 9:30). In a tandem postexilic indictment of Israel's long history of recalcitrance, Zechariah claims, "They made their hearts adamant in order not to hear the law and the words that the LORD of hosts had sent by his spirit through the former prophets. Therefore great wrath came from the LORD of hosts" (Zech. 7:12). Closer to the era of the early church, in the Dead Sea Scrolls, prophecy as a whole is linked to the spirit: "This is the study of the law wh[i]ch he commanded through the hand of Moses, in order to act in compliance with all that has been revealed from age to age, and according to what the prophets have revealed through his holy spirit" (*Community Rule* [1QS] 8.15-16). This association of the spirit with the entire succession of prophets continued in the early church; Stephen's last words include, "You stiff-necked people, uncircumcised in heart and ears, you are forever opposing the holy spirit, just as your ancestors used to do. Which of the prophets did your ancestors not persecute?" (Acts 7:51-52). These sweeping statements belie the dearth of references to the spirit and ecstatic experiences in most prophetic books — certainly in prophets dated prior to the return from exile in 539 BCE. Isaiah felt birth pangs, with a reeling mind and trembling (21:3). Habakkuk trembled within, and his lips quivered while his steps trembled (3:16). None of these details offers an incontrovertible picture of prophetic ecstasy. Emotional? Yes. Ecstatic? Not necessarily.

Even Hosea's criticism of Israel's disparagement of prophets, "The prophet is a fool, the man of the spirit is mad!" (9:7) may refer as much to the content of a prophet's teaching, which Israel rejected as madness, as to a prophet's ecstatic condition. Micah's ability to contrast the spirit of the LORD in him, alongside knowledge, justice, and might, with the false prophets' failed effort to receive revelation through visions, does offer a glimpse of ecstasy (Mic. 5:1-8). Yet these are *false* prophets, like the prophets of Baal who danced from foot to foot and cut themselves in a contest with Elijah (1 Kings 18). Israel's true prophets, Micah and Elijah, unlike their misguided opponents, do not resort to the ecstasy of visions or dance or self-impairment. Elijah even makes fun of their dancing. "How long will you go limping with two different opinions?" he asks in blatant mockery (1 Kings 18:21).[2]

The years leading up to Babylonian exile were more fertile, though only in the person of Ezekiel, who laid claim to spirit-inspired visions: "The spirit lifted me up," he says (3:12, 14); and in a vision "the spirit of the LORD fell upon me" (11:5). Not much, and certainly not an experience that characterized other prophets, but something at least is here: the association of the spirit with a vision trance. Ezekiel's contemporary, Jeremiah, despite the candor of his confessions, in which he laments his prophetic vocation (Jeremiah 20), barely mentions experiences that have a semblance of ecstasy: his heart beat wildly (4:19); he had an incurable wound (15:18). The prophet responsible for Isaiah 40–55 offers even less

---

2. The word translated by "limping" could just as well be translated by "dancing" — a possible indication of an ecstatic state or the attempt to induce an ecstatic state.

in his muted claims that the spirit rests upon God's servant (42:1) and that "the LORD God has sent me and his spirit" (48:16).[3]

Although Israel's prophets left only a few slivers that could conceivably be construed as ecstasy — and I think it is stretching the evidence to suppose they are — Israel's storytellers bequeathed a bit more. Balaam, we are told, saw Israel camping tribe by tribe. "Then the spirit of God came upon him, and he uttered his oracle . . ." (Num. 24:2-3). This is a laconic description of inspiration, though hardly a description of ecstasy, and Balaam's opening words (24:3-4) do not clarify the nature of his experience, due in part to difficulties in the Hebrew text.

The story of Saul contains a clearer picture of ecstatic prophesying. In experiences that function as bookends to his reign, Saul, overcome by the spirit, enters what seems to be an ecstatic state, which the storyteller describes with the verb *prophesy*. Samuel prepares Saul for his initial encounter: ". . . you will meet a band of prophets coming down from the shrine with harp, tambourine, flute, and lyre playing in front of them; they will prophesy. Then the spirit of the LORD will possess you, and you will prophesy along with them and be turned into a different person" (1 Sam. 10:5-6). Saul does exactly this: "a band of prophets met him; and the spirit of God possessed him, and he prophesied along with them. When all who knew him before saw how he prophesied with the prophets, the people said to one another, 'What has come over the son of Kish? Is Saul also among the prophets?' " (10:10-11). What happened to Saul is not entirely clear, though many translators make it so when they interpret the word *prophesy* as "fell into a prophetic frenzy." Fair enough, with music and instruments, particularly when in the final instance, nine chapters and what seems like a lifetime away, Saul, once again, overcome by the spirit of God, prophesies, though not before his messengers, whom he sent to capture David, succumb to a communal prophetic immobilization: "When they saw the company of prophets in a *frenzy* [literally: *prophesying*] with Samuel standing in charge of them, the spirit of God came upon the messengers of Saul, and they also prophesied" (19:20).

---

3. Key studies of ecstasy in Israelite literature include Johannes Lindblom, *Prophecy in Ancient Israel* (Philadelphia: Fortress, 1962); Robert R. Wilson, *Prophecy and Society in Ancient Israel* (Philadelphia: Fortress, 1980). I admit to the presence of many visions in the Jewish Bible, but the mechanics of the visionary experience are left unexplained, and often dreams, which take place while a subject is sleeping, are the mode by which God introduces revelation. None of the intricate discussions of divination that characterize Greco-Roman literature can be found in Israelite literature.

Predictably, Saul too succumbs, although not without a startling conclusion: he strips off his clothes and lies naked all day and night, prompting again the question, "Is Saul also among the prophets?" (19:23-24). This is a clear-cut instance of ecstasy, of being beside or out of oneself, of losing one's senses — in this instance, under the influence of communal ecstasy, induced perhaps by musical instruments.

What of the story in which Moses complains that the people are too much of a burden for him to carry? God reacts in turn by commanding Moses to gather seventy of the registered elders at the tent of meeting where, God promises, "I will come down and talk with you there; and I will take some of the spirit that is on you and *cause it to rest* on them; and they shall bear the burden of the people along with you so that you will not bear it all by yourself" (Num. 11:17). In due course, Moses "gathered seventy elders of the people, and placed them all around the tent. Then the LORD came down in the cloud and spoke to him, and took some of the spirit that was on him and put it on the seventy elders; and when the spirit rested upon them, they prophesied. But they did not do so again" (11:24-25). Two other elders, Eldad and Medad, failed to join the seventy at the tent of presence. Nonetheless, "the spirit rested on them . . . they prophesied in the camp" (11:26). After hearing this report, Joshua, appalled, asked Moses to have them stop. Moses responded with utter magnanimity, "Are you jealous for my sake? Would that all the LORD's people were prophets, and that the LORD would put his spirit on them" (11:29).

The nature of prophecy in this passage is typically identified as a form of ecstasy into which the elders fell — not unlike Saul. The recurrence of the verb *prophesy* in the stories of the elders (Numbers 11) and Saul (1 Samuel 10, 19) is the main piece of evidence used to argue that prophesying in the story of Moses is ecstatic. The presence of ecstatic prophesying, however, raises a severe difficulty for the interpretation of Numbers 11.[4] How do seventy-two elders caught in the throes of ecstasy, perhaps in a communal contagion of uncontrollability, solve Moses' problem by sharing the administrative burden with Moses? If we take Saul as a model, the scenario becomes laughable: a group of distinguished elders lying naked for several hours — if this is what prophesying entailed — are thought somehow to help Moses lead the people through the wilderness. This scenario makes no sense.

4. For a detailed analysis of Numbers 11, particularly the need to distinguish the prophesying of the elders (Numbers 11) from Saul's experience (1 Samuel 10, 19), see my "Prophecy in Ancient Israel: The Case of the Ecstatic Elders," *Catholic Biblical Quarterly* 65 (2003): 503-21.

This interpretation of prophesying, in light of Saul's experience, as unbridled ecstasy also ignores two other verbs in the story of Moses and the elders. On the one hand, God's promise to take or "withdraw" some of the spirit from Moses (Num. 11:17) is related to the word that is used of the seventy elders who accompany Moses on Mount Sinai. The elders at Mount Sinai are "the ones who withdraw" to receive a communal vision that confirms their authority alongside Moses (Exod. 24:11).[5] This recurrence of the same Hebrew root is hardly coincidental, as it draws together the stories of Moses and the elders at Sinai with the story of Moses and elders in the wilderness. The visionary experience authenticated the elders at Mount Sinai, and now, it would seem, a similar visionary experience authenticates them once again. In the next story, in fact, God speaks directly to Miriam and Aaron, Moses' sister and brother, and says, "When there are prophets among you, I the LORD make myself known to them in visions; I speak to them in dreams" (Num. 12:6).

On the other hand, the verb *to cause to rest* (Num. 11:25-26) mirrors the resting of the spirit of wisdom and understanding, counsel and might, knowledge and fear of the LORD upon the anointed messianic ruler of Isaiah's vision (Isa. 11:2). These concurrent verbs, *withdraw* and *rest,* cause the ambiguity of the word *prophesy* to evaporate: not Saul, but the anointed messianic ruler provides the key to interpreting the experience of the elders who aid Moses. They do not plunge into unbridled ecstasy but into a communal vision, with clear if undisclosed content, akin to the prior experience at Sinai; this second vision shores up their authority and lends to them qualities associated with leadership, which they can again share with Moses.

For one last possible eruption of ecstasy in the Hebrew Bible, we have to wait until the apocalyptic experiences described by the book of Daniel. Daniel's spirit was troubled and terrified (Dan. 7:15); he fell prostrate on the ground (8:17-18), lay down sick (8:27), lacked strength (10:8-9), and was speechless and prostrate (10:15-17). There is a problem, however, with all of these alleged experiences of ecstasy. As we will soon see, in the Greco-Roman world, to which the book of Daniel belongs as a product of the Maccabean era, these experiences ought to *precede* a vision; in the book of Daniel, these experiences *follow* visions. In these final few alleged instances of ecstasy in the Jewish scriptures, then, the experiences that normally would open a vista of visionary ecstasy are instead merely the aftershock of visionary tremors.

---

5. "Prophecy in Ancient Israel," pp. 514-16.

Ecstasy in the World of the New Testament

The book of Daniel, with hints of ecstasy that fail to materialize, is a reminder that ecstasy occupies a modest or minimal place in Israel's literature. In contrast, Hellenization, and Roman culture in its train, brought the allure of ecstasy to center stage. As early as the fifth century BCE, according to Plato, Socrates believed that "the greatest of blessings come to us through madness, when it is sent as a gift of the gods. For the prophetess at Delphi and the priestesses at Dodona when they have been mad have conferred many splendid benefits upon Greece both in private and in public affairs, but few or none when they have been in their right minds."[6] This sort of inspiration would overtake the poet and prophet as well. The poet, claimed Socrates, "is unable ever to indite until he has been inspired and put out of his senses, and his mind is no longer in him."[7] Composition of odes, dance songs, and verse are uttered "not by art . . . but by divine influence." Therefore, "God takes away the mind of these and uses them as his ministers, just as he does soothsayers and godly seers, in order that we who hear them may know that it is not they who utter these words of great price, but that it is God himself who speaks and addresses us through them."[8]

The most illustrious inspired figure held Greece spellbound by her words and fired the Greek imagination with her oracles. Enquirers at the temple of Delphi paid their consultation tax, offered their sacrifice, and, if the animal reacted as it should when sprinkled with water, entered the temple, offered another sacrifice, then entered, probably with the oracular interpreters, to the *adytum,* a space from which the priestess, or Pythia, was not visible. She, in turn, prepared herself by purification at the Castalian Spring and by burning laurel leaves and barley meal on the altar inside the temple. Crowned with laurel, she took her place on a tripod, was possessed by the god, shook a laurel branch, and prophesied. The interpreters, in some way that is still unclear, shaped her oracle for the enquirer.[9]

The experience of the Pythia at Delphi was shrouded in mystery, and

6. Plato, *Phaedrus* 244A-B.

7. Plato, *Ion* 534B.

8. Plato, *Ion* 534C-D.

9. Sarah Iles Johnston, *Ancient Greek Divination* (Malden, MA, and Oxford: Wiley-Blackwell, 2008); Sarah Iles Johnston and Peter T. Struck, eds., *Mantikê: Studies in Ancient Divination,* Religions in the Graeco-Roman World 155 (Leiden: Brill, 2005).

there may have been little historical reality to this conception of Delphic inspiration. Nevertheless, the mysterious figure of the Delphic Pythia riveted the attention of other Greek and Roman writers, who, in the shadow of Delphi, frequently associated filling with the spirit, whatever its precise nature, with uncontrolled but legitimate prophetic ecstasy. Strabo (born ca. 63 BCE) refers to an enthusiastic spirit *(pneuma enthousiastikon)* that causes the Pythia to speak while she sits on her tripod.[10] Pliny the Elder, a contemporary of Jesus' earliest followers (ca. 23-79 CE), attributes oracles to an intoxicating exhalation *(exhalatione temulenti)* from the earth in locations such as Delphi.[11] Iamblichus (ca. 245-325 CE) refers to a fiery *pneuma* that arises from the earth to envelop her.[12] Christian writer John Chrysostom (ca. 347-407 CE) derides the Pythia by contending that an evil *pneuma* entered her genitalia when she sat on the tripod.[13]

Plutarch (ca. 46-120 CE) had an intense interest in the mechanics of Delphic inspiration.[14] His dialogues are of real worth, not just because he had served as a priest at Delphi, but also because, in the spirit of the New Academy, Plutarch was less concerned with championing a single, definitive answer than with laying out alternative points of view. Consequently, he gathered several colorful characters around the conundrum of why, during his day, there occurred less oracular activity at Delphi than in prior eras. An important dialogue, *On the Obsolescence of Oracles,* offers several answers to the question of why, in Plutarch's era, Delphi was no longer in its heyday.

A key figure in *On the Obsolescence of Oracles,* Lamprias, summarizes the explanation of a certain Cleombrotus in this way: "When the demigods withdraw and forsake the oracles, these lie idle and inarticulate like the instruments of musicians."[15] Lamprias also summarizes — and criticizes — the answer a certain Ammonius gives: the god, like a ventriloquist who manipulates a dummy, "enters into the bodies of his prophets

---

10. Strabo 9.3.5.

11. *Natural History* 2.95.208.

12. Iamblichus, *On Mysteries* 3.11.

13. John Chrysostom, *Homily on 1 Corinthians* 29.1.

14. The treatises cited are included in Plutarch's *Moralia,* which consists of dialogues and essays on ethical, literary, and historical subjects, including such practical topics as *Advice to Married Couples.*

15. Cleombrotus's view of guardian spirits, it has been suggested, may represent Plutarch's own explanation of the decrease in oracles. See R. Flacelière, ed., *Sur la Disparition des Oracles* (Paris: Belles Lettres, 1947), p. 48; E. de Faye, *Origène, sa vie, son oeuvre, sa pensée,* vol. 2: *L'ambiance philosophique* (Paris: E. Leroux, 1927), p. 110.

and prompts their utterances, employing their mouths and voices as instruments."[16] The decrease in Delphic oracles during the first century, according to Lamprias's summaries of the positions held by Cleombrotus and Ammonius, is due to a lessened tendency of the gods to possess prophets and priestesses.[17]

This is the sort of inspiration that Philo, the prominent first-century Jewish philosopher from Alexandria, adopts to explain the inspiration of Israel's prophets. His interpretation of the word *ekstasis* in Genesis 15:12 (LXX) prompts him to describe the experience that "regularly befalls the fellowship of the prophets. The mind is evicted at the arrival of the divine Spirit [*tou theiou pneumatos*], but when that departs the mind returns to its tenancy. Mortal and immortal may not share the same home. And therefore the setting of reason and the darkness which surrounds it produce ecstasy and inspired frenzy."[18] When the prophet is inspired, "he is filled with inspiration [*enthousia*], as the reason withdraws and surrenders the citadel of the soul to a new visitor and tenant, the Divine Spirit which plays upon the vocal organism and dictates words which clearly express its prophetic message."[19]

In a signal of the extensive influence of this Greco-Roman point of view, in which infilling effects ecstasy, both Josephus and Philo adopt it, independently yet in stunning consonance, to resolve the problem that is raised in Numbers 22–24, when Balaam, the quintessential false prophet, delivers an oracular blessing upon Israel.[20] According to Philo, Balaam delivered his first oracle when "he became possessed, and there fell upon him the truly prophetic spirit which banished utterly from his soul his art of wizardry."[21] Later, "he was suddenly possessed, and, understanding nothing, his reason as it were roaming, uttered these prophetic words which were put into his mouth."[22] Josephus, writing on another Mediter-

16. Plutarch, *On the Obsolescence of Oracles* 414E.

17. This is, according to Lamprias (*On the Obsolescence of Oracles* 414E), a ridiculous position, for it fails to draw adequate distance between the divine and human worlds: "For if he [a god] allows himself to become entangled in people's needs, he is prodigal with his majesty and he does not observe the dignity and greatness of his preeminence."

18. Philo Judaeus, *Who Is the Heir?* 264-65.

19. Philo Judaeus, *On the Special Laws* 4.49.

20. Detailed analyses are available in my articles, "The Debut of the Divine Spirit in Josephus' *Antiquities*," *Harvard Theological Review* 87 (1994): 123-38, and "The Prophetic Spirit as an Angel according to Philo," *Harvard Theological Review* 88 (1995): 189-207.

21. Philo Judaeus, *Life of Moses* 1.277.

22. Philo Judaeus, *Life of Moses* 1.283.

ranean shore and close to a century later, offers a similar explanation of
Balaam's ability to speak a true oracle: "Such was the inspired utterance
of one who was no longer his own master but was overruled by the divine
spirit to deliver it."[23] Balaam himself confronts Balak: "Do you think that
it rests with us at all to be silent or to speak on such themes as these, when
we are possessed by the spirit of God? For that spirit gives utterance to
such language and words as it will, whereof we are all unconscious."[24]

Compare this onslaught of ecstasy with Israelite prophets, excepting
perhaps only Ezekiel, whose writings offer the barest sketches of their
experience. If there exists an inkling of ecstasy in this large literary corpus, it has been plunged beneath the surface of comprehensibility. Yet
Philo and, to some extent, Josephus, probe the mechanics of prophetic
inspiration. They discover in the rich veins of Greco-Roman discourse
a conception of inspiration which, though foreign to Israelite literature,
permits a full disclosure of prophetic inspiration: the divine spirit takes
hold of the prophet and produces, through his vocal cords, words and
sounds of God's choosing. The prophet, in this process, is little more
than a vehicle, like a musical instrument through whom a divine being
blows. It is a measure of the value of ecstasy that both Philo of Alexandria, during the early first century, and Josephus of Rome, during the
late first century, incorporate views strikingly similar to those held by
Ammonius to explain how a despicable Mesopotamian seer delivered a
magnificent blessing of Israel.

Because early Jewish authors who wrote during the Greco-Roman
era could not excavate sufficient resources in their own sacred texts to explain the mechanics of inspiration, at least some of these Jewish authors,
such as Philo and Josephus, opted to import inspired ecstasy, understood
in Greco-Roman terms, into their own portrayals of inspiration. More
surprising is that this proclivity is evident in the *Liber antiquitatum biblicarum*, a Palestinian reinvention of biblical narratives from Adam and
Eve to Samuel.

Take, for instance, an embellishment of the story of Kenaz, an obscure biblical figure who is the father of the judge Othniel (actually the
author merges the first judge, Othniel, with his father, Kenaz). The author of the *Liber antiquitatum biblicarum*, who is normally referred to as
Pseudo-Philo because the manuscript was falsely attributed to Philo, de-

23. Josephus, *Antiquities of the Jews* 4.118.
24. Josephus, *Antiquities of the Jews* 4.119.

81

votes inordinate space to Kenaz. Nearly spinning a tale out of thin air, he tells the story of a remarkable vision that Kenaz experiences. Although *Liber antiquitatum biblicarum* exists only in a Latin translation, which creates all sorts of difficulties, the essential lines of what prompts this vision are discernible at the start: "And when they [Israelite prophets and elders of Israel] had sat down, [a][25] holy spirit came upon Kenaz and dwelled in him and elevated his mind [put him in ecstasy], and he began to prophesy, saying . . ."[26] This brief snippet offers, from an unexpected quarter, a quintessential expression of the association between infilling by *pneuma* and an ecstatic loss of control.

The vision ends with a similar indication of ecstasy: "And when Kenaz had spoken these words, he was awakened, and his senses came back to him. *But he did not know what he had said or what he had seen.*"[27] Kenaz, while seeing a vision, lost his senses, which had to be returned to him. He also, afterwards, lost the ability to recall what he had experienced under ecstasy (though he actually describes in detail what he saw). This element of the story owes its origin to Plato's *Apology* 22C and *Meno* 99C, in which Plato contends that inspired poets do not know what they are saying. This view, which we will return to later, spawned interpretations in which the inability to recall what was said during a bout of ecstasy authenticated the prophetic condition.[28]

From the mere mention of a name in Judges 3 and a few formulaic words, "The spirit of the LORD came upon him" (Judg. 3:10), Pseudo-Philo has spun an episode of inspiration that is a mirror of the Greco-Roman world. Kenaz's vision begins when the spirit leaps upon him, in-

25. Daniel Harrington (*The Old Testament Pseudepigrapha*, 2 vols., ed. James H. Charlesworth [Garden City, NY: Doubleday, 1983, 1985], 2:374) translates *spiritus* with the indefinite article "a." M. R. James (*The Biblical Antiquities of Philo* [New York: Ktav, 1968], p. 235) translates "the spirit"; and C. Dietzfelbinger (*Pseudo-Philo: Antiquitates Biblicae*, Jüdische Schriften aus hellenistisch-römischer Zeit 2.2 [Gütersloh: Gerd Mohn, 1975], p. 257) translates "der heilige Geist." On *Liber antiquitatum biblicarum* in general, see Howard Jacobson, *A Commentary on Pseudo-Philo*, 2 vols., Arbeiten zur Geschichte des Antiken Judentums und des Urchristentums 31 (Leiden: Brill, 1996).

26. *Liber antiquitatum biblicarum* 28.6. Latin, *Et dum sederent, insiluit spiritus sanctus habitans in Cenez, et extulit sensum eius, et cepit prophetare dicens. . . .* The association between Kenaz's ability to prophesy and possession of the spirit is drawn from biblical roots, particularly 1 Samuel 10:5-6, 10-13; 19:20-24.

27. *Liber antiquitatum biblicarum* 28.10.

28. See my *Filled with the Spirit* (Grand Rapids: Eerdmans, 2009), pp. 164-68, for details.

dwells him, and causes his mind to ascend or to leave altogether.[29] It ends when Kenaz's senses are restored, though the impact of ecstasy remains when he cannot recall what he saw or said. This sort of ecstasy Greco-Roman authors identify as "enthusiasm."[30] It corresponds to what, in Philo's view, "regularly befalls the fellowship of the prophets. The mind is evicted at the arrival of the divine Spirit, but when that departs the mind returns to its tenancy."[31]

We will not linger any longer in the Greco-Roman world, but I hope that the few examples of ecstasy I have identified will demonstrate the influence it exercised over the imagination of Greeks and Romans, including Jewish authors from Egypt, Rome, and Palestine. This interest, which bordered for some authors on obsession, contrasts sharply with the Jewish Bible, with its faint hints of ecstasy, which I think are fool's gold anyway. The Greeks and Romans, in contrast, were eager to impute ecstasy to their prophets, priests, poets, and pythia. These figures, especially the virgin priestess at Delphi, were like sirens, from whom many Greco-Roman writers could not look away. Nor, would it seem, could Jewish writers of the Greco-Roman era. Philo describes the entire race of Israelite prophets as ecstatics, whose minds are ousted when the divine spirit takes up its tenancy. He and Josephus even manage to solve a fundamental conundrum by importing the Greco-Roman view that God — in Balaam's instance, the divine spirit — enters into a prophet and takes hold of his or her vocal cords; this explains how Balaam, a false diviner, was able to bless Israel. Even a Palestinian author could, from start to finish, color Israel's first judge in the hues of Greco-Roman ecstasy.

Ecstasy in the New Testament

Against the background of its Greco-Roman context, inspired ecstasy shrinks dramatically in the early church. The word *ekstasis* and its cognate verb, *existēmi,* nearly always communicate amazement, such as the crowds' amazement at Jesus' teaching and healing.[32] They rarely connote a loss of mental control. In Mark's Gospel, Jesus' relatives claim he has lost

29. Latin, *extulit sensum eius,* in *Liber antiquitatum biblicarum* 28.6.

30. See Plutarch, *Amatorius* 758E.

31. Philo Judaeus, *Who Is the Heir?* 264-65.

32. Matthew 12:23; Mark 2:12; 5:42; 6:51; 16:8; Luke 2:47; 5:26; 8:56; 24:22; Acts 2:7; 2:12; 3:10; 8:9-13; 9:21; 10:45; and 12:16.

his mind, and scribes pronounce him possessed;[33] this is obviously not the inspired ecstasy that Plato, Plutarch, and Philo praise. Paul's claim, "if we are beside ourselves [*exestēmen*], it is for God; if we are in our right mind, it is for you," probably refers not so much to ecstasy as to ministry; his actions, crazed or sane, are constrained by a love for Christ.[34] He is, in short, a fool for Christ.

Only in visions do the word *ekstasis* and the related verb *existēmi* possibly refer to ecstasy.[35] The word *ekstasis,* however, need not be present to describe an ecstatic experience. Before looking at some of these experiences, it is necessary to draw two distinctions — one ancient, the other modern. First, for the modern distinction. Social anthropologists (e.g., I. M. Lewis) distinguish central from peripheral contexts of ecstasy.[36] Ecstasy in central contexts gives divine support to the status quo. This sort of ecstatic behavior occurs in a well-defined social order, including a strict hierarchy of ecstatic figures. The Korekore Shona, for example, represent "a clearly defined morality cult in which the spirits that watch over the conduct of men and control their interests make known their wishes through a group of chosen agents who are organized in a clearly structured shamanistic hierarchy. Inspiration here is virtually a male monopoly."[37] Ecstasy in peripheral contexts, in contrast, ultimately enhances the marginal status of the ecstatic; this person is able to challenge the status quo from the margins and with divine approval. In Numbers 11, when the seventy-two elders enter a visionary trance that authenticates their ability to stand alongside Moses, they are experiencing ecstasy in what social anthropologists might identify as a central context: their experience supports the status quo, including a male hierarchy (though the experiences of Eldad and Medad throw a twist into the works). In the early church, ecstasy occurs exclusively in peripheral contexts. For example, female prophets at Corinth, whom Paul tells to have some sort of "authority" or control on their heads, appear to experience ecstasy in socially peripheral contexts; this enhances their own status and allows them to speak with divine imprimatur outside the normal conduit of their husbands' authority (1 Cor. 11:4, 10).

33. Mark 3:21-22.

34. 2 Corinthians 5:13-14.

35. Acts 10:10; 11:5; and 22:17.

36. I. M. Lewis, *Ecstatic Religion: A Study of Shamanism and Spirit Possession,* 2nd ed. (London/New York: Routledge, 1989), pp. 59-113, especially 62-64, 90-113.

37. Lewis, *Ecstatic Religion,* p. 124; see further pp. 115-33.

Now for the ancient distinction. Greco-Roman writers distinguished between artificial and natural divination. Artificial divination, such as seeking omens by examining the organs of dead animals or bird formations in the sky or patterns in the smoke of sacrifices, played no role in experiences of ecstasy in the early church. Natural divination, on the other hand, entailed frenzy or ecstasy, as well as dreams and pre-death visions, when the soul could most easily withdraw from the body. We noticed already that Plutarch described natural divination in detail. Lamprias, for instance, believed that external impulses, including breezes in groves or *pneuma* carried through air, prompted these experiences.[38]

In the New Testament, the most valuable data for determining the character of natural divination occur in the book of Acts, which contains a triad of visions. These visions play a pivotal role in Acts, though the mechanics of visions, and thus the nature of ecstasy, are not entirely clear. The first of the three, Stephen's vision of Jesus, occurs before his death (7:55-56); this fits Greco-Roman discussions of natural divination, in which the soul or spirit or mind is freer from the body, and thus more open to visions, in sleep or prior to death. Cicero, in *On Divination,* explains that the soul's "power to divine is much enhanced by the approach of death."[39] Whether Stephen's is presented as an ecstatic vision we cannot say with certainty, though it does look like an ecstatic vision trance.

The second in the triad, Peter's vision of unclean foods, transpires while *ekstasis* comes upon him — Luke actually adopts the word — though this could mean anything from an afternoon nap to an ecstatic trance (Acts 10:10). On the one hand, Peter's ability to recount the vision suggests the absence of ecstasy, since often a key indicator of ecstasy was the inability to recall experiences that took place in an ecstatic state. In the second century CE, a noted public speaker and man of letters, Aelius Aristides, claimed that the priestesses of Zeus had no idea of the oracles they were about to receive, "nor afterwards do they know anything which they have said, but all inquirers understand it better than they."[40] Second- or third-century Christian author Pseudo-Justinus compared the sibyl, a female prophet, with poets, who were able to spend time polishing their writing. The sibyl had no such opportunity because "as soon as the inspiration ceased, there ceased also the remembrance of all she had said."[41]

---

38. Plutarch, *On the Obsolescence of Oracles* 432C-D.
39. Cicero, *On Divination* 1.63.
40. Aelius Aristides, *In Defense of Oratory* 43.
41. Pseudo-Justinus, *Cohortatio ad Graecos* 37.2; in 37.3, he writes, "the prophetess

Peter's ability to recollect the content of his vision, in contrast, may suggest that he was not in an ecstatic state. On the other hand, Peter's subsequent description suggests that the vision may have been ecstatic. He recollects that in Joppa "I was . . . praying, and *in ecstasy* I saw a *vision*" (Acts 11:5). This could mean, of course, that he fell asleep, though more could be meant, particularly because both Peter and Stephen before him (6:55) "stare" *(atenizein)* during their visions — indications, perhaps, of an altered state of consciousness.

In a later episode, Paul recollects in terms similar to Peter's vision that, while he was praying in the Jerusalem temple, Jesus "put me into ecstasy, and I saw him saying to me . . ." (Acts 22:17). These three visions create a possible web of ecstatic experiences in the book of Acts: Stephen and Peter *stare* and see a *vision;* Peter and Paul *pray,* are *in ecstasy* (or, less dramatically, asleep), and see a *vision;* Stephen and Paul both see the risen Jesus.

What of Paul's letters? Paul's claim to visions and revelations, to being "caught up to the third heaven — whether in the body or out of the body I do not know," may reflect similar ecstatic experiences in a peripheral social context (2 Cor. 12:1-10). Certainly he cites "extraordinary revelations" to raise his status in the Corinthians' eyes, while his inability to recall whether his experiences were physical or not possibly may point to ecstasy. His visions of the risen Jesus may also have occurred while he was in an ecstatic state (1 Cor. 9:1; 15:8), though Paul gives too few details to allow us to arrive at any certain conclusion.

In the four visions of Revelation, each marked by the phrase "in the spirit" (Rev. 1:10; 4:2; 17:3; 21:10), ecstasy is, once again, ambiguous.[42] The author of Revelation remembers everything with utter clarity, signaling perhaps the absence of ecstasy; the words *in the spirit* may function, therefore, primarily as a literary device as much as a signal of a psychological state, since they evoke a salient literary precursor to Revelation:

---

having no remembrance of what she had said. . . ." For other texts and a fuller discussion of the inability to recall the contents of an ecstatic experience, see *Filled with the Spirit,* pp. 164-68.

42. These observations are based upon David Aune's excellent discussion of the phrase "in the spirit," which makes this ambiguity evident. See David E. Aune, *Revelation,* 3 vols., Word Biblical Commentary 52A (Dallas: Word, 1997), pp. 82-83. Aune does not understand spirit as the divine spirit; the phrase rather is "an idiom that refers to the fact that John's revelatory experiences took place not 'in the body' but rather 'in the spirit,' i.e., in a vision trance."

the prophetic book of Ezekiel.[43] Yet the visions take John out of body, e.g., to the heavenly court; this may capture the essence of ecstasy, as Cicero describes it: "Those, then, whose souls, spurning their bodies, take wings and fly abroad — inflamed and aroused by a sort of passion — these, I say, certainly see the things which they foretell in their prophecies." Recall in this regard Cicero's explanation: "When, therefore, the soul has been withdrawn by sleep from contact with sensual ties, then does it recall the past, comprehend the present, and foresee the future."[44] The book of Revelation does all three: it absorbs the past by transforming the visions of Daniel and Ezekiel; it praises and blames churches of the author's day (Revelation 2–3) and offers a trenchant critique of Rome; and it predicts "what must soon take place" (Rev. 1:1).

Where do these observations leave us? In the span of New Testament literature, precious little can be identified without question as an indication of ecstasy. For all of its claims to the spirit, to miracles (Gal. 3:1-5), to charismatic gifts (1 Corinthians 12–14), to prophets and prophecies (e.g., Acts 11:27-30; 1 John 4:1-6), a disproportionately low occurrence of ecstatic phenomena rises to the surface.[45] Three visions in Acts, Paul's own visions, and visions in the book of Revelation — this is likely the totality of possible references to ecstasy in the New Testament. It is absolutely essential to note that there is no ecstasy where there are no visions. Yet even where there are visions, these visions contain clear content and the ability to remember, a fact that may call the embrace of ecstasy into question — the risen Jesus (Stephen and Paul in Acts, and perhaps Paul's own letters), the sheet with forbidden food (Peter), words in paradise to be left unspoken (Paul), and four visions told in daring detail in the book of Revelation. Visions, and visions alone, may be the sole effect of ecstasy in the early church, and the product of these visions is, without exception, memorable, comprehensible, and communicable content.[46]

---

43. E.g., Ezekiel 3:14; 11:5.

44. Cicero, *On Divination* 1.63.

45. On prophecy, see also *Didache* 11:12-13.

46. In Acts 16:16-19, a slave girl has a pythonic *(pythona)* spirit. This is quintessential ecstasy — admittedly a maligned form of ecstasy — in which a pythonic spirit acts as a ventriloquist by controlling her vocal cords. The slave girl illustrates the ambiguity of New Testament ecstasy. She occupies a peripheral social context, speaks in ecstasy under the control of a suspect spirit, yet even she tells the truth: "These men are slaves of the most high God, who proclaim to you (a) way of salvation" (16:17). For a detailed discussion of this text in relation to the story of Pentecost, see *Filled with the Spirit*, pp. 317-25. For critiques of my interpretation, see Blaine Charette, "'And Now for Something Completely

Speaking in Tongues

Hermann Gunkel, more than a century ago, and Pentecostals ever since claim the charismatic gift of *glossolalia,* or speaking in tongues, to be the *sine qua non* of Christian experience.[47] The experience of speaking in tongues rises explicitly to the surface of the apostle Paul's letters once, and three times in the book of Acts.[48] What we find in the relevant texts may surprise us. Speaking in tongues, understood from the perspective of Paul's response to the Corinthians and the book of Acts, rather than from the errant practices of *glossolalia* in the church at Corinth, is invariably associated with intelligent speech. Ecstasy and comprehension, in the New Testament, are not-so-strange bedfellows after all.

Paul's Letter to the Corinthians

The apostle Paul's response to the Corinthians' question about spiritual gifts is a model of pastoral leadership. While responding to egregious Corinthian errors, he still manages to affirm them while correcting them. His is a remarkable feat, for he redirects their parody of a principal spiritual gift, *glossolalia,* without dismissing the gift altogether. On top of this, he is engaging in spiritual triage from afar: in a letter rather than in person, he tries to stanch the bleeding of a fractured and frazzled church in Corinth.[49]

Different': A 'Pythonic' Reading of Pentecost?" *Pneuma* 33 (2011): 59-62; and James B. Shelton, "Delphi and Jerusalem: Two Spirits or Holy Spirit? A Review of John R. Levison's *Filled with the Spirit,*" *Pneuma* 33 (2011): 51-53.

47. See Hermann Gunkel, *The Influence of the Holy Spirit: The Popular View of the Apostolic Age and the Teaching of the Apostle Paul,* 3rd ed. (Philadelphia: Fortress, 1979; paperback edition, 2008), p. 88. For a thorough analysis of Gunkel's legacy, with accompanying bibliography, see *Filled with the Spirit,* pp. xiv-xxvii, 3-13, 109-17, 225-35, 428-29; for a single coherent statement, see my "Assessing the Origins of Modern Pneumatology: The Life and Legacy of Hermann Gunkel," in *Christian Body, Christian Self: Concepts of Early Christian Personhood,* ed. Clare K. Rothschild and Trevor W. Thompson, Wissenschaftliche Untersuchungen zum Neuen Testament 284 (Tübingen: Mohr Siebeck, 2011), pp. 313-31.

48. The intercession of the spirit in "sighs too deep for words" (Rom. 8:26) may refer to a form of *glossolalia,* but Paul does not describe the experience as one of *glossolalia,* as he does in 1 Corinthians 12–14. For a detailed discussion, see Gordon Fee, *God's Empowering Presence: The Holy Spirit in the Letters of Paul* (Peabody, MA: Hendrickson, 1994), pp. 575-86.

49. See also my entry, "Tongues, Gift of," in *The New Interpreter's Dictionary of the Bible,* ed. Katharine Doob Sakenfeld, 5 vols. (Nashville: Abingdon, 2007), 5:625-26; *Filled*

Despite the problems it has clearly precipitated among the Corinthians — not least a spiritual pecking order — Paul heartily embraces the ecstasy of speaking in tongues. According to his letter to the Corinthians, Paul does not deride the experience of speaking in tongues even though it excludes the activity of the mind. It is a form of prayer in which, observes Paul, "my spirit prays but my mind is unproductive" (1 Cor. 14:14). It is the essence of ecstasy, of being outside oneself. His description of speaking in tongues parallels Philo's description of Israel's prophets, in which a prophet "is filled with inspiration, as the reason withdraws and surrenders the citadel of the soul to a new visitor and tenant, the Divine Spirit which plays upon the vocal organism and dictates words which clearly express its prophetic message."[50]

Such mindlessness, Paul recognizes, can disintegrate into meaninglessness. Speaking in tongues, at worst, consists of mindless chatter that benefits no one but the person who speaks: "nobody understands them, since they are speaking mysteries in the spirit" (1 Cor. 14:2). Like a military bugle that bungles the battle cry with an indistinct sound, tongues is "speech that is not intelligible," "speaking into the air" (14:8-9), an act in which the speaker is a foreigner to the hearer and the hearer a foreigner to the speaker (14:11). Speaking in tongues cannot even evoke the response of "amen" because no one understands the words (14:16). In fact, unbelievers who participate in a church in which tongues are spoken by all will be driven away from faith and conclude, "you are out of your mind" (14:23).

No matter how distorted speaking in tongues becomes in the clumsy hands of the Corinthians, Paul is unwilling to throw this experience away. He does, however, offer several sensitive correctives in an effort to draw the Corinthians away from their obsession with ecstasy and toward an appreciation of the power of comprehension. The first of these subtle corrections occurs in a list of spiritual gifts, where Paul refers first to wisdom and knowledge and last to speaking in tongues and their interpretation (1 Cor. 12:4-11). This late placement of speaking in tongues corrects the assumption that communication through a dormant mind is preeminent. Speaking in tongues, this order implies, is not the principal source of inspired wisdom and knowledge. In another list, Paul again sets speaking in

with the Spirit, pp. 336-40; and, in a more popular vein, *Fresh Air: The Holy Spirit for an Inspired Life* (Brewster, MA: Paraclete, 2012), pp. 178-84.

50. Philo Judaeus, *On the Special Laws* 4.49.

tongues and their interpretation in secondary positions, perhaps to imply that no worship experience, not even speaking in tongues, is powerful enough to reverse the proper order of the church: first apostles, second prophets, third teachers, then powers, then gifts of healing, assistance, and leadership, and then various kinds of speaking in tongues (12:27-28). Apostles, prophets, and teachers, who offer capable and comprehensible leadership, are the anchors of the "greater gifts" (12:31). In other lists, in Romans 12:3-8 and Ephesians 4:11-12, there is no mention of speaking in tongues at all.

Later in his letter, Paul also subtly topples the Corinthians' priorities by advising them to pursue prophecy rather than tongues in order to build up the community: "for those who speak in a tongue do not speak to other people but to God; for nobody understands them, since they are speaking mysteries in the spirit. On the other hand, those who prophesy speak to other people for their upbuilding and encouragement and consolation. Those who speak in a tongue build up themselves, but those who prophesy build up the church" (1 Cor. 14:2-4).

Although Paul appears to opt for restraint rather than ecstasy, for lucid speech rather than *glossolalia,* from this point on in his letter, throughout chapter 14, he embraces the interplay between both, between ecstasy and comprehension, as he shifts from speaking in tongues to the *interpretation* of speaking in tongues. He is now less troubled by speaking in tongues than by speaking in tongues without an interpreter. Paul prefers prophecy, it would seem — "I would like all of you to speak in tongues, but even more to prophesy" — yet he concedes that prophesying is greater than tongues "unless someone interprets, so that the church may be built up" (1 Cor. 14:6). The tongues-speaker, advises Paul, should pray for the power *to interpret,* so that those around may say amen in agreement, may be built up, may be instructed (14:13-19).

At this point Paul poses his own question to the Corinthians — a question suggesting he wants them to pursue an experience that is both ecstatic and comprehensible. Not one or the other but *both:* "What should I do then? I will pray with the spirit, but I will pray with the mind also; I will sing praise with the spirit, but I will sing praise with the mind also." And why? So that others can listen, agree, say "Amen!" and be edified (1 Cor. 14:15-16).

Later still in his letter, in order to draw the Corinthians to the clear priority that everything should be done "for building up" the community (1 Cor. 14:26), Paul turns to extremely practical advice: every gift in worship should be exercised one at a time, that is, in an orderly fashion. He even implies that interpretation and speaking in tongues are controllable acts when he advises tongues-speakers to keep it to themselves, and to God, if there is no interpreter present (14:27-28). There is an indispensable element of control in the exercise of spiritual gifts. Whether speaking in tongues or prophesying or singing hymns or offering revelations — these must take place in due order, while everyone else remains silent (14:26-33).

Finally, based on his own experience, Paul suggests that the clearest arena for the exercise of speaking in tongues is private, personal prayer. In a thinly veiled boast, Paul thanks God that he speaks in tongues more than all of the Corinthians. Despite the vitality of his personal prayer life, however, Paul would prefer to speak five words in public with his mind intact "in order to instruct others also" (1 Cor. 14:18-20).

When Paul is forced to confront the Corinthians' fraying order, based in part upon their mistaken hierarchy of spiritual gifts, his advice is magnanimous. Rather than getting rid of troublesome ecstasy altogether, instead of dismissing tongues out of hand, Paul tempers the potential disintegration of speaking in tongues with restraint by supplying a series of subtle signals that speaking in tongues, if it is to be of value in building up the church, must be joined at the hip to comprehensible speech. When Paul makes this case, step by nuanced step, he demonstrates that ecstasy without restraint is a menace to the church's life and that order without ecstasy is simply unthinkable, for ecstatic and comprehensible speech are inseparable companions. They are, quite simply, made for one another.

Pentecost and Beyond in the Book of Acts

At three key junctures in the book of Acts — the beginning of the church (Acts 2:4), the inclusion of Gentiles (10:44-46), and the completion of John's promise of baptism with the holy spirit in chapter 19 (19:6) — there is a lucid association of speaking in tongues with comprehensible speech. In each of these critical junctures in the book of Acts, Luke offers much more than an instance of unintelligible speaking in tongues; he champions instead a model of inspiration that unites ecstasy with comprehension.

Ecstasy and comprehension fuse in the fiery experience of Pentecost. The way Luke tells the story, the cosmos stirred at Pentecost:

When the day of Pentecost had come, they were all together in one place. And suddenly from heaven there came a sound like the rush of a violent wind, and it filled the entire house where they were sitting. Divided tongues, as of fire, appeared among them, and a tongue rested on each of them. All of them were filled with the holy spirit and began to speak in other languages, as the spirit gave them ability. (Acts 2:1-4)

THE ADVENT OF ECSTASY

At first blush, the experience of Jesus' followers exhibits the characteristics of Greco-Roman ecstasy: fire, filling, and the appearance of drunkenness. It would have been difficult, if not impossible, for a Greco-Roman reader (including Jews) to have heard about tongues as of fire, filling with (the) spirit, and the charge of drunkenness without discerning in them the presence of ecstasy.[51]

Pneuma was a primary source of inspiration according to many Greco-Roman writers. In particular, enthusiasm — a state of ecstatic loss of control — was traced to the inspiring *pneuma*. Return for a moment to Plutarch's *On the Obsolescence of Oracles,* where Lamprias, one of those in heated conversation with Cleombrotus and Ammonius, attributes the decrease in oracular activity at Delphi to a disappearance of a vapor that in the past rose from the ground to inspire the Delphic Pythia; this vapor has stopped due to changes in sun and earth.[52] Under such physical influences, which once were plentiful, explains Lamprias, "the reasoning and thinking faculty of the souls is relaxed and released from their present state as they range amid the irrational and imaginative realms of the future."[53] The principal catalyst for such inspiration is *pneuma,* a physical entity that enters the body and produces a condition free of mental restraint — enthusiasm. Lamprias clarifies:

Often the body of itself alone attains this disposition. Moreover the earth sends forth for people streams of many other potencies, some of them producing derangements, diseases, or deaths; others helpful, benignant, and beneficial, as is plain from the experience of persons who

---

51. For a detailed analysis of this point, see *Filled with the Spirit,* pp. 325-35.

52. Plutarch, *On the Obsolescence of Oracles* 431E-434C. On the theory of the vapors, see J. Fontenrose, *The Delphic Oracle: Its Responses and Operations* (Berkeley: University of California Press, 1978); H. W. Parke and D. E. W. Wormell, *The Delphic Oracle,* vol. 1: *The History* (Oxford: Blackwell, 1956), pp. 19-26.

53. Plutarch, *On the Obsolescence of Oracles* 432C.

have come upon them. But the prophetic current and breath [*pneuma*] is most divine and holy, whether it issue by itself through the air or come in the company of running waters; for when it is instilled into the body, it creates in souls an unaccustomed and unusual temperament, the peculiarity of which it is hard to describe with exactness.[54]

There is no need to rehearse the point that Greeks and Romans often traced inspiration to *pneuma*. Israelite authors did as well, long before the Greeks entered the picture. Yet the presence of fire alongside *pneuma* is less at home in the literature of Israel than in Greco-Roman discussions of inspiration. According to a first-century poetic description, the Delphic Pythia "boils over with fierce fire" while Apollo is allowed to "dart flame into her vitals."[55] This highly sexualized version of inspiration is a far cry from Luke's story of Pentecost, but the imagery of fire is not. Cicero too associates fire with inspiration and the Delphic *pneuma* when he writes, "Those, then, whose souls, spurning their bodies, take wings and fly abroad — inflamed and aroused by a sort of passion — there were certain subterranean vapors which had the effect of inspiring persons to utter oracles."[56]

Then, of course, there is the charge of drunkenness that some in the crowd lodge against the followers of Jesus. This is a patently false charge, Peter explains, but it is not for that reason incredible, at least not in the presence of a crowd that came from the far-flung corners of the Roman Empire. Such a crowd was familiar with Bacchic ritual. Drinking new wine in honor of Bacchus was integral to the festival of Anthesteria, which took place in late February and early March and became extremely popular in Greece, especially in Athens. The charge leveled against Jesus' followers, that they were drunk in the morning on new wine, may in this light comprise only a thinly veiled accusation that they were acting like the devotees of Bacchus, who entered an ecstatic state through inordinate drinking.[57] Understood from this perspective, the charge at Pentecost may have been less a denial of their inspiration than the accusation that they were indeed inspired, but through new wine drunk in honor

54. Plutarch, *On the Obsolescence of Oracles* 432D.
55. Lucan, *On the Civil War* 5.118, 120.
56. Cicero, *On Divination* 1.114.
57. For a plethora of parallels, see Pieter van der Horst, "Hellenistic Parallels to the Acts of the Apostles (2.1-47)," *Journal for the Study of the New Testament* 25 (1985): 54-55.

of another popular god who would have been unacceptable to the Jews gathered at Pentecost.[58]

Plutarch, too, probed the nature of inspiration by comparing it with the fiery effects of wine, especially wine drunk in Bacchic frenzy. "It is likely that by warmth and diffusion it [*pneuma*] opens up certain passages through which impressions of the future are transmitted, just as wine, when its fumes rise to the head, reveals many unusual movements and also words stored away and unperceived. 'For Bacchic rout/And frenzied mind contain much prophecy,' according to Euripides, when the soul becomes hot and fiery, and throws aside the caution that human intelligence lays upon it, and thus often diverts and extinguishes the inspiration."

Luke's story of Pentecost, then, contains three elements of ecstasy that were familiar to his Greco-Roman readers — and all of his readers were Greco-Roman, since they read the story in Greek: fire; filling with *pneuma;* and apparent drunkenness. It looks, on the surface, as if the followers of Jesus succumbed to the ecstatic impulse. Yet this is only a surface reading. In fact, Luke sets these elements into a remarkable story of miraculous comprehension.

THE INEVITABILITY OF COMPREHENSION

Comprehension is evident, first of all, in what Luke actually writes: not that the earliest followers of Jesus "spoke in tongues" but that they "spoke in *other* tongues." The underlying element of ecstasy that is inherent in the phrase "speaking in tongues" is broken by the word *other,* which points to comprehensible dialects. The inspired ability to speak in other languages prompts the hearers, "who were bewildered because each one heard them speaking in the native language of each," to ask, "And how is it that we hear, each of us, in our own native language?" (Acts 2:6-7). Comprehension — what Michael Welker calls the miracle of ultra-comprehensibility — rules the day of Pentecost. Luke tells us so in both third person narrative (2:4) and direct speech (2:7-8). It is hard to miss the comprehensible impact of the holy spirit.[59]

---

58. For a detailed discussion, see H. Lewy, *Sobria Ebrietas: Untersuchungen zur Geschichte der antiken Mystik,* Beihefte zur Zeitschrift für die neutestamentliche Wissenschaft und die Kunde der älteren Kirche 9 (Giessen: Töpelmann [now Walter de Gruyter], 1929), pp. 42-72; also Raniero Cantalamessa, *Sober Intoxication of the Spirit: Filled with the Fullness of God* (Cincinnati: St. Anthony Messenger Press, 2005), pp. 1-10.

59. Michael Welker (*God the Spirit* [Minneapolis: Fortress, 1994], p. 233) showcases the ultra-comprehensibility of Pentecost.

Comprehension is apparent, second, when Luke reveals the content of speaking in other tongues: the praiseworthy acts of God. "Praiseworthy acts" is a shorthand expression for God's powerful acts in Israel's history.[60] These acts begin with creation, traverse the storied experience of the exodus, and continue through the reigns of faithful monarchs.

Comprehension is evident, third, in the verb Luke adopts to describe the disciples' speech — a word, *apophthengesthai*, translated inadequately at the end of Acts 2:4 as "gave them ability" (NRSV) or "enabled" (NIV) or "gave them utterance" (ESV). In the book of Acts, this word means much more. A few short lines later, Peter will stand up and deliver an inspired sermon that brings thousands to repentance. This grand speech is introduced by the word *apophthengesthai* (2:14). Peter "uttered" his explanation of Pentecost by stitching together scriptural allusions and citations. All of these texts provide certainty "that God has made him both Lord and Messiah, this Jesus whom you crucified" (2:36). Luke takes up this verb a third time when he depicts Paul in dire straits, left to languish in prison and itching for an appearance before the Roman governor. In the course of his appearance, Paul is accused, "You are out of your mind, Paul! Too much learning is driving you insane!" Paul responds, "I am not out of my mind, most excellent Festus, but I am speaking the sober truth" (26:24-25). The verb Paul adopts to underscore the utter veracity of his claims is *apophthengesthai*. Of all the words Luke might have chosen to express Paul's sanity, of all the ways in which Luke might have contrasted madness with mental composure, he chooses to contrast, in the clearest of terms, two expressions: "I am not mad" and "I *utter* [*apophthengesthai*] true and sober words." The verb earlier used of the Pentecostal believers (2:4) and Peter the preacher (2:14) occurs here to communicate complete and utter sanity (26:25).

If there is a verb in Acts that expresses intellectual acuity, it is this verb, *apophthengesthai*. The selection of this verb in the context of the Pentecost story blunts the hard edge of ecstasy while maintaining the rhetorical clout that the ecstatic dimension conveyed within the confines of the Greco-Roman world. In a dazzling world of disarray overflowing with violent winds, filling with spirit, tongues as of fire, and the appearance of drunkenness, there occurs a trustworthy utterance of scripture. These believers, like Paul before Agrippa and Festus much later in the story, are not mad or drunk; their proclamation, like Peter's in quick succession

---

60. See, for example, Deuteronomy 11:2-5 and Psalm 105:1-2.

and Paul's later, contains a fresh — Luke would say inspired — interpretation of scripture that is, through and through, the essence of sobriety and truth.

THE SYMBIOSIS OF ECSTASY AND COMPREHENSION

Yet that is not the end of the story. The experience of speaking in tongues occurs twice more in the ongoing narrative of the early church. When, in the second instance, which is often called the Gentile Pentecost, the holy spirit comes upon Cornelius and his Gentile friends, Peter and his coterie hear them "speaking in tongues and praising God." The association of speaking in tongues with praise draws us back to speaking in other tongues in Acts 2 because the verb *praise* in Acts 10:46, *megalunein,* is related to the comprehensible "praiseworthy acts," *megaleia,* of Pentecost (Acts 2:11). The so-called Gentile Pentecost, like its Pentecostal predecessor, combines comprehensible praise with the ecstasy of speaking in tongues.

In the third instance of speaking in tongues, Paul meets a band of "disciples" who have not heard of the holy spirit (Acts 19:1-7); when he laid his hands upon them, "the holy spirit came upon them, and they spoke in tongues and prophesied." Prophesying throughout Acts, like praise, is comprehensible. Prophets punctuate the history of the early church with occasional but certain clarity about the future. For example, the prophet Agabus correctly predicts a famine (11:27-28). Judas and Silas, themselves prophets, are sent to Antioch with a letter to communicate the Jerusalem Council's decision (15:22, 27, 32). In Acts 19, then, speaking in tongues is combined with comprehensible prophetic speech when Paul lays his hands on disciples who have, prior to this moment, no awareness of the holy spirit.

Luke has composed a remarkable triad of speaking in tongues, which leads to the simultaneous embrace of ecstasy and comprehension. When the earliest believers are filled with the holy spirit, they speak the praiseworthy acts of God in comprehensible foreign tongues. When Gentiles speak in tongues, they participate actively in praise, as had the followers of Jesus during Pentecost. When a group of disciples speak in tongues, they prophesy — an activity that is, throughout Acts, practical and understandable. Three times Luke unites in a single moment a form of inspiration — speaking in (other) tongues — that rides the edge of ecstasy while proclaiming in clear and comprehensible ways words of praise and prophecy.

Luke's portrayal of speaking in tongues, then, joins enigmatic with intelligent speech — sober truth — in a way that embraces the love of learning which the church's ancestors — people such as Daniel and Beza-lel — had cherished before them. God's praiseworthy acts, in particular, lead back to the heart of Israel's scriptures. The psalmist asks, "You who have done *praiseworthy acts,* O God, who is like you?" (Ps. 71:19).[61] The sign of the spirit, Luke is clear, is not an unbridled loss of control, a fiery experience like drunkenness. The spirit is present in an experience that is too unaccountable, too extraordinary to be pinned down as ecstasy.

Yet it would be misleading to emphasize comprehensibility at the expense of ecstasy. Notwithstanding the heightened comprehension that comprises an impressive façade for the story of Pentecost, bubbling under the surface are the accoutrements of ecstasy. Any one of these elements — filling, fire, intoxication, and tongues — is enough to suggest that something of the ecstatic or uncontrollable may be at play here.

It is a pity that interpreters tend to line up on one side of the debate or the other, according to whether they understand speaking in tongues *either* as speech in comprehensible foreign dialects *or* as incomprehensible speech.[62] What Luke does is more subtle than to opt for *either* ecstatic tongues speech *or* comprehensible foreign languages. The power of Pentecost may lie, in Luke's estimation, not in either incomprehensibility or apprehension, but in the early believers' ability to straddle both worlds. The holy spirit combines both in the alchemy of inspiration in order to create one magnificent experience.

The Holy Spirit and the Power of Reflection

If Pentecost provides a salient illustration of striking a balance between ecstasy and comprehension, other stories in the book of Acts embrace this symbiosis in different guises. To put ecstasy in its place, its proper place, we will benefit from exploring a few of those stories in a good measure of detail: Paul's vision of the risen Jesus and his later retelling

61. My translation, instead of "great things." For the Greek, *megaleia,* see LXX Psalm 70:19.

62. Joseph Fitzmyer (*The Acts of the Apostles,* Anchor Bible 31 [Garden City, NY: Doubleday, 1998], p. 239) offers an extensive list of scholars who understand this phenomenon *either* as an ecstatic experience of speaking in tongues *or* as xenolalia, speaking in foreign tongues.

of the story in the presence of King Agrippa (Acts 9; 26);[63] Peter's vision of illicit foods and his interpretation of the vision (Acts 10–11, 15); the groundwork that led to an inspired word in the church at Antioch and the interpretation of that word (Acts 13); and what led to the decision of the Jerusalem Council which, according to a letter from James, "seemed good to the holy spirit and to us" (Acts 15). These stories have the power to illuminate the work of the holy spirit in relation to, and beyond the boundaries of, inspired ecstasy.

Paul, Ananias, and a Mission Ahead

The text Peter chooses to explain the miracle of Pentecost he extracts from the prophetic book of Joel, in which Joel sees a day when "your sons and your daughters shall prophesy, and your young men shall see visions, and your old men shall dream dreams. Even upon my slaves, both men and women, in those days I will pour out my spirit; and they shall prophesy" (Acts 2:17-18; Joel 2:28-29). Dreams. Visions. Prophetic oracles. These, during the Greco-Roman era, were the palpable evidence of ecstasy.

Very little of this actually occurs in the book of Acts. The only daughters who prophesy are Philip's, though we have no trace of what they said (Acts 21:9). The only slave who prophesies is a girl inspired, not by the holy spirit, but by a pythonic spirit, a foreign spirit whom Paul tells to leave because he is annoyed by the girl's constant shouts (Acts 16:16-18). The only significant dreams and visions in the book of Acts belong, not to young men, but to established ones, like Paul, Peter, and Cornelius. What we learn from these visions — from the sole experiences that Luke describes with the word *ekstasis* — is that ecstasy, if it is present at all in visionary experiences, has its place, and that place is alongside the thoughts and reflections of people who are *compos mentis*.

By way of starters, a brief look at the story of Paul's Damascus Road vision, which Paul retells twice, will make this point clear. Paul's experience on the road, as Luke tells it, consisted of a vision, a sudden light from heaven that dropped Paul to the ground. Those around Paul heard the voice of the risen Jesus but did not see the vision; Paul alone did, and he left the scene of this encounter blinded (Acts 9:3-9). The content of

---

63. At this point in the story of Acts, Paul is still referred to as Saul. I opt for the name Paul simply because it is less confusing.

this vision is straightforward. Jesus says, "Saul, Saul, why do you perse-cute me?" Paul asks, "Who are you, Lord?" The reply comes, "I am Jesus, whom you are persecuting. But get up and enter the city, and you will be told what you are to do" (9:4-6). Essentially, the vision consists of a ques-tion, a response in which Jesus identifies himself with those whom Paul persecutes, and practical instructions.

The purpose of Paul's vision does not arise so much from his own ex-perience as from a tandem vision, where the Lord gives Ananias instruc-tions. Two things emerge from Ananias's vision that do not from Paul's. First, the Lord tells Ananias — but apparently not Paul — that Paul "has seen in a vision a man named Ananias come in and lay his hands on him so that he might regain his sight" (Acts 9:12). Second, Ananias — but ap-parently not Paul — learns what Paul's vocation will be; God tells Ananias, "Go, for he is an instrument whom I have chosen to bring my name before Gentiles and kings and before the people of Israel. I myself will show him how much he must suffer for the sake of my name" (9:15-16). This second bit of information is explosive in part because Luke tells us something that even Paul, at this point in the story, does not yet know.

This information is explosive as well because, right from the start, it takes a reader to the heart of Paul's vocation. The mission to Gentiles and Israel, accompanied by suffering, takes our eyes to the servant of Isaiah 40–55, who will suffer as he brings teaching to the coastlands. This mis-sion, as it is explained to Ananias, leads us also to Simeon's revelation, in which Jesus will be "a light for revelation to the Gentiles and for glory to your people Israel," though the whole while Jesus is a sign that would pro-voke opposition (Luke 2:28-35). The mission of Paul also connects him to believers before him, such as Stephen, whose suffering arose in part from his belief that faith could be disconnected from the temple and the land of Israel; with this theology, Stephen paved the way for Gentiles to believe — and for his own martyrdom. Paul had championed Stephen's martyrdom; now Paul would join him in the shadow of martyrdom. The vocation of Paul, in short, would follow suit from the suffering servant of Isaiah, the suffering messiah, and the suffering community of believers who followed in his train.

None of this, as far as we can tell, is communicated to Paul while he lies on the ground in a visionary state. None of it. Ananias learns of Paul's vocation in a separate vision altogether.

Yet much later in the book of Acts, in his defense before King Agrippa, Paul tells the story of his vision differently. This later version reflects elements from Ananias's vision that may not have been part of his own. Paul tells Agrippa that Jesus said, "I am Jesus whom you are persecuting. But get up and stand on your feet; for I have appeared to you for this purpose, to appoint you to serve and testify to the things in which you have seen me and to those in which I will appear to you. I will rescue you from your people and from the Gentiles — to whom I am sending you to open their eyes so that they may turn from darkness to light and from the power of Satan to God, so that they may receive forgiveness of sins and a place among those who are sanctified by faith in me" (Acts 26:15-18).[64] There is much more here than in Paul's original vision. There is much more even than in Ananias's original vision. What are we to make of the difference?[65]

One possibility is to say that Luke withheld this in his initial story of the vision. This is possible, though difficult to determine why. A much better suggestion is this: Paul reflected subsequently on his possibly ec-static experience. On what did he reflect? Scripture. At least his version of the experience in Acts 26:14-18 points to the Jewish Bible (or its Greek translation). The words *get up and stand on your feet* may reflect the influence of Ezekiel 2:1. The promise of rescue may reflect the influence of Jeremiah 1:7-8. The association of *your people* and *Gentiles* has roots in Isaiah 42:7, while *turning from darkness to light* picks up the language of Isaiah 42:16 (which Simeon in turn picked up in his words about Jesus in Luke 2:32).

So many allusions in this later version of Paul's vision, none of which appeared in the original story of his vision! These allusions suggest that Paul had reflected on his original vision in light of the Jewish scriptures. In short, he put ecstasy in its place: in the crucible of scripture, in the context of prophetic calls.

What prompted Paul to reflect on his vision in light of the scriptures? Perhaps this was just a natural tendency for him, a penchant he simply was unable to circumvent. Trained as a Pharisee, committed to the in-terpretation of scripture, Paul inevitably turned there to understand his own ecstatic experience. Yet we can take one more step. Recall Ananias's

64. Although much has been written on the so-called conversion of Saul, a good place to start an analysis is with Seyoon Kim, *The Origin of Paul's Gospel* (Grand Rapids: Eerdmans, 1981; paperback edition, Eugene, OR: Wipf & Stock, 2007).

65. Luke does not as a rule withhold elements of visions. Cornelius's recounting of his vision (Acts 10:30-32), for example, is similar to Luke's account of it (10:3-5). The angel becomes a man in dazzling clothes; otherwise, the details, though in paraphrase, remain much the same.

vision, which contained the seeds of Paul's vocation: "he is an instrument whom I have chosen to bring my name before Gentiles and kings and before the people of Israel" (Acts 9:15). Ananias became Paul's mentor, his advocate, his colleague. It is likely, in the compass of the story, as Luke tells it, that Ananias communicated to Paul the substance of his own vision. In short, Ananias provides an unspoken link between Saul of Acts 9 and Paul of Acts 26. Ananias may have taught Paul in the first place that his fate would follow from the servant's fate, from Jesus', and from his predecessors' in the church. Ananias, after all, had garnered the essence of this perspective on Paul's vocation from his own vision.

Once again, therefore, ecstasy is not left to stand alone. Its place is alongside the power of study and learning. Through the power of a mentor, the further study of scripture, and Paul's later life experience of suffering for Jesus' sake, ecstasy finds its purpose: to bring light to the nations in the grit of mission.

Peter, Cornelius, and the Outpouring Ahead

Another pair of visions sets up an equally astounding tremor in the foundations of the church. A devout centurion, Cornelius, one afternoon at three o'clock, "had a vision in which he clearly saw an angel of God coming in" and telling him to send men to Peter in Joppa. Accustomed to taking and giving orders, Cornelius sent two slaves and a devout soldier — a soldier presumably devoted to the practice of Jewish faith — to find Peter in Joppa (Acts 10:1-8).

The second vision, which took place about twenty-one hours later, was also a quiet and private work (Acts 10:9-16). At lunchtime the next day, the leader of the Jerusalem church, Peter, was grabbing a few moments alone to pray on a roof. The small detail, *Peter was praying,* is a reminder of Daniel and Simeon, for whom sheer discipline provided the context for a startling and world-changing experience of the spirit.

While Peter was praying, a few things happened all at once. First, while he was hungry and waiting for lunch to be prepared, he went to the roof to pray, and he had a vision — literally, *ekstasis* came upon him (Acts 10:9). Though the word can mean, as we saw, that Peter fell asleep, more likely this means ecstasy came upon him, since he immediately experienced a vision and, notably, did not need to wake up, as if he had been sleeping. As soon as he was no longer under the power of ecstasy, he "was greatly puzzled about what to make of the vision that he had seen" (10:17). Second, while Peter was puzzling over what to make of this vision, the two slaves and soldier sent by Cornelius arrived at the door; they asked for Peter (10:17-18). Third, "while Peter was still thinking about the vision, the spirit said to him, 'Look, three men are searching for you. Now get up, go down, and go with them without hesitation; for I have sent them'" (10:19-20). No time for musing here; the spirit had practical orders to deliver, not unlike those the spirit had earlier given to Paul and Ananias (9:6; 9:11) and, just the day before, to Cornelius (10:5-6). It was quite an afternoon for Peter, with a vision, a visit, a voice, but apparently no lunch — all because he showed up for private prayer.

The result of Cornelius's vision and Peter's ecstasy — Cornelius's vision should perhaps also be construed as ecstasy, given its pairing with Peter's — was the obliteration of the barrier between Jew and Gentile. After his vision, Peter went down from the roof and accompanied the men to Caesarea, where Cornelius told him about his own vision. Peter responded in character by preaching, though his sermon was interrupted by the work of the holy spirit:

> While Peter was still speaking, the holy spirit fell upon all who heard the word. The circumcised believers who had come with Peter were astounded that the gift of the holy spirit had been poured out even on the Gentiles, for they heard them speaking in tongues and praising God. Then Peter said, "Can anyone withhold the water for baptizing these people who have received the holy spirit just as we have?" So he ordered them to be baptized in the name of Jesus Christ. Then they invited him to stay for several days. (Acts 10:44-48)

This is a remarkable state of affairs, and the need for tandem visions to occasion it is hardly baffling. In an unnatural but divinely ordained impulse, traditional borders are broken, Gentiles and Jews brought into contact. All heaven had broken loose, and a new community was in the making.

When Peter returned to Jerusalem, he asked the Jewish followers of Jesus there, "If then God gave them the same gift that he gave us when we believed in the Lord Jesus Christ, who was I that I could hinder God?" Apparently his baffled audience was convinced, because, "when they heard this, they were silenced. And they praised God, saying, 'Then God has given even to the Gentiles the repentance that leads to life'" (Acts 11:17-18).

This is the outer shell of the story, the framework of a seismic shift in the early church. Yet other transformations take place under the surface, two significant ones in particular.

MEANING MATTERS

The first under-the-surface transformation unfolds in Peter's response to the vision that took place while *ekstasis* was upon him. The surfeit of meaning unfolds in three closely related parts.

Part one: Peter is puzzled over this vision, though God's command to eat unclean foods seems obvious enough. Still, he is deep in thought when Cornelius's emissaries appear at his door. This verb, *puzzle,* is important. Peter searches for meaning in a vision that took place under ecstasy or sleep. He is not interested in physical transport or emotional catharsis or basking in ecstasy; he wants *meaning.*

Peter does not have the luxury of arriving at the meaning of his vision because Cornelius's emissaries interrupt his perplexity, and he travels with them to Caesarea, where a sequence of events arrests his attention: the spirit is poured out upon Gentiles, who invite Peter to stay for several days — eating, perhaps, profane foods (Acts 10:48), after which he returns to Jerusalem to explain all that happened. This begins phase two.

Part two: once Peter returns to Jerusalem, he retells his vision and the subsequent events in response to their questions, "Why did you go to uncircumcised men and eat with them?" (Acts 11:3). Surprisingly, Peter does not connect the outpouring of the spirit upon Gentiles to his vision. Instead he turns to the words of Jesus to explain the events in Caesarea: "John baptized with water, but you will be baptized with the holy spirit" (11:16). The logic of Peter's actions and explanation are framed by the words of Jesus — and not by his vision.

Part three: Peter continues, "If then God gave them the same gift that he gave us when we believed in the Lord Jesus Christ, who was I that I could hinder God?" (Acts 11:17). After appealing to the words of Jesus, Peter appeals to the experience of his community. The close correspondence between the experiences of Jew and Gentile validates the work of the holy spirit among the nations.

We do not yet see Peter arrive at the meaning of his vision, but we do see a model for dealing with the aftermath of ecstatic visions. First, Peter *puzzles over* what his vision might mean. Second, Peter turns to the *words of Jesus.* Third, Peter compares events with the experience of his own community.

Part four: Only later still does Peter incorporate the insight of his vision. After Paul and Barnabas return from traveling to the island of Cyprus and on to interior regions along the northern coast of the Mediterranean Sea, where they encounter myriad more receptive Gentiles, who "were glad and praised the word of the Lord" (Acts 13:48), does Peter begin to make the connection between his vision and God's work among the Gentiles. He makes the connection, in fact, only when Paul is pressed — and pressed hard by followers of Jesus who belong to members of a sect of the Pharisees. Some of these believers say, "It is necessary for them to be circumcised and ordered to keep the law of Moses" (15:5). A fierce debate follows, after which Peter stands and says that God has appointed him to go to the Gentiles. "And God," he continues, "who knows the human heart, testified to them by giving them the holy spirit, just as he did to us; and in cleansing their hearts by faith he has made no distinction between them and us. Now therefore why are you putting God to the test by placing on the neck of the disciples a yoke that neither our ancestors nor we have been able to bear?" (15:8-10). Peter now understands, not only that there is no distinction between Jew and Gentile, but also that neither Jew nor Gentile needs to conform to the regulations of Torah. The importance of Torah, and Peter's opposition to its imposition on Gentiles, goes to the heart of his vision about unclean foods.

Peter's understanding of his vision has expanded in its aftermath. He knows it was not about him alone; the vision was about others. He knows it was not about Cornelius's emissaries, who arrived just after the vision ended; the vision was about all Gentiles. He knows it was not even only about all Gentiles; all Jews too need not be burdened by a heavy yoke. And he knows it was not only about food but Gentiles — people — who are not unclean. This vision, Peter now grasps, is about the salvation of humankind, the liberation of both Jew and Gentile: "we believe that we will be saved through the grace of the Lord Jesus, just as they will" (Acts 15:11). We and they, Jew and Gentile, are saved exclusively by the grace of the Lord Jesus. This is not, to be sure, the original content of the vision over which Peter initially puzzled. Yet, in light of his puzzling, in light of the words of Jesus, in light of the uncanny similarities between the experience of Jewish and Gentile followers of Jesus, in light of his encounter with Cornelius and the report from Paul and Barnabas, Peter comes to the conclusion — an expansive conclusion that goes far beyond the actual content and words of his vision — that it is universal in scope and global in importance.

Obviously, *meaning matters.* The purpose of ecstasy, at least in relation to Peter's vision, is full of meaning, rife with transformation, rich in barrier-breaking. And this happens through pondering and *puzzling,* through recollection of the *words of Jesus,* through an embrace of *unexpected experiences,* and through *immersion in an alien world.*

OLD WORD, NEW MEANING

Another transformation occurs in the aftermath of Peter's vision; Luke signals this transformation through the recurrence of a single Greek word. At the start of it all, the spirit ordered Peter to "go with them without hesitating" (10:20). *Without hesitation.* Something new is afoot — the embodiment of Joel's vision, in fact, though Peter does not know this yet — and Peter must not enter it with his feet dragging.

The verb that is translated as *hesitating (diakrinomenos)* in Acts 10:20, just after Peter had his vision of profane foods, can also mean *discriminating,* and this is how Peter understood the spirit's word after he followed the spirit's directions and traveled to Caesarea, where he unexpectedly saw the holy spirit poured out on Gentiles, on non-Jews, who went on to speak in tongues and to praise God, just as the Jewish followers of Jesus had experienced the holy spirit on the day of Pentecost. When Peter returned to Jerusalem, he retold the story to the Jewish followers of Jesus there: "The spirit told me to go with them *without discriminating* between them and us" (11:12). Notice that Peter adopted the same verb, *diakrinein,* which the spirit had used when Cornelius's emissaries arrived on the scene — but with a different meaning. Now Peter understood that the spirit had not told him to get up and go *without hesitating,* but to get up and go *without discriminating* between Jews and non-Jews, between the believers in Jerusalem and those in Caesarea.

Later still, when the Jerusalem community comes together to decide what Torah obligations to impose upon Gentile followers of Jesus, Peter picks up this verb yet again, "And God, who knows the human heart, testified to them by giving them the holy spirit, just as he did to us; and in cleansing their hearts by faith, he [God] has not discriminated [*diakrinen*] between them and us" (Acts 15:8-9).[66]

This is a powerful interpretation of the spirit's words to Peter. Peter does not take a minimalist approach to revelation. He does not sit tight with the directions of the spirit. He does not grasp, white-knuckled, the

---

66. My translation. NRSV reads, "has made no distinction."

command to go *without hesitating* (Acts 10:20). He realizes subsequently that the spirit was commanding him to go *without discriminating* between them and us — between Jews like himself and Cornelius's slaves and soldier (11:12). Yet this is not the end of Peter's excavation of the spirit's word. In the third occurrence of the verb, *diakrinein,* Peter transforms the word spoken just to him in particular historical circumstances — the appearance of Cornelius's trio at his door — into a theological agenda: "And God, who knows the human heart, testified to them by giving them the holy spirit, just as he did to us; and in cleansing their hearts by faith, he [God] has not discriminated between them and us" (15:8-9). What began as a "get your butt in gear" statement of the spirit has become, through the experience of Peter with believing Gentiles, an agenda for the entire church of every age.

The Church in Antioch and the Frontier of Mission

Our foray into the work of the spirit has led us to two coordinated sets of visions. In the visions of Ananias and Cornelius, the holy spirit directs traffic with clarity and concreteness: Ananias is told exactly how to meet Paul, while Cornelius is told exactly how to meet Peter. The visions of Paul and Peter are more open-ended, lending themselves to interpretation, and both visionaries do a sizeable amount of interpretation. Paul gradually understands that his Damascus Road encounter with the risen Jesus was a prophetic call that would cost him dearly. This interpretation of Paul's vision becomes explicit through several means: his relationship with Ananias, to whom the spirit spoke the kernel of this message; the study of scripture, especially Israel's prophetic texts; and his own experience, as he labored among the Gentiles. Peter, too, gradually arrives at an expansive interpretation of his vision. Initially puzzled by what the vision might mean, he then sets his vision in the context of Jesus' promise of the holy spirit and in his experience of the impact of the holy spirit on the Gentiles. This combination of study, recollection, and experiences leads Peter to recognize that the vision was about Torah or, more accurately, *not-Torah* for Jew and Gentile.

Peter also receives a word of the spirit once he is no longer in an ecstatic state. The spirit tells him not to hesitate to go with Cornelius's emissaries. Yet Peter expands (as he did with the vision itself) the meaning of the word *diakrinesthai,* or hesitate. He uses the word differently, as if he understands that the spirit was telling him not to *discriminate* between himself and Cornelius's people. Even this is not enough, however, and Peter comes to a fuller realization that discrimination cuts against the grain of God's will for the entire human race, God's great design for the salvation of all people.

THE INDISPENSABILITY OF PREPARATION

Apart from a couple of details — Peter prayed, while Cornelius prayed and gave alms — we learn very little about preparation for potentially ecstatic experiences. Paul was totally unprepared; he was caught up short by the vision. We know little more about Ananias except that he was a disciple (Acts 9:10). Yet Luke is not silent about preparation for receiving, if not an ecstatic experience, at least a revelatory word of the spirit. In a story that follows shortly after the visions of Paul, Ananias, Peter, and Cornelius — in fact, right after Peter tells the community in Jerusalem about the Gentile Pentecost — we hear of a church that was particularly receptive to a word of prophecy. Luke writes:

> at that time prophets came down from Jerusalem to Antioch. One of them named Agabus stood up and predicted by the spirit that there would be a severe famine over all the world; and this took place during the reign of Claudius. The disciples determined that according to their ability, each would send relief to the believers living in Judea; this they did, sending it to the elders by Barnabas and Saul. (Acts 11:27-30)

The church in Antioch responded with concrete acts of giving to the word of a prophet they had not even met before. Agabus was not one of their own; he had come from Jerusalem, a city far away.

Yet this response is only the tip of the iceberg. A flurry of activity took place even before Agabus arrived in Antioch. Believers scattered by the persecution in Jerusalem visited, and the numbers of new believers swelled (Acts 11:21). The church in Jerusalem sent Barnabas, who found Paul and brought him to Antioch. "So it was that for an entire year they met with the church and taught a great many people" (11:26). The church was the locus of learning both for its own people and for a huge crowd.

What prepared the church in Antioch to receive a prophetic word was not a flurry of prophetic words or a spell of ecstatic experiences or an outbreak of the spirit with uncontrollable physical symptoms. What prepared the church in Antioch to receive a prophetic word was learning. Not superficial learning, a few scattered verses memorized here or there, desultory interest in the words of Jesus, a sermon from a preacher once a week. For an entire year, Paul and Barnabas devoted themselves to teaching a church and the huge crowd gathered with it. In short, *intensive learning* prepared the church in Antioch to respond to a prophetic word.

And they responded to Agabus's prediction of a famine with *extreme generosity*. "The disciples determined that according to their ability, each would send relief to the believers living in Judea; this they did, sending it to the elders by Barnabas and Saul" (Acts 11:29-30). This simple statement says a great deal about the quality of their generosity. Notice, first, that the church in Antioch did not wait for a famine to hit before responding, before calculating how much the believers in Jerusalem might need. They gave before there was a famine. Second, they did not simply give what was needed. They gave on the basis of what they had to give. Their generosity, in other words, came from their sense of well-being, of having enough, even more than enough. The Greek words translated, "according to their ability," to describe how much they would donate, can also be translated, "as anyone had plenty." *Plenty* is a relative term. Apparently Christians in Antioch felt they had, not just enough, but plenty, so they sent help to followers of Jesus in Judea. And third, they gave of their own free will. Agabus did nothing more than announce the famine; he did not, it seems, order them to give, or tell them who should give, or how much. The believers in Antioch decided to give, each who had plenty, on the basis of the news that a severe famine would blanket Jerusalem. This was a generous church.

Another quality of the church in Antioch prepared them to respond to distant need. Recall that the whole scenario began because people scattered by the persecution in Jerusalem traveled north. Most spoke only to Jews, "but among them were some men of Cyprus and Cyrene who, on coming to Antioch, spoke to the Hellenists also, proclaiming the Lord Jesus. The hand of the Lord was with them, and a great number became believers and turned to the Lord" (Acts 11:20-21). These men did not limit their preaching to Jews; they spoke as well to Greeks, and with great success. Antioch, therefore, was a church that absorbed people from foreign cities and islands. Agabus's arrival from Jerusalem was no novelty; many had arrived before him, and the church in Antioch was already an amalgamation of Jews and Greeks, island and inland dwellers, Hebrew and Greek speakers. They were poised, therefore, to respond to a prophet from a distant city with news of a distant disaster.

It is one thing to receive a prophetic word of the spirit. It is quite another to respond to that word in the right way. Antioch knew how to respond to Agabus's prediction because they had particular virtues. They had received a sustained education during a year of intense learning at the feet of Barnabas and Paul. They were a generous church, a church that understood the meaning of having enough — and knowing that "enough" is "plenty" when others, even faraway others, are, or soon will be, in desperate need. And the church in Antioch was a multicultural church with the capacity to absorb a prophet who hailed from far away.

COMMUNAL VIRTUE AND RECEPTIVITY TO REVELATION

These qualities of learning, generosity, and cultural openness go a long way to explain why, a few stories later in the book of Acts, Antioch became the launching pad for a vibrant mission. In deceptively few words, Luke reports:

> Now in the church at Antioch there were prophets and teachers: Barnabas, Simeon who was called Niger, Lucius of Cyrene, Manaen a member of the court of Herod the ruler, and Saul. While they were worshiping the Lord and fasting, the holy spirit said, "Set apart for me Barnabas and Saul for the work to which I have called them." Then after fasting and praying they laid their hands on them and sent them off. So, being sent out by the holy spirit, they went down to Seleucia; and from there they sailed to Cyprus. (Acts 13:1-5)

Luke's economy of words here belies the explosive significance of this snippet: the church at Antioch was the starting-point for a full-fledged mission of the church to the Gentiles.

There is a direct correlation between the preparation of the church and the inspired word it receives. First of all, the leaders in the church were teachers and prophets. Teachers take the lead in the process of learning — something we saw clearly in Barnabas and Paul's yearlong teaching stint in Antioch. Prophets take the lead in transforming teaching into practical directions. It's likely that the holy spirit spoke through prophets in this scenario with a concrete word: set apart Paul and Barnabas for the work to which the holy spirit has called them.[67]

---

67. The book of Acts does not allow us to do this with absolute certainty, but we may be able to piece together the relationship that existed between prophets and teachers at Antioch. Teachers communicated the whole tapestry of scripture, including the expansive

The second quality that prepared the church in Antioch to receive a word of the holy spirit was their generosity, which they had already exercised in sending provisions to Jerusalem in advance of a famine. Now they exercise this generosity again. Paul and Barnabas immediately went to the nearby town of Seleucia and sailed to Cyprus. Luke makes no mention of provisions or tickets, but someone in the church must have provided them. Then, when the mission was complete, the pair returned to Antioch, "where they had been commended to the grace of God" (Acts 14:26), and stayed with the disciples in Antioch "for some time" (14:28). Once again, Paul and Barnabas were shown hospitality by the church with whom they had earlier spent an entire year.

The third quality that made Antioch the perfect starting-point for a divinely directed mission was its multicultural character. We noticed that Antioch was the seedbed of a multicultural church. Now we see that the leadership team reflected this composition; it was ethnically and economically diverse. Barnabas no longer owned what he once did, since he sold his property and laid the proceeds at the apostles' feet in Jerusalem (Acts 4:36-37). Simeon, "the black one," was probably from North Africa. Lucius was from Cyrene, on the northern coast of Africa. Manaen was — or had been at one time — wealthy and Herod Antipas's friend from youth. Paul, from Tarsus, a coastal city in Asia Minor, claimed to be a Pharisee.[68] This church was not a homogeneous unit, held together by ethnic or social or economic uniformity. Antioch was led by a multicultural team. Its prophets and teachers stemmed from different shores of the Mediterranean world. Its leaders represented different economic strata. This was the ideal base for a mission that would break through cultural barriers.

Learning, generosity, and a multicultural makeup do not exhaust the qualities that prepared Antioch to respond efficiently and effectively to a word of the holy spirit. These qualities combined with still others. The spirit's word came to the church at Antioch while they were worshiping (the Greek word could also mean serving, as in serving the poor, though

---

vision that God would appoint servants, like the servant of Isaiah, to be a light to the nations. Prophets, in the context of worship and fasting, took those visions into the future — in this case in the calling of Saul and Barnabas to take on the mission of becoming Isaiah's light to the nations. The church then returned to fasting and prayer in order to discern the truth of the prophecy and to determine a road map for action, such as sending Saul and Barnabas to Cyprus — something the spirit did not say. In this way, prophets and teachers worked in tandem with one another and the church.

68. See Acts 22:3; 23:6; Philippians 3:5.

worship is more likely in this context) and fasting: *"while they were worshiping and fasting, the spirit said."* The church, in short, practiced communal disciplines.

These disciplines did more than prepare the church to receive this word. They provided the crucible for discerning implications of this word. These worshipers did not immediately ship Paul and Barnabas off to their work. The Christians in Antioch returned to the practice of fasting — now with the addition of prayer — before laying their hands on Barnabas and Paul and sending them off.[69] The Antioch Christians had to pray more because the holy spirit gave no overt directions. The spirit said only that the pair were to be set apart for the work to which God had called them. The call was clear, but its contents were left to the church in Antioch to figure out, and this they did, at least in part, through further fasting and prayer, along with the laying on of hands.

The whole of these qualities — a commitment to learning, generosity, a multicultural church and leadership team, along with the communal practices of worship, fasting, and prayer — is greater than the sum of its parts. Together, these qualities transformed Antioch into a source of favor and grace. When Barnabas first arrived in Antioch, "he came and saw the grace of God" (Acts 11:23). With their mission complete, Paul and Barnabas "sailed back to Antioch, where they had been handed over to *the grace of God* for the work they had completed" (14:26). Their generosity was not compulsory. Their prayer was not token. Their worship was not obligatory. Their fasting was not ostentatious. This church was a conduit of the grace of God, a spring of hospitality, a place Paul and Barnabas would naturally return to when their work was done and, as Luke puts it, stay there for some time.

It is not serendipitous that the holy spirit spoke a word to a church that was gathered for worship in Antioch. This particular church had set the groundwork for such a profound word. The spirit spoke to a church that was prepared by its knowledge, its generosity, its multicultural character, and its practice of communal disciplines. Nevertheless, despite the clarity of this word, it was incomplete, or at least inchoate. So the church returned to its disciplines, adding prayer to the mix, and discerned the

---

69. Where there is prophecy, there must be a discernment process to understand the prophetic word fully. Paul, in his letters, insists on the need for discernment. In a letter to the Corinthians, he gives explicit instructions about how to exercise the gift of prophecy (1 Corinthians 14), and to another Greek church he writes, "Do not despise the words of prophets, but test everything" (1 Thess. 5:20).

specific directions this work should take — directions that would have an inescapable impact on the church far beyond the confines of this coastal city.

Spirit, Conflict Resolution, and Collective Virtue: The Jerusalem Council

Biblical authors, unlike so many of their Greco-Roman counterparts, including Jewish authors like Philo, did not dissect experiences of ecstasy to any appreciable extent, so the contours of ecstasy are blurry. When we, so many years later, attempt to probe the mechanics of ecstasy, we are like the blind man in the gospels whom Jesus heals twice (Mark 8:22-26). On his first healing, the man sees people, but they look like trees walking. We are like that man at this stage of his healing — able to see the outline of ecstasy but certainly without surgical precision.

Such is the case with the experience of the church in Antioch. Although it came to a church engaged in worship and fasting — possibly as prolegomena to prophecy — and although prophets may have communicated the word, the word that came to Antioch was not necessarily given by people in an ecstatic state or to people in a state of ecstasy. Nor can we assume that the presence of the spirit entails ecstasy in the next episode we will explore: the story of the so-called Jerusalem Council (Acts 15). Still, the leader of the church in Jerusalem attributes the decision to which the Council comes to a combination of divine and human effort: "For it has seemed good to the holy spirit and to us" (Acts 15:28). This combination of divine and human cooperation provides us with an excellent episode with which to continue our study of the relationship between ecstasy, virtue, learning, and the holy spirit.

The story begins when a group tied to the Pharisees states their case: "It is necessary for them [Gentiles] to be circumcised and ordered to keep the law of Moses" (Acts 15:5). Peter takes up the opposing position, arguing instead, "And God, who knows the human heart, testified to them [the Gentiles] by giving them the holy spirit, just as he did to us; and in cleansing their hearts by faith he has made no distinction between them and us. Now therefore why are you putting God to the test by placing on the neck of the disciples a yoke that neither our ancestors nor we have been able to bear? On the contrary, we believe that we will be saved through the grace of the Lord Jesus, just as they will" (15:8-11). James takes a mediating position, though one that tilts toward Peter's position: "Simeon [or Simon] has related how God first looked favorably on the Gentiles, to take from among them a people for his name" (15:14). James concludes, "Therefore I have reached the decision that we should not trouble those Gentiles who are turning to God," except for abstention from things polluted by idols, from fornication, from strangled animals, and from blood (15:19-20).

This is well and good: a clear compromise reasonably made by a mediating leader in the early church. Yet that is not the whole of the story. What emerges subsequently is the belief that this is an inspired and inspiring moment in the life of the church. James writes in a letter to the church at Antioch, where the issue took root, *"For it has seemed good to the holy spirit and to us* to impose on you no further burden than these essentials: that you abstain from what has been sacrificed to idols and from blood and from what is strangled and from fornication. If you keep yourselves from these, you will do well" (Acts 15:28-29). This is a striking shift. What was earlier described as a reasonable decision *("I have decided")* is attributed in the letter to the holy spirit *("to the holy spirit")*. What was earlier depicted as James's individual decision ("*I* have reached the decision") is portrayed in the letter as a communal event ("to the holy spirit and to *us*"). The rhetorical force of this is clear: this is a communal, inspired decision of the church at Jerusalem; it is not the whim of a single leader, however well respected he may be. The importance of this communal decision is buttressed by envoys who bring the letter: not just Paul and Barnabas, but Judas and Silas, prophets from the Jerusalem community, who, James promises, "will tell you the same things by word of mouth" (15:27).

James does not simply attribute the decision to the holy spirit, as if it came in a thunderbolt of revelation. Nor does he claim to have decided on his own. He says, instead, that this decision "seemed good to the holy spirit *and* to us." His statement, brief as it is, encapsulates the cooperation that exists between the inspiration of the holy spirit and the tough, gritty work of conflict resolution. Under the surface of the story, in fact, we can discern how inspiration for this decision lay in a combination of experience, scripture, and difficult deliberation.

EXPERIENCE

One lesson of the Jerusalem Council is that inspiration incorporates experience. Several experiences clash with one another in this decision-making process.

Some of the believers who are Pharisees say simply, "It is necessary" to impose circumcision and adherence to Torah. None of the typical argumentation that we find in the writings of their descendants, the rabbis, is here. No ample citation of scripture. No connection of a detail in one scripture to another. No rabbinic logic: if the heavier matter took place, then of course the lighter matter will as well. No appeal to the tradition of other rabbis, such as "Rabbi Hillel says this, but Rabbi Shammai says that." Simply, "It is necessary." These Pharisaic believers are, quite simply, appealing to what they know, what they have experienced: believers, Jewish or Gentile, follow Torah (Acts 15:5).

Peter responds by appealing to his own experience. God called him to be the messenger to the Gentiles. This claim refers to his vision on the roof during lunchtime (Acts 15:7; 10:9-23); though the vision was ostensibly about food, Peter understood that it was actually about people. Peter continues with his experience of the outpouring of the spirit upon Gentiles in Caesarea: "And God . . . testified to them by giving them the holy spirit, just as he did to us" (15:8; 10:44-48).

The meeting continues with a recitation of the experiences of Paul and Barnabas, who "told of all the signs and wonders that God had done through them among the Gentiles" (Acts 15:12). This, too, is an explicit appeal to experience.

When James claims, "it seemed good to the holy spirit and to us," he incorporates the varied experiences of the believers in Jerusalem that led to a decision. How their divergent experiences led to this conclusion, however, was not the work of a single inspired — or peaceable — moment.

HEATED DELIBERATION

When James writes simply, "It seemed good to the holy spirit and to us," he butts inspiration ("to the holy spirit") up against deliberation ("to us") rather than driving a wedge between revelation and human effort. Deliberation actually began in Antioch. Luke notes, "And after Paul and Barnabas had no small dissension and debate with them [the Pharisaic believers], Paul and Barnabas and some of the others were appointed to go up to Jerusalem to discuss this question with the apostles and the elders" (Acts 15:2). The word *dissension (stasis)* is elsewhere in Acts associated with riots in Ephesus (19:40) or the rigid division that divided Pharisees from Sadducees over belief in resurrection; this dissension turned violent (23:7, 10). While Luke does not say whether the dissension turned violent in Antioch, we know it was "no small" dissension that led people there to resort to sending a delegation to Jerusalem. This was not civil debate. It was heated — so heated that it could not be solved in Antioch.

What ensues in Jerusalem is "much debate" (Acts 15:7). This *debate* [*zētēsis*], which had occurred earlier in Antioch (15:2), continues in Jerusalem. The word *debate* may suggest the process of investigation more than argument or dissension. Later in Acts, for example, Festus consults with King Agrippa over Paul's status. He tells him, "Since I was at a loss *about the investigation* [*zētēsis*] of these questions, I asked whether he [Paul] wished to go to Jerusalem and be tried there on these charges" (25:20). In this light, what occurred in Antioch and now in Jerusalem is not a random, undisciplined argument, ignorant head-butting, but the intense investigation of a particular question: the obligations of believing Gentiles to observe Torah. The churches in Antioch and Jerusalem are involved in an intense investigation of this question.

Once again, a great deal of tortured interaction lies behind the simple words, "it seemed good to the holy spirit and to us." Different experiences of believers in Antioch led to a dissension that seems to have turned violent; a great deal, after all, was at stake. The work of resolution required concentrated examination of the issue at stake. According to the story of the Jerusalem Council, then, the holy spirit inspires communities by means of, rather than apart from, the rigors of the mind, the sustained and scrupulous examination of an important issue that expresses — and determines — the character of the church.

SCRIPTURE

James first and foremost appeals to *experience* to make his decision. He sides with Peter by agreeing that God looked favorably upon the Gentiles (Acts 15:14). Yet he then turns to scripture to support this decision, citing Amos 9:11-12 in a version that agrees with the Greek translation rather than the Hebrew, followed by a few words of Isaiah 45:21.[70] The point he wishes to make, on the basis of scripture, is that the nations, the Gentiles, are part of God's rebuilding.

---

70. The "remnant of Edom" in the Hebrew of Amos was understood in the Septuagint as "all the nations" because the Hebrew *edom* resembles *adam,* which means, of course, humankind.

Summary

This story splits the book of Acts. It is its exact center. This is true by a sheer counting of words. It is also important because Peter's words are his last in the book of Acts; the Jerusalem apostles' input will now evaporate, eclipsed by Paul and his travel companions. At this decisive moment, this critical transition, James connects the work of the holy spirit with the experience of believers, intense argument and deliberation, and scripture. The decision to include Gentiles with negligible adherence to Torah is made, not on the basis of scripture alone, however authoritative it may have been, nor by reason alone, however well exercised it may have been, nor by experience alone, however persuasive it may have been, nor by inspiration alone, however overwhelming the holy spirit may have been. This crucial decision in the church required rigorous and rancorous — we might say violent — analysis and disagreement. This decision entailed a scriptural foothold in Israel's prophetic tradition. And this decision arose from clear claims to experience, both personal and communal. This is the triangle — experience, deliberation, and scripture — that led to the most significant decision in the early church.

What unites the points of this triangle is a firm belief in the holy spirit: *it seemed good to the holy spirit and to us.* The experience of Peter is rooted in the outpouring of the spirit on Gentiles. The scripture James cited is an inspired text.[71] Even rigorous deliberation is suffused with inspiration, grounded in inspired teaching, aimed at weighing the Torah-driven experience of the Pharisaic believers against the spirit-driven experience of Peter and Paul. The core and content of this triangle is the holy spirit, whose presence permeates the experience that precedes, the scripture that supports, and the deliberation that is required to make the best decision in these peculiar and unprecedented circumstances.

Is this an inspired communal compromise? Yes, because deeply divided factions in the church do not finally win the day, but unity dawns, and a new, diverse community emerges.

Is this learning? Yes, because indispensable to this decision is violent

---

71. Throughout the book of Acts, Israel's scriptures are a product of inspiration. At the start of the book, Peter says, "Friends, the scripture had to be fulfilled, which the holy spirit through David foretold concerning Judas" (1:16). Toward the end of the book, Paul says, "The holy spirit was right in saying to your ancestors through the prophet Isaiah" (28:25). By citing scripture, therefore, James claims to cite the words of the holy spirit.

debate, a painstaking investigation of the issue, and knowledge of scripture.

Is this inspiration? Yes, because at the heart and soul of this imbroglio James discerns the work of the spirit. Not apart from, but in the bruising process of decision-making, the holy spirit does one of its greatest works — and certainly one of its most inclusive — in the history of the church.

The Significance of Putting Ecstasy in Its Place

The thrust of this chapter is this: *an emphasis on ecstasy without an emphasis on comprehension is a distortion of the experience of the early church.* As we saw, ecstasy finds hardly a toehold in Israelite literature and the New Testament. We find a far greater emphasis upon ecstasy in the literature of the Greco-Roman period *outside the New Testament.* The Corinthians seem to have taken their cue from their culture, in this regard, rather than from apostolic teaching and practice.

We can turn this around: *an emphasis on comprehension without an equal emphasis on ecstasy is a distortion of the experience of the early church.* The literature of the New Testament makes it crystal clear that the spirit of God led through visions, from Jesus' baptism to the calling of Paul on the Damascus Road to the visions of Revelation — that is, from the very first pages of the New Testament to its last, the spirit reveals God's work in the world (and beyond, in the case of Revelation) through experiences that transcend intellect alone, whether or not those experiences are ecstatic or what we might prefer to call semi-ecstatic. (Early Christian visionaries recalled what they saw and heard in their visions, for example, unlike ecstatic prophets in the Greco-Roman and Greco-Jewish world.) We also learn from Paul's response to the Corinthians that ecstasy is not a problem when it is accompanied by interpretation; Paul refuses to throw out the baby with the bathwater. He clearly prefers to permit ecstasy when it is balanced by comprehensibility.

This balance is essential to the portrayal of the early church in the New Testament. Ecstasy without intellect is impermissible. Intellect without ecstasy — or, more accurately, semi-ecstatic experiences, or just inspiration — is inconceivable. Strange bedfellows, inspiration and extreme discipline may be, but they are bedfellows nonetheless. This realization has serious implications for several aspects of the Christian faith: (1) how borders are crossed; (2) how Christians prepare for the work of the holy spirit; (3) how believers respond to the work of the holy spirit; and (4) how churches arrive at inspired compromises.

How Borders Are Crossed

When the holy spirit acts, when ecstasy — or something akin to ecstasy, such as visions — comes into play, believers cross boundaries. That is the primary insight we can derive from each of the five stories we have identified in the book of Acts. On the day of Pentecost, the holy spirit fills Galileans, who proclaim with utter clarity *(apophthengesthai)* the praiseworthy acts of God in the varied dialects of Diaspora Jews, whose presence in Jerusalem represents a gathering of pilgrims from far-flung corners of the inhabited world.

Later, after Paul meets the risen Jesus on the Damascus Road, he is met by Ananias, who has learned in his own vision that Paul is an instrument chosen to bring God's name before Gentiles, kings, and — only last — his own people, Israel. Paul, in short, will take on the role of the servant of Isaiah 42 to become a light to the nations.

Peter's vision crashes through boundaries from the start. Told not to eat profane food, he soon travels with two slaves and a soldier to Cornelius, where he is able to observe the marvel of another Pentecost, when the spirit is poured out on Gentiles.

The community in Antioch receives a word of the holy spirit that authorizes the first full mission in the history of the church. This mission will carry Paul and Barnabas to both Jews and Gentiles in the heart of Gentile territory.

The story of the Jerusalem Council signs, seals, and delivers all of this boundary-breaking: a decision that seems good to the holy spirit and the church in Jerusalem makes sure that Gentiles need only observe the merest of regulations in Torah — and certainly not circumcision.

None of these boundaries is broken merely by intellectual effort, by reasoning God's plan, by examining God's design. As I have been at pains to demonstrate, intellectual effort and human endeavor are there in these border crossings. Yet human skill and thought are not the totality of the radical movement of the church beyond its borders. An essential part of that movement in each case is the work of the holy spirit and visions, which lead the church beyond where it would naturally remain and stagnate.

It may help to think here of three experiences in quick succession that move the church from Jerusalem to Rome. Think of Philip, whom the spirit directed to meet an Ethiopian eunuch — an African excluded from temple worship by his sexual status (Acts 8:29). Think of Paul, confronted by Jesus on the road to Damascus and sent to the Gentiles at the ends of the earth to suffer on Jesus' behalf. Think of Peter and a vision at lunchtime that would shatter cherished borders and childhood eating habits, leading Peter to an alien world beyond the familiar culture in which he was comfortable. In three chapters in a row (Acts 8–10), the church changes and misplaced borders crumble when believers are led, not by intellect alone, to unforeseen and once unpalatable people.

How Christians Prepare for the Work of the Holy Spirit

An experience of the holy spirit can take place spontaneously, but that is not typically the pattern in the New Testament. Even Paul, when he gets down to brass tacks on the practicalities of worship, asks, "What should be done then, my friends [brothers and sisters]?" His answer is simple: "When you come together, each one has a hymn, a lesson, a revelation, a tongue, or an interpretation. Let all things be done for building up" (1 Cor. 14:26). Presumably individual believers know their responsibility: to come to worship with something. They are to *prepare* for worship.

The book of Acts offers a similar scenario. Pentecost may be an eruption — or irruption — of the holy spirit, but it does not occur without serious preparation. After Jesus left, the disciples returned to Jerusalem. "All these were constantly devoting themselves to prayer, together with certain women, including Mary the mother of Jesus, as well as his brothers" (Acts 1:14). Though it is parenthetical, Luke mentions as well that there was a total of 120 believers (1:15). However large, the group devoted itself "in absolute unity."[72] Concord and prayer marked the community that received the holy spirit and spoke God's praiseworthy acts in other tongues.

Cornelius's vision is the result of a soldierly diligence. Luke describes Cornelius as "a devout man who feared God with all his household," which means he worshiped with Jews, as he was able, despite his not being born a Jew. His devotion took shape in generous almsgiving and constant prayer (Acts 10:2). In response to this dogged devotion, the

---

72. I prefer this translation to "constantly."

angel of the vision says, "Your prayers and your alms have ascended as a memorial before God" (10:4). The vision, in short, is a direct response to Cornelius's practiced devotion. The next day, Peter's vision takes place over lunch, while he is on the roof in prayer (10:9). With a sense of humor, Luke explains that ecstasy came on Peter while he was hungry; naturally, he had a vision of food. These visions, Cornelius's and Peter's, occur because both men are actively in prayer and, consequently, in a condition to receive a vision that would break traditional boundaries.

The church in Antioch is committed to similar disciplines, though in a communal effort. Quite apart from extreme generosity, openness to prophecy, and an entire year of intense learning — virtues we learn about in an earlier story featuring Antioch — the church is also committed to worship and fasting, in the context of which the church hears a word of the holy spirit. Once again, disciplines are the crucible of inspiration, practiced devotion the context of revelation.

How Believers Respond to the Work of the Holy Spirit

Once the vision is over or an inspired word has gone silent, much of the work has yet to begin. We see this again in Paul's letter to the Corinthians. Speaking in tongues must be followed by an interpretation; otherwise "if there is no one to interpret, let them be silent in church and speak to themselves and to God" (1 Cor. 14:28). Similarly, after a prophetic word, there must be discernment: "let others weigh what is said" (14:29). Those who hear the prophecy have a responsibility to listen and learn: "For you can all prophesy one by one, so that all may learn and all be encouraged" (14:31).

At Pentecost, the work begins with the reception of the holy spirit. Clarity of utterance must win the day, with a recitation of the praise-worthy acts of God. Peter's sermon is an example of this recitation; it contains several scriptural texts sewn together to demonstrate that the death, resurrection, and ascension of Jesus, as well as the outpouring of the spirit at Pentecost, are the heart and soul of God's design for Israel. In the community that emerges from an overwhelming response to the events of Pentecost and Peter's sermon, disciplines reign supreme; the believers "devoted themselves to the apostles' teaching and fellowship, to the breaking of bread and the prayers" (Acts 2:42). The church also engaged in an equitable distribution of wealth to support the pilgrims who now followed Jesus; because they had "all things in common, they would sell their possessions and goods and distribute the proceeds to all, as any had need" (2:44-45). High ideals, indeed, though ones that brought about glad and sincere hearts, as the believers spent time together in the temple, shared meals, and praised God (2:46-47).

If concord and prayer paved the way for the marvelous events of Pentecost, the upshot was a web of communal disciplines — educational, spiritual, and economic — that kept that initial experience of the spirit alive. A few chapters later, in fact, the church is once again hard at prayer for boldness in speech, accompanied by signs and wonders performed through the name of Jesus. "When they had prayed, the place in which they were gathered together was shaken; and they were all filled with the holy spirit and spoke the word of God with boldness" (Acts 4:31). Their prayer was answered, then, with a continuation of Pentecost, including even the distribution of wealth, which Luke mentions in the very next line (4:32).

For Paul and Peter, a different sort of work begins with a vision. Paul, we saw, is told very little about what he is to do on the Damascus Road. In a tandem vision, Ananias, but not Paul, is told the purpose of Paul's vision: to embody the vocation of the servant described by Isaiah 42. What then is Paul's work? Apparently he must learn from Ananias the purpose of the vision on the Damascus Road. This we know he does, because much later Paul is clear that his call to the Gentiles is rooted in Isaiah 42. Yet what Paul says goes much further than what Ananias was told; Paul devotes serious reflection to his experience of suffering in relation to Israel's prophetic literature, including Isaiah 42. The vision on the Damascus Road, therefore, is just the beginning. Paul must learn its meaning from Ananias, experience it firsthand, reflect upon that experience, and understand his encounter with the risen Jesus in light of his ongoing study of Israel's sacred literature.

Peter's work is simpler but no less difficult. We see the transformation in Peter via the recurrence of a single verb, *diakrinein*. At first, he assumes apparently that this word, spoken by the spirit, is telling him not to *hesitate*. Yet his experience with Cornelius's entourage and the Gentiles, on whom the spirit is poured, calls for a transformation of the meaning of this word — a transformation that reflects a change in Peter. In the second instance, therefore, he understands that the spirit was telling him not to *discriminate* between Jew and Gentile. And in the third instance, the word is part and parcel of God's great salvific plan for the Gentiles: no one should *discriminate* between them and the Jews because God saves all by grace. So Peter, like Paul, must think through the meaning of the vision. He does, and this reflection leads him to a shift in the tectonic plates of the early church, which expanded its borders in ways that Peter, on his own, could never have imagined.

Reflection also takes place on the communal level when the church in Antioch receives a word of the spirit. They do not simply set apart Barnabas and Paul, as they are told, but they return to further fasting and prayer before laying hands on them and sending them off. No doubt part of this is the simple task of discerning the truth of the prophetic word. Yet another part is the need to explore the practical implications of the word. What is the work? To what exactly are Paul and Barnabas called? As it turns out, the work leads to a nearby port and the island of Cyprus and the first mission to both Jew and Gentile outside of the mainland. At Antioch, then, the practice of communal disciplines yields a word of the spirit, which yields the practice of still further communal discipline, which brings about a tangible result: a pioneering mission.

Still another response to the holy spirit occurs following the Jerusalem Council. A flurry of activity follows the work of the holy spirit. James, first of all, writes a letter to churches in Antioch, Syria, and Cilicia, which they receive as a word of encouragement and a cause for joy (Acts 15:31). In his letter, James promises that two prophets, Judas and Silas, will "tell you the same things by word of mouth" (15:27). They do much more; they, in fact, say "much to encourage and strengthen the believers" (15:32). Even after Silas and Judas leave, Paul and Barnabas remain in Antioch, and there, with many others, teach and proclaim "the word of the Lord" (15:35).

Proclamation. Prayer. Distribution of wealth. Communal meals. Absorbing the apostles' teaching. Reflection on experience. Connecting experience to scripture. Discernment. Prayer and fasting. Letter writing. Encouragement. Strengthening. Teaching and more proclamation. The lesson is clear: *disciplines, individual and communal, pave the way for an experience of the holy spirit, and the enduring work of the holy spirit begins after the intensity of that experience ebbs.*

How Churches Can Come to Inspired Compromises

The association of the holy spirit with human effort crescendoes in a pivotal story that emblematizes the inclusive qualities of the early church: the Jerusalem Council. The church gathers to crack a conundrum. The scene, though tidy on the surface, is messy. The words Luke selects to describe the process that prompts James eventually to link human effort and inspiration, "it seemed good to the holy spirit and to us," hint at heated, even violent debate. Experiences at odds with one another breed bitter discussions, angry arguments *(stasis),* accompanied by painstaking investigation *(zētēsis).* It is essential to remind ourselves that investigation takes place in Jerusalem alongside dissension; debate does not entail the lobbing of ignorant, unexamined opinions at one another. When James finally emerges with an appeal to scripture, he completes a triangle that began with divisive experiences and bitter but informed arguments. He gathers the shards of potential schism, of rupture, into a single satchel of inspiration. What has happened, James knows, occurred neither apart from the spirit nor along a track parallel to inspiration. James knows that the holy spirit is palpable in an odd assortment of human experiences, heated debate, and meticulous analysis.

James, as Luke portrays him, is a remarkable model of leadership — irenic, conciliatory, but not naïve. Most of all, James is willing to recognize the spirit's presence in the dirty work of the church. His brief words, "to the holy spirit and to us," encapsulate the combination of inspiration and intellectual willpower. Human experience, dissension in tandem with thorough investigation, and scripture are the ingredients of inspired compromise.

The spirit in this story takes believers to the mat, where they wrestle until the match is over, until they come to a communal compromise, until they take others' experiences seriously, until arguments are angrily laid out, until scripture is carefully considered. Bruised, battered, but not beaten by schism, the church then rolls on and rolls out a compromise that, in the end, seems good to the holy spirit and to them because, however difficult it may have been to arrive at, this compromise enlarges the boundaries of the church.

CHAPTER THREE

The Spirit and the Interpretation of Scripture

On January 24, 1885, the front page of *The New York Times* carried an unlikely story about a little-known evangelist who held sway in a relatively unknown town situated in red-barn farmland, roughly midway between Indianapolis and Fort Wayne, Indiana. Born in 1844 as the fourth daughter in a family of eight children in rural Ohio, Maria Woodworth-Etter entered the fray of evangelism at the age of thirty-five.[1] What drew crowds — and reporters — to Hartford City, Indiana, was the mystery and magic of trances. Over the years, the number of people at her evangelistic meetings swelled, and she even outgrew her grand tent, which accommodated a stunning crowd of eight thousand people.[2]

Woodworth-Etter refused to prepare her sermons in advance. She determined rather to "take a text and trust God to lead me in his own way."[3] Sometimes she stood to preach without even having a biblical text in mind, but just in time, she recalled, God revealed a text to her, as well as the place to find it. "I opened the meeting and repeated the text. As

1. For an excellent introduction to Maria Woodworth-Etter, including extensive excerpts from her autobiography, see Priscilla Pope-Levison, *Turn the Pulpit Loose: Two Centuries of American Women Evangelists* (New York: Palgrave Macmillan, 2004), pp. 96-109. For extensive detail, see Wayne E. Warner, *The Woman Evangelist: The Life and Times of Charismatic Evangelist Maria B. Woodworth-Etter,* Studies in Evangelicalism 8 (Metuchen, NJ: Scarecrow, 1986).

2. By 1912, Woodworth-Etter made her way into Pentecostal circles, when F. F. Bosworth, a prominent Pentecostal evangelist, invited her to hold evangelistic meetings for six months in his Dallas church. From then on, she was a regularly featured evangelist on Pentecostal platforms across the country. See Pope-Levison, *Turn the Pulpit Loose,* pp. 103-4.

3. Maria B. Woodworth, *The Life and Experience of Maria B. Woodworth* (Dayton, OH: United Brethren Publishing House, 1885), p. 45.

I did so the power came, and it seemed that all I had to do was to open my mouth."[4] On one occasion, she preached in this way for seventy-five minutes.

No doubt many a preacher over the years would join Maria Woodworth-Etter in her desire to have the spirit speak through him or her for a week of inspired preaching. An inspired sermon without the drudgery of exegesis crammed into the fray of pastoral responsibilities, even for a week, or a week of Sundays, would be welcome, I imagine, to the men and women who occupy the pulpit week after week.

Underneath the natural desire to be free of the hard work of Bible study and sermon preparation lies a dichotomy that, at least in part, characterizes vast tracts of Christianity, including segments of American Christianity. The dichotomy takes various guises: education versus faith, letter versus spirit, liturgy versus spontaneity. I was warned not to learn too much in college and graduate school so as to preserve my faith. I was told not to study too hard so as to live in the spirit. I was cautioned not to succumb to rote prayers so as to maintain the vitality of worship. Whatever one calls this dichotomy, however one labels it, it consists of this: *the polarization of preparation and inspiration.* Maria Woodworth-Etter, the trance evangelist, as she was known, opted for inspiration without any preparation whatsoever. This sort of speaking, utterly spontaneous preaching, was, she came to believe, as much a sign of the holy spirit as her trances, her healing, and her ability to perform miracles.

If you have read from the beginning of this book, you know that I am intent upon breaking down dichotomies: the misguided breach between the breath of God and the spirit of God; the harmful rift between ecstasy and comprehension; and now the pointless divide between preparation and inspiration. My primary reason for breaking down the dividing-wall inherent in these dichotomies is that they are not biblical. I do not think that Jewish and Christian scripture support these dichotomies, and I believe we carry them into our lives to our detriment.

My second reason is professional. I am dogged in my commitment to cultivating the life of my students' minds — a life that entails intense learning. Years ago I preached a sermon at North Park University that featured Martin Luther King Jr.'s sermon, "A Tough Mind and a Tender Heart."[5] I talked of the competence and care of the nurses in the Pediatric Inten-

---

4. Woodworth, *Life and Experience,* p. 46.
5. Martin Luther King Jr., *Strength to Love* (Minneapolis: Fortress, 1981), pp. 13-20.

sive Care unit of Chicago North Shore Hospital — nurses who tended our daughter, Chloe, with extraordinary competence during the first week of her life. Few of us want a nurse who can insert a needle but not be compassionate; few of us want a nurse who can be kind but careless with a needle. Why, then, should we want to distinguish knowledge from piety, study from the holy spirit? Yet we do — some of us all the time or all of us some of the time. Even one of my favorite students a few years back, a young woman with appreciable intellectual gifts, did this. She approached me about being the faculty sponsor for an independent housing unit on campus. As I asked her for details, she responded, "I haven't worked that out; I want to leave it to the spirit." Normally, I would have understood this as an admission of nonchalance, even carelessness. Yet she was not an indolent student. She genuinely embraced a tacit dichotomy between preparation and inspiration. She believed too much planning would impede the work of the holy spirit.

There is a third reason for this book — this chapter in particular — and that reason is personal. In the autumn of 1974, a professor entered the classroom in which I sat, turned without a word, and wrote one line of Greek on the chalkboard. He explained that these Greek words came from Philippians 4:13, which is usually translated something like, "I can do all things through Christ who strengthens me." He suggested another translation: "I can face anything through the one who gives me power." After all, we cannot "do" calculus through Christ, he quipped, but we can (some of us just barely) face its challenges through Christ. At that moment, as a college professor of Greek opened a single line of scripture, I felt the movement of the holy spirit deep in my gut. The whole of my life changed, and my love affair with learning took wings. This impulse led me in a lifelong effort to understand the roots of the holy spirit in the ancient world and the early church.

The roots of the holy spirit, I intend to demonstrate in this chapter, take us to a symbiosis between sustained study and the experience of the holy spirit — not to a division between them. Those who cautioned me not to build up a cache of knowledge, for fear I would lose my faith, had no need to worry. A life of study and life in the spirit, in my view, go hand in hand, at least from a biblical perspective. While I do not intend to denigrate preachers like Maria Woodworth-Etter, I want to point out that hers was not a *biblical* experience.

To make this point effectively, we will explore together one further practice that the holy spirit was believed to ignite: the interpretation of scripture. Although we could spend an entire book on the subject — that is how ample the ancient resources are — I will select only a few key texts. These, I hope, will be enough to compel you to see that, more than any other experience of the spirit, the interpretation of scripture permeates Israelite, Jewish, and early Christian literature. Therefore, a return to the serious and sustained study of scripture as the locus of inspiration may rekindle the experience that fired the engine of the early church.

Despite its promise, this effort to locate the presence of the holy spirit in the practice of studying scripture may seem anticlimactic or disappointing. It may appear to do away with the sound of a rushing wind, tongues as of fire, miracles, ecstasy, and the exquisite abundance of the spirit-filled life. On the contrary. These experiences have not disappeared. They have not evaporated. The gifts of the spirit remain essential. The fruits of the spirit are still indispensable. Yet the truth of the matter is this: all of these are fed, according to the varied testimonies gathered in the Bible, by the inspired knowledge of scripture. The inspired interpretation of scripture does not disqualify or discount other experiences; it feeds them.

Inspired Interpretation in Israelite Literature

Commitment to the inspired interpretation of scripture in the early church grew from the rich soil of Israelite experience, particularly after the return from Babylonian exile, in the 530s BCE. Israel needed to rebuild Jerusalem, reestablish the temple as the center of worship, and rekindle loyalty to Torah. This third commitment was combined, in the minds of some, with the presence of the spirit.

The interpretation and fresh application of ancient traditions was not, of course, a new creation of the postexilic era. When Amos, during the eighth century BCE, held up a plumb line to an errant Israel, this consisted of the expectations of Torah. When Ezekiel portrayed God on an impossibly mobile throne, his vision was a reinterpretation of God on a stationary throne in Isaiah's vision a century and a half earlier.[6] When Jeremiah claimed that God had never demanded sacrifices, he was tweaking, perhaps with a heap of irony, the entirety of Torah, in which God had indeed prescribed sacrifices.[7]

---

6. Compare Ezekiel 1:4-28 with Isaiah 6:1-8.
7. See Jeremiah 7:22.

Yet it was during the postexilic era, when a small band of refugees returned to the diminutive province of Judea, that the relationship between the interpretation of scripture and the holy spirit came into the open. Several examples of this relationship feature in the books of Nehemiah and 1-2 Chronicles; we will glance at three of them.

Ezra

In the prayer of Ezra in Nehemiah 9, Ezra connects the spirit that God had given to the Israelites in the wilderness with instruction: "You gave your good spirit to instruct them, and did not withhold your manna from their mouths, and gave them water for their thirst" (9:20). This fragment of Israel's history in Nehemiah 9:19-25 mirrors Nehemiah 9:12-15 — parallel portions divided by an account of Israelite rebellion (9:16-18). The reiteration of the elements of Nehemiah 9:12-15 in Nehemiah 9:19-25 is striking:

the pillars of cloud and fire:	9:12	&	9:19
good laws or instruction:	9:13-14	&	9:20a
physical provision of manna and water:	9:15a	&	9:20b-21
promise and possession of the land:	9:15b	&	9:22-25

This repetition produces a direct correspondence between the giving of Torah in the wilderness (9:13-14) and the giving of the spirit in the wilderness (9:20). Nehemiah 9:13-14 recounts the giving of Torah at Sinai: "You came down also upon Mount Sinai, and spoke with them from heaven, and gave them right ordinances and true laws, good statutes and commandments, and you made known your holy Sabbath to them and gave them commandments and statutes and a law through your servant Moses." Its counterpart, Nehemiah 9:20a, reads, "You gave your good spirit to instruct them. . . ." Alongside the gift of Torah, then, came the gift of the good spirit for interpreting Torah.[8]

---

8. For a detailed discussion of Nehemiah 9:20, its context, and its antecedents, see my *The Spirit in First-Century Judaism* (Leiden: Brill, 1997; paperback edition, 2002), pp. 194-97.

INSPIRED

Amasai

The innumerable lines of genealogy that provide entrée to the books of
1-2 Chronicles hardly promise a trove of spiritual vitality. Nor does the
way in which this postexilic author adapts earlier sources, particularly
1-2 Samuel and 1-2 Kings. 1-2 Chronicles, for example, contains no trace of
Saul's dramatic surrender to spirits, both good and evil (1 Samuel 10–19).
Nor does a burnished David receive the spirit, as in 1 Samuel 16:13. It is
startling that no less than four times the spirit comes to unknown figures,
whose footprints are otherwise negligible in the sands of Israel's history.
All four are fascinating instances of inspiration; we will limit ourselves to
two of them.

The first of these is "Amasai, chief of the Thirty." Apparently some
Benjaminites and Judahites approach David, who is uncertain about their
loyalty. "If you have come to me in peace, to help me, then my heart will
be knit to you," David says, "but if you have come to betray me to my ad-
versaries, though my hands have done no wrong, then may the God of our
ancestors see and give judgment." Into this breach steps an inspired Amasai: "Then the spirit clothed Amasai . . ." (1 Chron. 12:18; Hebrew 12:19).
We know almost nothing about Amasai, apart from his leading the Thirty,
a group of warriors that was earlier led by valiant military leaders.[9] Yet we
know what to expect: Amasai, clothed with the spirit, should fight. After
all, the spirit had clothed Gideon centuries earlier, and he defeated the
Midianites.

What actually transpires is disconcerting. This warrior of warriors
turns poet, expressing his support for David:

We are yours, O David;
and with you, O son of Jesse!
Peace, peace to you,
and peace to the one who helps you!
For your God is the one who helps you.

Without hesitation, "David received them, and made them officers of his
troops" (1 Chron. 12:16-18).[10] This is stunning. Amasai has not only *not*

9. See Gary N. Knoppers (*1 Chronicles 10–29,* Anchor Yale Bible Commentaries 12A
[New Haven: Yale University Press, 2004], pp. 564-65) for interesting alternatives on the
identification of Amasai.
10. Hebrew 1 Chronicles 12:17-19.

taken up arms against David; instead he poetically pledges loyalty to David. What a bizarre little scene! Equally bizarre, David believes him without a moment's hesitation.

Amasai's effective poetry seems to be the product of inspired spontaneity, not unlike Maria Woodworth-Etter's trance-induced sermons. In reality, it is a piece of hard-edged politics that resurrects Israel's traditions. For example, the tandem pairing of "David" and "son of Jesse" hearkens back to Nabal's refusal to give food to David's men. Nabal had responded to David's servants, after they had requested food, "Who is David? Who is the son of Jesse? There are many servants today who are breaking away from their masters" (1 Sam. 25:10).[11] Amasai too pairs "David" with "son of Jesse," but he erases any hint of disloyalty, such as characterizes 1 Samuel 25:10, by opening his abbreviated speech with a pledge of loyalty to David, son of Jesse.

Amasai continues by picking up the word *peace* from David's initial response, "If you have come to me in peace . . ." Three times he pronounces "peace" upon David and the one who helps him. Peace is of the essence. Amasai continues by rhapsodizing, "For your God is the one who helps you." His choice of the words "your God," rather than the traditional "God of our ancestors," an expression David himself had just used, is at once inspired and deliberate, a nod in the direction of the centrality of David in God's scheme (1 Chron. 12:17).[12]

This is not an extemporaneous inspired speech. Amasai offers David a finely crafted speech, rooted in tradition and the exigencies of the present, tense moment. In a swift inspired poem, Amasai transforms an anti-Davidic sentiment in Israel's sacred tradition, dispels the suspense prompted by David's ambivalence, exudes the requisite tone of deference, and acknowledges that David's God is the source of victory. At the end of the day, the inspired poem wins over the king.

11. See also 2 Samuel 20:1, where a so-called scoundrel, Sheba, expresses the sentiments of a Benjaminite revolt against David: "We have no portion in David, no share in the son of Jesse! Everyone to your tents, O Israel!" This sentiment came to a head following the death of Solomon, when the kingdom divided: "When all Israel saw that the king [Rehoboam, Solomon's son] would not listen to them, the people answered the king, 'What share do we have in David? We have no inheritance in the son of Jesse. To your tents, O Israel! Look now to your own house, O David.' So Israel went away to their tents" (1 Kings 12:16 [2 Chron. 10:16]).

12. Hebrew 1 Chronicles 12:18.

Jahaziel

The full flowering of inspired speech comes about slightly later, as "all Judah stood before the Lord, with the little ones, their wives, and their children" (2 Chron. 20:13). The author, in predictable language, notes that "the spirit of the Lord came upon Jahaziel" (20:14), but the speech is anything but predictable.

Jahaziel's speech gives clear military direction. He said, "Listen, all Judah and inhabitants of Jerusalem, and King Jehoshaphat: Thus says the Lord to you: 'Do not fear or be dismayed at this great multitude; for the battle is not yours but God's. Tomorrow go down against them; they will come up by the ascent of Ziz; you will find them at the end of the valley, before the wilderness of Jeruel. This battle is not for you to fight; take your position, stand still, and see the victory of the Lord on your behalf, O Judah and Jerusalem.' Do not fear or be dismayed; tomorrow go out against them, and the Lord will be with you" (2 Chron. 20:15-17). The precision in this speech is noteworthy, including the precise location of the enemy: the ascent of Ziz. This is one of the clearest examples in all of Israelite literature of prediction; it is offered with even more precision than Micaiah ben Imlah's prediction that King Ahab would die in battle (1 Kings 22:17).

Yet this speech does not principally consist of prediction. Jahaziel's concern is less with the ins and outs of battle than with delivering a prescribed priestly speech before battle. The encouragement not to fear, the promise of victory, coupled with the realization that the battle is not Judah's to fight but God's, embodies the core concerns of his instruction. This is priestly instruction. According to Deuteronomy, the priest is told to speak to the troops prior to battle against superior armies: "Before you engage in battle, the priest shall come forward and speak to the troops, and shall say to them: 'Hear, O Israel! Today you are drawing near to do battle against your enemies. Do not lose heart, or be afraid, or panic, or be in dread of them; for it is the Lord your God who goes with you, to fight for you against your enemies, to give you victory'" (Deut. 20:2-4). When the spirit comes upon Jahaziel, he speaks in the role of the Deuteronomic priest by gathering the essential ingredients of the priestly instructions that must be delivered prior to battle. He is the inspired keeper of the priestly tradition, and he does so by integrating the prescribed priestly speech, to be delivered prior to battle, into his own speech prior to battle.

This prescribed priestly speech contains as well elements of traditional oracles of salvation, as in Isaiah 41:8-13, which addresses hearers, begins with a formula, such as "fear not," offers reasons why there is no need to fear, and concludes with a reiteration of the encouragement not to fear. Its form, in other words, is patently prophetic. There are, in addition, specific allusions to Israelite texts. The words "the battle is not yours but God's" recall David's final words to Goliath before he kills the giant: "the battle is the LORD's" (1 Sam. 17:47). The command "Do not fear . . . This battle is not for you to fight; take your position, stand still, and see the victory of the LORD on your behalf," recollects Moses' monumental words to Israel on the cusp of the sea, with Egyptian horses and chariots in hot pursuit: "But Moses said to the people, 'Do not be afraid, stand firm, and see the deliverance that the LORD will accomplish for you to-day'" (Exod. 14:13).

What makes the precision of the speech and the tradition it incorporates so surprising is that Jahaziel is one of Israel's trained musicians, a member of the Levitic line, the sons of Asaph; David and the officers of his army earlier "set apart for the service the sons of Asaph, and of Heman, and of Jeduthun, who should prophesy with lyres, harps, and cymbals" (1 Chron. 25:1). These musicians "were all under the direction of their father for the music in the house of the LORD with cymbals, harps, and lyres for the service of the house of God. Asaph, Jeduthun, and Heman were under the order of the king. They and their kindred, who were trained in singing to the LORD, all of whom were skillful, numbered two hundred eighty-eight" (1 Chron. 25:6).

This scenario exhibits the characteristics that we have so often seen in our study. On the one hand, prophesying in the context of a community of musicians is reminiscent of the community of prophets to whose ecstatic state Saul and his emissaries succumbed. On the other hand, the military precision of Jahaziel's speech contains studied allusions to Israel's literature. Two ends of the experiential spectrum coalesce in this single episode — in this single speech. To return to the language of the last chapter: ecstasy and comprehension are tied at the hip.[13]

---

13. The king responds by bowing down, face to the ground, as do all of Judah and the inhabitants of Jerusalem, in worship. The Levites and others stand "to praise the LORD, the God of Israel, with a very loud voice" (2 Chron. 20:18-19). Such praise no doubt takes place in song, for, in the next scene, Jehoshaphat "appointed those who were to sing to the LORD and praise God in holy splendor, as they went before the army." Then, "as they began to sing and praise, the LORD set an ambush against the Ammonites, Moab, and Mount Seir" (20:20-22). The victory is won without battle, and after spending three days taking the spoil, they return to Jerusalem "with harps and lyres and trumpets" (20:24-28). This is a

Summary

We have come a long way from the inspiration of the judges, despite verbal clues, such as clothing with the spirit. In Judges, the spirit inspired astonishing acts of liberation through figures such as Othniel, Gideon, Jephthah, and Samson; in 1-2 Chronicles, the spirit inspires a prophet to urge the people of Judah *not* to fight. In Judges, the spirit was associated with action; in 1-2 Chronicles, the spirit inspires speech, perhaps accompanied by musical instruments. In Judges, the spirit appeared in arenas that were outside the corridors of power; in 1-2 Chronicles, the spirit speaks in the arena of politics to kings and those gathered around him. In Judges, unexpected leaders received the spirit — the feeble Gideon, the bastard Jephthah, the fickle Samson; in 1-2 Chronicles, though relatively unknown, those who receive the spirit are people of pedigree — Amasai, chief of the Thirty warriors (2 Chron. 12:18), and Jahaziel, a descendant of Asaph (2 Chron. 20:14), who combines the prerogatives of priest and prophet.[14]

In 1-2 Chronicles, inspired speakers deliver speeches that are rich in tradition, rife with citations and allusions, and, in the case of Jahaziel, set in the context of a priestly mandate. While the author is loath to indicate what exactly happens to these speakers when the spirit clothes or comes upon them — there are no details such as accompany Saul's experience of the spirit — there are enough literary clues to suggest that the primary purpose of inspiration by the spirit is to bring Israel's traditions to bear upon a contemporary situation. At the base of the speeches lies Ezra's conviction that God gives Torah, but not just Torah; God gives the spirit as well to instruct Israel in Torah. In fact, in Chronicles, the full scope of scripture is incorporated in speeches that are at one and the same time inspired and instructive, spirit-directed and full of a nuanced application of scripture tapered to the demands of a new, concrete situation.

---

stunning series of episodes. (1) A son of Asaph, when the spirit of God came upon him, predicted what would happen in the middle of an assembly of men, women, children. (2) The Levites led the people in songs of praise prior to battle. (3) Set for battle, the people sang and praised God while they watched the miraculous ambush. (4) The victors, who lifted voices rather than a finger against the enemy, returned to the temple, laden with the spoils and weapons of war — harps, lyres, and trumpets — "for the Lord had enabled them to rejoice over their enemies" (20:27-28).

14. See also the story of Azariah, upon whom "the spirit of God came." He delivered words of "prophecy" directly to the king (2 Chron. 15:7).

The Inspired Interpretation of Scripture in Judaism

This postexilic impulse to associate the spirit with the interpretation of scripture — or more accurately, valued literature, since there was not yet scripture as such — gathered strength among Jewish authors of the Greco-Roman era. From Egypt to Palestine to Rome, we can trace the belief that the spirit is the source of an adequate and reliable interpretation of scripture.

Ben Sira and the Inspired Scribe

During a period of calm before the storm that erupted with the rise of the ruthless Syrian ruler, Antiochus IV Epiphanes, in 175 BCE, whose reign of terror launched the Maccabean Rebellion and the grand drama of Hanukkah, a scholar by the name of Jesus ben Sira directed a scribal academy in a relatively violence-free Jerusalem. In a lengthy collection of his diverse sayings, which his grandson translated from Hebrew to Greek in 132 BCE, occurs a memorable description of the successful scribe, which no doubt contains a dose of autobiography:

> If the Lord Almighty desires,
> he [the scribe] will be filled by (a) spirit of understanding;[15]
> he will pour out his own words of wisdom
> and by prayer he will give thanks to the Lord.
> He will direct his counsel and knowledge
> And he will reflect upon hidden matters.
> He will make known the instruction of what he has learned
> and boast in the law of the covenant of the Lord. (Sirach 39:6-8)

This is the inspired scribe, pure and simple. Filled with a spirit of understanding, he will gush with words of his own wisdom. Yet the font of this outpouring of wisdom is not navel-gazing. The source of the inspired scribe's wisdom is Torah, the Torah of the covenant of the Lord. In fact, the marvel of his teaching lies in the knowledge he has of "hidden matters," the mysteries of Torah. The image is of a classroom full of scribal hopefuls who are waiting with baited breath for the inspired scribe to unlock the mysteries that they cannot themselves resolve.

15. The Greek is anarthrous, making interpretation difficult.

How is this scribe filled with (a) spirit of understanding? Most interpreters take the words "filled by [a] spirit of understanding" to signal a charismatic endowment of the spirit.[16] After all, the phraseology of inspiration sounds very much like filling with the spirit in the New Testament. Peter, for example, filled with the spirit, preaches to members of the Jewish Sanhedrin (Acts 4:8-12), who are awestruck by Peter's teaching. Taken in this way, the spirit, at a particular point in time, inspires a scribe to grasp the true meaning of scripture and to reveal this meaning to his (or her) students.

The phrase "filled with a spirit of understanding," however, could lead in a different direction — into the world of Joseph, Bezalel, and Daniel, in which case Ben Sira understands inspiration, not as a gift of the spirit at a particular moment in time, but as the lifelong presence of God within that a scribe can cultivate.[17] Taken in this way, God does not fill the scribe with a rich but temporary dollop of the spirit; God instead tops up, through study, prayer, and travel, the spirit of understanding that already exists in Ben Sira's sage. The inspired scribe, full to the brim, pours out his own words of wisdom.

Either interpretation of inspiration or a combination of both — a charismatic endowment, a lifelong cultivation of an understanding spirit, or a lifelong cultivation of this spirit capped by an extraordinary experience of the spirit — is possible. Underlying all of these is the firm association between the spirit and the rigor required to study scripture. Ben Sira

---

16. For example, Friedrich Büchsel, *Der Geist Gottes im Neuen Testament* (Gütersloh: Bertelsmann, 1926), pp. 58-59; H. Stadelmann, *Ben Sira als Schriftgelehrter: Eine Untersuchung zum Berufsbild des vor-makkabäischen Sôfer unter Berücksichtigung seines Verhältnisses zu Priester-, Propheten- und Weisheitslehrertum,* Wissenschaftliche Untersuchungen zum Neuen Testament 2.6 (Tübingen: Mohr Siebeck, 1980), pp. 216-46; David Orton, *The Understanding Scribe: Matthew and the Apocalyptic Ideal,* Journal for the Study of the New Testament Supplement Series 25 (Sheffield, UK: Sheffield Academic, 1989), pp. 70-71; Cornelis Bennema, *The Saving Power of Wisdom: An Investigation of Spirit and Wisdom in Relation to the Soteriology of the Fourth Gospel,* Wissenschaftliche Untersuchungen zum Neuen Testament 2.148 (Tübingen: Mohr Siebeck, 2002), pp. 55-60.

17. I accepted the interpretation of Sirach 39:6-8 as a charismatic endowment in my *Spirit in First-Century Judaism,* pp. 198-99, but in *Filled with the Spirit* (Grand Rapids: Eerdmans, 2009), pp. 118-25, I understand the spirit of understanding as a lifelong endowment that fills the mature scribe to overflowing. See also Jan Liesen, who suggests (in *Full of Praise: An Exegetical Study of Sir 39,12-35,* Supplements to the Journal for the Study of Judaism 64 [Leiden: Brill, 2000], p. 64) that the understanding the scribe of Sirach 39:6 exhibits is not a miraculous superadditum that distinguishes him from inferior scribes and all other people but "the creational endowements *[sic]* come to full fruition. . . ."

tenders this clearheaded advice to his students: "If you are willing, child, you can be taught, and if you devote your soul (to it), you can be clever." His students must love to listen, pay attention, stand in the company of elders, seek mentors, take note of every godly discourse, let no wise proverb escape their notice, rise early to meet an intelligent person, and — in what is a delightful image of tenacity — let their feet wear out their mentors' doorsteps. The student must "reflect on the statutes of the Lord, and meditate at all times on his commandments. . . ." Once all of this is done, and done tenaciously, the Lord "will give insight to your mind, and your desire for wisdom will be granted" (Sir. 6:32-37). This promise plunges divine insight into the rigor of listening and studying and devoting oneself to a mentor, whether at the end there will be a special endowment with a spirit of understanding or an eruption of knowledge that has built up in the scribe's spirit of understanding.[18]

In whatever form inspiration takes place, Ben Sira is certain about the practices from which inspired wisdom does not arise. He rejects the quick fixes of divination. "The senseless have vain and false hopes," he writes, "and dreams give wings to fools. As one who catches a shadow and pursues the wind, so is anyone who believes in dreams. . . . Divinations and omens and dreams are unreal . . ." (Sir. 34:1-2, 5a). Ben Sira counts himself in no uncertain terms among the circle of those who are learned in Torah rather than in the arts of divination: "For dreams have deceived many, and those who put their hope in them have perished. Without such deceptions the law [Torah] will be fulfilled, and wisdom comes to completion in the mouth of the faithful" (34:7-8). The source of inspiration is not the *pneuma* of the ecstatic prophet, the Delphic priestess who flails under the inspiration of *pneuma,* or Cassandra, who feels the fire of Apollo in her belly. For Ben Sira, the devoted headmaster, shortcuts such as dreams and visions, as well as the search for omens, are bastard forms of inspiration. The font of the spirit of understanding lies elsewhere: in *intense discipline and the study of scripture.*

---

18. The scribe is different from the businessperson, the farmer, the painter, the blacksmith, and the potter. "How different," continues Ben Sira, "is the one who devotes himself to the study of the law of the Most High! He seeks out the wisdom of all the ancients, and is concerned with prophecies; he preserves the sayings of the famous and penetrates the subtleties of parables; he seeks out the hidden meanings of proverbs . . ." (39:1-3). He also "serves among the great and appears before rulers; he travels in foreign lands and learns what is good and evil in the human lot" (39:4) and rises early to pray and to ask pardon for his sins (39:5).

The Qumran Hymns

During the decades that followed the Maccabean Rebellion, the splinter group of Jews that gathered along the shores of the Dead Sea developed an alternative Israel, with its own rules of ritual order, its own priestly hierarchy, and its own methods of interpretation. Initiates at Qumran were obligated to take an oath to follow Torah as it was interpreted by means of revelation at Qumran.[19]

We catch a glimpse of inspiration, among other places, in the Scrolls, especially in the Hymn Scroll. For the most part, the poet is pessimistic, reflecting on Genesis 2, "And I, from dust [I] have been gathered, [and from clay] I have been [fo]rmed to be a source of impurity, and of vile filth, a pile of dust, mixed with [water, . . .] a lodging of darkness" (1QH 20.24-26). Dust though he may be, the poet does have something to say because God has revealed to him the meaning of scripture:

> And I, the Instructor, have known you, my God,
>   through the spirit which you gave (in)to me,
>   and I have listened loyally to your wonderful secret through
>   your holy spirit.
> You have opened within me
>   knowledge of the mystery of your wisdom,
>   the source of your power. . . . (1QH 20.11-12)

These brief lines evoke powerful images of inspired knowledge and wisdom.

The hymn writer cements the association of inspiration and interpretation by sandwiching "your holy spirit" between references to "your wonderful secret" and "knowledge of the mystery of your wisdom." The word *mystery*, furthermore, refers throughout the Habakkuk Commentary to "the mysteries of the words of his servants, the prophets," that is, to prophetic texts which the Teacher of Righteousness interprets with divine aid.[20]

---

19. See 1QS 5.9. On inspired interpretation in the Dead Sea Scrolls, see Otto Betz, *Offenbarung und Schriftforschung in der Qumransekte,* Wissenschaftliche Untersuchungen zum Neuen Testament 6 (Tübingen: Mohr, 1960); David E. Aune, "Charismatic Exegesis in Early Judaism and Early Christianity," in *The Pseudepigrapha and Early Biblical Interpretation,* ed. James H. Charlesworth and Craig A. Evans, Journal for the Study of the Pseudepigrapha Supplement Series 14 (Sheffield, UK: JSOT, 1993), pp. 126-50; Orton, *The Understanding Scribe,* pp. 121-33.

20. See 1QpHab 7.5.

For a community so steeped in the biblical tradition that truth cannot be conceived of without recourse to biblical conceptions and phraseology, a community in which the holy spirit can be a means of knowing God, God's secrets, God's mysteries (1QH 20.11-12), a community whose initiates are obligated to follow a particular interpretation of Torah (1QS 5.9), a community whose central figure receives divine aid to interpret prophetic texts (1QpHab 7.4) — this community lies under the authority of an *instructor,* who functions like Ezra the scribe before him, who *instructed* the returned exiles (Neh. 8:8, 13), and like Ben Sira, who rooted inspiration in the serious task of study. If the teacher at Qumran is able to instruct his own people, if he holds the interpretive key to the divine secrets and mysteries, he does so exclusively because God has given to him the holy spirit, the good spirit that had instructed Israel.

Philo Judaeus

The association of inspiration with interpretation burgeons in the brilliant hues of Philo's self-portraits. Philo's palette is textured, a studied concoction of ecstasy and inspired interpretation that yields no less than three distinct descriptions of the inspired interpretation of scripture.

(1) In a moment of autobiographical reflection, Philo describes occasions of dryness when he is bereft of insight. During these momentary lapses, he often comes up empty. However, "On other occasions, I have approached my work empty and suddenly become full, the ideas falling in a shower from above and being sown invisibly, so that under the influence of the Divine I have been filled with corybantic frenzy and been unconscious of anything, place, persons present, myself, words spoken, lines written. For I obtained language, ideas, an enjoyment of light, keenest vision, pellucid distinctiveness of objects, such as might be received through the eyes as the result of clearest shewing."[21] This is meaningful self-disclosure, not only because Philo admits to periods of dryness, but because he describes himself as filled with the movement of Corybants, nature spirits who dance about the newborn Zeus[22] or to the sound of flutes in the orgiastic cults of Dionysus[23] and Cybele.[24] Philo refers to

21. Philo Judaeus, *On the Migration of Abraham* 35.
22. See Pausanius 8.37.6.
23. See Strabo 10.3.11.
24. See Diodorus Siculus 5.49.

nothing less than the most pagan of dances to describe what happens to him on those occasions when he is utterly stumped by the interpretation of Torah, those moments when God steps in to offer him an ecstatic unawareness of anything but a brilliant vision.

(2) On other occasions, the divine spirit intensifies Philo's intellectual powers. While in the throes of a full-fledged allegorical interpretation of scripture, Philo pauses to describe his experience: "I hear once more the voice of the invisible spirit, the customary secret tenant, saying, 'Friend, it would seem that there is a matter great and precious of which thou knowest nothing, and this I will ungrudgingly shew thee, for many other well-timed lessons have I given thee."[25] In this autobiographical snippet, Philo tells his readers that he can interpret Jerusalem allegorically as a "vision of peace" because the spirit communicates directly with his mind. Philo signals this by describing the spirit as "customary" — precisely the word Socrates and his admirers used to describe the daemon that regularly inspired him.[26] According to a late first-century discussion of Socrates' inspiration, "What reached him was not spoken language, but the unuttered words of a daemon, making voiceless contact with his intelligence by their sense alone."[27] By adopting the word *customary* to indicate that he, like Socrates, hears the voice of a daemonic presence, Philo steers clear, in this instance, of ecstasy. Not with a mad spree of

25. Philo Judaeus, *On Dreams* 2.252.

26. His selection of the evocative word *customary* to describe the spirit could scarcely have been read without reminding Philo's readers of Socrates' daemon, whom, according to Plato, Socrates himself appealed to as "the customary prophetic inspiration of the daemon" (Plato, *Apology* 40A), "the daemonic and customary sign" (Plato, *Phaedrus* 242B), and "my customary daemonic sign" (Plato, *Euthydemus* 272E; see also Plato, *Euthyphro* 3B). This resonance between Socrates' customary daemon and Philo's divine spirit has resounding implications for apprehending Philo's description of inspired interpretation, which characterizes Moses' inspiration in Philo's *On the Life of Moses* 2.264-65 as well. In Plutarch's *On the Sign of Socrates,* which addresses "the problem of the nature and mode of operation of the so-called sign of Socrates" (588B), a certain Simmias ventures: "Socrates . . . had an understanding which, being pure and free from passion, and commingling with the body but little, for necessary ends, was so sensitive and delicate as to respond at once to what reached him. What reached him, one would conjecture, was not spoken language, but the unuttered words of a daemon, making voiceless contact with his intelligence by their sense alone" (588D-E). For further discussion, see my "The Prophetic Spirit as an Angel According to Philo," *Harvard Theological Review* 88 (1995): 195-206. For an extensive analysis of Philo's writings, see my "Inspiration and the Divine Spirit in the Writings of Philo Judaeus," *Journal for the Study of Judaism* 26 (1995): 271-323.

27. Plutarch, *On the Sign of Socrates* 588E.

frenzy but by listening to the voice of the invisible spirit, his customary friend, as it addresses his pure intellect, is Philo able to interpret Israel's scripture.

On a similar occasion, while puzzling over the question of why two cherubim rather than one were required to guard paradise, according to Genesis 3:24, Philo had a comparable experience of inspiration, when he received a "higher word," that is, an allegorical interpretation of the two cherubim: "But there is a higher thought than these. It comes from a voice in my own soul, which oftentimes is god-possessed and divines where it does not know. This thought I will record in words if I can. The voice told me that while God is indeed one, his highest and chiefest powers are two, even goodness and sovereignty. . . . O then, my mind, admit the image unalloyed of the two Cherubim, that having learnt its clear lesson of the sovereignty, and beneficence of the Cause, thou mayest reap the fruits of a happy lot."[28] Philo's ability to discover that there are two cherubim because they represent dual divine qualities — the sovereignty and beneficence of God — is due to a voice within, a possession that does not obviate his intellectual powers, even though he is in an inspired state. The voice tells Philo — better yet, Philo's mind — the meaning of the mystery. In this way, *On the Cherubim* and *On Dreams* are of a piece.[29] According to both, while studying scripture, Philo encounters difficulties in Torah that require explanation. He ponders them and is led to a solution when he listens to the voice of another within him, which he identifies in *On Dreams* as "the customary unseen spirit."[30]

(3) Philo's untamed enthusiasm about the inspired interpretation of Torah leads him to take his experiences in still another direction in *On the Special Laws* 3.1-6, where he borrows the famed language of the ascent of the soul from Plato's *Phaedrus* to describe his uncanny ability to interpret scripture.[31] When on occasion Philo is able to "obtain a spell of fine

---

28. Philo Judaeus, *On the Cherubim* 27-29.

29. Both *On Dreams* 2.252 and *On the Cherubim* 27-29 exhibit similar formal features: an introduction that identifies the source (soul; spirit) and means (prompting; divining) of inspiration; a description of the content of teaching; and a concluding self-directed exhortation ("Receive the image unalloyed . . ." and "Let it then be . . .").

30. Philo recounts yet another encounter with an exegetical difficulty in *On Rewards and Punishments* 50. Compare also the teachings of "Consideration," one of Philo's personified virtues, in *On Flight and Finding* 53-58.

31. Plato, *Phaedrus* 246A-53C. For further discussion, see my *Spirit in First-Century Judaism*, pp. 151-58, 208-9.

weather and a calm from civil turmoils," he is able to "open the soul's eyes," to be wafted on the winds of knowledge, and to become "irradiated by the light of wisdom." During these rare moments of respite, Philo finds himself "daring, not only to read the sacred pages of Moses, but also in my love of knowledge to peer into each of them and unfold and reveal what is not known to the multitude."

This reflection contains a striking correspondence between the ascent of the philosopher's mind and the discernment of an interpreter's mind. His experience as an interpreter of scripture mirrors the experience of the philosopher. The passage begins with philosophical ascent and possession (*On the Special Laws* 3.1-2), is interrupted by a plunge into the ocean of civil cares (3.3-4), and concludes with an ascent on the winds of knowledge to interpret Torah (3.5-6). Within this structure, the initial ascent to contemplate the upper air corresponds to the final ascent to interpret Torah. Philo reinforces this correlation between philosopher and interpreter by employing the same verb, "to stoop," to describe the experiences of ascent and interpretation. The words "Ah then I stooped [gazed down] from the upper air . . ." (3.2) correspond to "Behold me daring . . . to stoop [peer] into each of them [the sacred messages of Moses] and unfold . . ." (3.6).[32]

In *On the Special Laws,* Philo depicts an ecstatic rapture, a form of possession, an experience of the spirit that is very much like how he understands prophetic inspiration — though not exactly. Prophets speak when they fall under the power of ecstasy and divine possession, "when the mind is evicted at the arrival of the divine Spirit."[33] In contrast, his experience in *On the Special Laws* is preceded by preparation, knowledge, and contemplation at moments when he is free of civil responsibilities, and his mind becomes more alert, not less, as his ability to interpret Torah intensifies rather than diminishes.

The sheer variety of Philo's portrayals of inspiration is testimony to his conviction that the interpretation of scripture, especially on an allegorical plane, is due to the presence of the divine spirit. Whether due to the sway of ecstasy and Corybantic dance, the quiet whisper of the

32. On the illuminating relationship between *On the Special Laws* 3.5-6, *On Planting* 22-24, and *On the Giants* 53-54, see my "Inspiration and the Divine Spirit," pp. 288-98. The correlation between Philo as an inspired interpreter and Moses as an inspired teacher is apparent in *On the Cherubim* 48, which includes what is implicit in *On the Special Laws* 3.6. For further analysis, see my *Filled with the Spirit,* p. 194 note 29.

33. Philo Judaeus, *Who Is the Heir?* 265.

customary spirit, or the upsurge of contemplation, Philo becomes, to his own mind at least, an exceptional and inspired interpreter of Moses' writings.

Josephus

Josephus offers his own set of autobiographical reflections. Once a Jewish general, Josephus joined the Romans for the duration of the Jewish War in 66-73 CE. To defend his traitorous turn, Josephus recalls that, when he

> overheard the threats of the hostile crowd, suddenly there came back into his mind those nightly dreams, in which God had foretold to him the impending fate of the Jews and the destinies of the Roman sovereigns. He was an interpreter of dreams and skilled in divining the meaning of ambiguous utterances of the Deity; a priest himself and of priestly descent, he was not ignorant of the prophecies in the sacred books. At that hour he was inspired to read their meaning, and, re-calling the dreadful images of his recent dreams, he offered up a silent prayer to God.[34]

Josephus musters a potent partnership of skills — dream interpretation and the ability to determine the meaning of sacred texts — to validate his decision to surrender to the Romans rather than to commit suicide with his Jewish compatriots. His ability to interpret dreams recalls, of course, his namesake, Joseph, as well as Daniel, whom Josephus elsewhere designates "one of the greatest prophets," whose "memory lives on eternally."[35] His ability to interpret prophetic texts in an effort to persuade the Jews to acquiesce to the Romans even recalls Jeremiah's prophetic appeal to the Israelites to capitulate to Babylon.[36] Josephus, in short, belongs to a long line of Jewish luminaries.

According to his testimony, two modes of revelation compelled Josephus to surrender. One was a nightly diet of dreams. The other was an inspired reading of biblical prophecies. The particular phrase Josephus employs to describe his inspiration, "becoming enthused," is ambigu-

---

34. Josephus, *Wars of the Jews* 3.351-53.

35. Josephus, *Antiquities* 10.266.

36. See Louis H. Feldman, "Prophets and Prophecy in Josephus," *Journal of Theological Studies* 41 (1990): 388, 404.

ous.[37] On the one hand, the word *enthused* may point to a heightening of Josephus's native ability, according to the *Antiquities,* such as when Vespasian, "like one inspired," prompted extraordinary courage and resolve in his soldiers,[38] when Saul, inspired, dismissed citizens of Jabis with a promise to come to their aid,[39] or when Elijah, inspired, kept pace with Ahab's chariot.[40] Such a word, on the other hand, may evoke the impression of an ecstatic experience, such as when Elisha, under the influence of a harp, prophesied, ordering certain kings to dig pits in a stream,[41] or when Samuel predicted that Saul would become inspired and prophesy with an assembly of prophets.[42] Whether the expression "become enthused" or "inspired" entails a heightening of innate interpretative abilities or the onset of ecstasy, Josephus's self-serving autobiographical account of his decision to surrender provides another early Jewish example of the conviction that the correct (to Josephus's mind, at least) interpretation of ancient texts rests upon an experience of inspiration.

Summary

These Jewish authors are worth considering. One of them led an elite academy for scribal students in Jerusalem, and another composed hymns for an isolated community that fled Jerusalem and sequestered itself from other Jews. One was an Egyptian philosopher and civic leader who commented voluminously upon Torah. One was a Jewish general who tried to redeem himself by writing copiously in defense of the Jews and revising for Roman palates the entirety of Jewish scripture. In innumerable respects these authors have very little in common. The dates of their compositions span as many as nearly thirty decades. Their attitudes to Greece

37. The word *enthused* or *inspired,* employed adjectivally, may connote reliability, as in the case of a (nonbiblical) prophetic text, which may be one of the texts Josephus interpreted to persuade him to surrender: "For there was an ancient saying of inspired men that the city would be taken and the sanctuary burnt to the ground by right of war . . ." (Josephus, *Wars of the Jews* 4.388).

38. Josephus, *Wars of the Jews* 4.33.

39. Josephus, *Antiquities* 6.76.

40. Josephus, *Antiquities* 8.346.

41. Josephus, *Antiquities* 9.35-36.

42. Josephus, *Antiquities* 6.56. Josephus also employs the adverb "enthusiastically" to depict simply the uncontrollable love of Herod for Mariamme in *Antiquities* 15.240.

and Rome could hardly be more disparate. Ben Sira evinced a nationalistic strain without vilifying Greek and Syrian overlords. The people of the Scrolls expressed revulsion toward foreign nations. Philo of Alexandria included volumes of Greek ideas in his writings and even made an official visit to the Roman emperor, Gaius. Josephus's patrons belonged to the wealthy Roman family, the Flavians.

These differences serve to underline what these Jewish authors hold in common: the conviction that the spirit inspires the interpretation of scripture. Ben Sira tells his students that "if the Lord Almighty desires, he [the scribe] will be filled by a spirit of understanding; he will pour out his own words of wisdom and by prayer he will give thanks to the Lord." The Qumran hymn writer claims, "and I have listened loyally to your wonderful secret through your holy spirit." Philo hears an inner "voice," the "customary friend," and, in a condition of rapt possession, floats on the breezes of knowledge and peers into every page of Moses' writings. Josephus turns traitor on the basis of a daily diet of dreams and the enthusiasm that reveals the hidden meaning of ancient prophetic oracles. Despite their differences — and they were sizeable geographically, chronologically, and ideologically — these authors together attest to the Jewish conviction that the spirit, whether the spirit given at birth or later in life or both, inspires the interpretation of scripture.

The Inspired Interpretation of Scripture in the New Testament

We call them early Christians, but the followers of Jesus chose not to forfeit their Jewish roots. In the pages to follow, we can detect how, and how much, the early church cherished Israelite literature, so much so that they believed the spirit to be ardent and active in the process of its interpretation. We begin with the song of Simeon, a virtually unknown old man whose poetry permeates church liturgy; then we continue with the Gospel of John, the book of Acts, the letter to the Hebrews, and the letters of Paul. No sooner do I create this list of New Testament texts than I suppress the urge to apologize for all that we are not studying — texts such as the book of Revelation. I have opted, nonetheless, to keep this study fairly short, nearly anecdotal, but long enough, I trust, to uncover a dimension of pneumatology that has the distinction of being left to languish, to this day, in the halls of scholarship.

Simeon's Song

Our study of the inspired interpretation of scripture begins in an unlikely corner of Jerusalem, where peasant parents from Galilee, so poor that they cannot afford the offering of sheep for purification after birth, bring two turtledoves as an offering for their son (Lev. 12:1-8; Luke 2:22-24). The Pharisees do not come to celebrate the occasion. Nor do the priests populate the picture. The Sadducees, despite their vested interest in the temple, have not rolled out the red carpet. The couple receives very few courtiers, apart from an old and expectant widow, Anna the prophet (2:36-38), and a solitary man, about whom we know almost nothing — except that he was disciplined in devotion, hopeful, versed in scripture, and receptive to the holy spirit: "Now there was a man in Jerusalem whose name was Simeon; this man was righteous and devout, looking forward to the consolation of Israel, and the holy spirit rested on him. It had been revealed to him by the holy spirit that he would not see death before he had seen the Lord's messiah. Guided by the spirit, Simeon came into the temple ..." (Luke 2:25-27). This old man, though invisible to the Jewish and Roman authorities, was inspired. The spirit rested "on him." He had received a revelation "by the holy spirit." And he came to the temple, guided "by the spirit." Three references to the spirit are clumped around this otherwise undistinguished and indistinguishable man.[43]

When Simeon sees the peasants' child, he cradles the baby in his arms and praises God: "Master, now you are dismissing your servant in peace, according to your word; for my eyes have seen your salvation, which you have prepared in the presence of all peoples, a light for revelation to the Gentiles and for glory to your people Israel" (Luke 2:28-32). Though it seems extemporaneous, this prayer is actually drenched in the language of Isaiah 40–55.[44] Simeon's anticipation of "the consolation of Israel," of comfort for his people, connects this old man to words that open the curtain of hope to Israelites long battered by exile in Babylon: "Comfort,

---

43. For further discussion, see my "The Spirit, Simeon, and the Songs of the Servant," in *The Spirit and Christ in the New Testament and Christian Theology: Essays in Honor of Max Turner,* ed. I. H. Marshall, V. Rabens, and C. Bennema (Grand Rapids: Eerdmans, 2012), pp. 18-34.

44. These sixteen chapters of prophetic poems were probably written during the dire days of Babylonian exile, when Israel was weary to the bone, mired in hopelessness. Into the dark of national defeat, a nameless prophet flashed the brilliance of the expectation that God's people were on the cusp of liberation.

O comfort my people, says your God. Speak tenderly to Jerusalem, and cry to her that she has served her term, that her penalty is paid, that she has received from the LORD's hand double for all her sins" (Isa. 40:1-2). Simeon understands that the advent of the baby is the inauguration of the liberation that this prophet of the exile had announced. The "salvation" that "you [God] have prepared in the presence of all nations," which Simeon sees in front of him, is rooted in Isaiah 52:10, which imagines that "The LORD has bared his holy arm before the eyes of all the nations; and all the ends of the earth shall see the salvation of our God." Yet the roots of Simeon's song spread more broadly, for his belief that this salvation will be "a light for revelation to the nations" is embedded in Isaiah 42:6, "I have given you as. . . . a light to the nations," as well as Isaiah 49:6, "It is too light a thing that you should be my servant to raise up the tribes of Jacob and to restore the survivors of Israel; I will give you as a light to the nations, that my salvation may reach to the end of the earth." Even Simeon's belief that this salvation is also "for glory to your people Israel" is rooted in Isaiah 46:13, "I bring near my deliverance, it is not far off, and my salvation will not tarry; I will put salvation in Zion, for Israel my glory."

This prayer is not just a smattering of allusions to Jewish scripture. It offers a clear vision of Jesus' vocation. Simeon's second speech, spoken privately to the baby's young mother, also reveals that he has the whole of Isaiah 40–55 in mind when he speaks. To Mary, and to Mary alone, he says, "This child is destined for the falling and the rising of many in Israel, and to be a sign that will be opposed. . . ." Opposition will be the hallmark of the child's destiny. He will become, in short, the servant, the suffering servant, whose uncompromising expansion of God's reign to all nations — not just Israel — will lead to rejection (Isa. 53:3), to unspoken personal anguish (42:2-3), to the torment of having his beard torn out (50:6) and his back beaten (53:4-5, 7), and to an early, ignominious, and silent death (53:7-12). Simeon, in a few words, captures the majesty of Jesus' ministry — he will be a light to the nations — and the misery of his death, like the servant long before him.

This story of Simeon encapsulates the symbiosis that exists between the spirit and scripture in no less than three ways. First, Simeon is disciplined. The first two words that Luke adopts to describe Simeon tell us this much. He was "just" and "godly." Both words are an indication of Simeon's disciplined adherence to a godly way of life. He is like Elizabeth and Zechariah, whom Luke describes, in the first occurrence of the word, as just *(dikaios)*. They are just because they live "blamelessly according to all the commandments and regulations of the Lord" (Luke 1:6). Simeon, with Elizabeth and

Zechariah before him, is a Torah-follower. Second, Simeon knows scripture. Nearly every line in his public prayer and private words to Mary is suffused with scripture. When he finally speaks, after years of waiting, he speaks in the language of Isaiah's vision, not merely in a general sense, but with actual words, clear allusions, that go to the heart of the matter: this baby will turn out to be the suffering servant of Isaiah's vision. Third, Simeon is receptive to the holy spirit. The spirit is upon him, the spirit reveals knowledge to him, and he enters the temple in the spirit.

Simeon combines the discipline of keeping Torah, the study of scripture, and inspiration by the holy spirit. He has waited, obeyed, and studied. He has immersed himself in ancient texts, memorized scripture with an eye toward that single significant inspired moment in his life when all that he has studied will combust. And that moment arrives when, under the inspiration of the holy spirit, he recognizes the openhanded, expansive, and perilous salvation of God in the baby carried to the temple by a pair of peasants.

The Promised Paraclete

A rich web of shared imagery between Wisdom and Jesus permeates the Fourth Gospel.[45] The opening lines, in which the *logos* is with God in the beginning, sets the tone by evoking Wisdom personified, who existed with God from the beginning, even prior to the creation of the earth.[46] Wisdom and Jesus alike descended from heaven to live among human beings.[47] Both busy themselves with teaching.[48] In both wisdom literature and the Fourth Gospel, teaching is depicted vividly as life-giving food.[49]

In this atmosphere of learning, Jesus promises the presence of the

45. For a concise survey of these correspondences, see Raymond E. Brown, *The Gospel according to John I–XII*, 2nd ed., Anchor Bible 29 (Garden City, NY: Doubleday, 1982), pp. cxxii-cxxv.

46. See John 1:1, 17:5; see Proverbs 8:22-23; Sirach 24:9; Wisdom of Solomon 6:22.

47. See John 1:14, 3:31, 6:38, 16:28; Proverbs 8:31; Sirach 24:8; Baruch 3:37; Wisdom of Solomon 9:10. Compare John 3:13 with Baruch 3:29 and Wisdom of Solomon 9:16-17.

48. Cor Bennema (*The Power of Saving Wisdom: An Investigation of Spirit and Wisdom in Relation to the Soteriology of the Fourth Gospel*, Wissenschaftliche Untersuchungen zum Neuen Testament 2.148 [Tübingen: Mohr Siebeck, 2002], pp. 228-34) provides a good discussion of the teaching vocation of the paraclete, including studies of key verbs. See also Max Turner, *The Holy Spirit and Spiritual Gifts in the New Testament Church and Today* (Peabody, MA: Hendrickson, 1998), pp. 82-85.

49. See John 6:48-51 and Proverbs 9:5-6.

spirit of truth, another paraclete, whose vocation will be what Jesus' own vocation has been throughout the Fourth Gospel — to teach: "But the paraclete, the holy spirit, whom the father will send in my name, will teach you everything" (John 14:26).[50] In a final saying about the spirit, Jesus promises that "when the spirit of truth comes, it will guide you into/ in all the truth . . ." (16:13).[51] Such promises are redolent of the psalmists' prayers, "Lead me in your truth, and teach me, for you are the God of my salvation" (Ps. 25:5), and "Teach me to do your will, for you are my God. Let your good spirit lead me on a level path" (143:10).

Yet Jesus promises more than a vague sensation of guidance and teaching. He promises that the spirit will teach the disciples *all* things, will guide them into (or in) *all* the truth. This appears to be a fantastic promise, a voyage into the unknown realms of the future. Notwithstanding the blank check that Jesus appears to offer the disciples, there is a more pedestrian but also a more essential strain to the promise, the scope of which is constrained by the rationale Jesus gives for the promise: "I still have many things to say to you, but you cannot bear them now. When the spirit of truth comes, he will guide you into [in] all the truth . . ." (John 16:13). The "many things" that Jesus has yet to say consist of what he did not say when he was with the disciples: "I did not say these things to you from the beginning, because I was with you" (16:4). Now that he has begun to say them, his disciples have become despondent: "But because I have said these things to you, sorrow has filled your hearts" (16:6). In short, the disciples "cannot bear them now" (16:12). What they cannot bear are sayings that have to do exclusively with Jesus' imminent departure. This is where the spirit of truth enters the picture: what Jesus cannot now say about his impending death because of the disciples' heavy-heartedness, the spirit of truth will say on his behalf. Because the disciples cannot at this moment prior to Jesus' death accept any more of his teaching, the spirit of truth, the paraclete, will lead the disciples in retrospect into all the truth about his departure.

---

50. For an excellent introduction to the holy spirit in the Fourth Gospel, with a keen eye to secondary literature, Jewish literature, and the coherence of the Fourth Gospel itself (which scholars often subdivide by separating chapters 1–12 from the farewell discourses in 13–17), see Marianne Meye Thompson, *The God of the Gospel of John* (Grand Rapids: Eerdmans, 2001), pp. 145-88.

51. Textual uncertainty makes it difficult to determine whether the spirit, in the original text, is said to lead "in" or "into" truth. Of the major codices, Alexandrinus and Vaticanus read "into," while Sinaiticus and Bezae read "in."

Within the perspective of the farewell discourses, then, "the things to come" are not events that lie in the disciples' future after they receive the spirit; it is not these teachings that the disciples cannot bear to hear because of the sorrow they generate. The "things to come" are those events that lie in Jesus' immediate future, events that, from Jesus' perspective at this moment in the narrative of the Fourth Gospel, are still to come — his death, his departure, his glorification. Because they cannot any longer endure such teaching, the paraclete, when it is given, will teach the disciples about Jesus' glorification — what Jesus would have taught — in precisely the way that Jesus would have done because "he will take what is mine and declare it to you."[52]

To construe the paraclete's vocation as unrestrained prophetic prediction, therefore, is to misconstrue Jesus' promise by neglecting the constraints that the context places upon it. The focus of the paraclete's vocation is not to predict but to recollect. The spirit within will faithfully draw the disciples back to Jesus, particularly to those events that are soon to take place following their last night together. The nature of this peculiar vocation of recollection is clear in what Jesus says in the second promise about the paraclete in the farewell discourses. The holy spirit "will teach you all and remind you of all that I have said to you" (John 14:26). The *all* that the holy spirit will teach is the *all* that Jesus himself has said and accomplished. The holy spirit, in brief, will teach by reminding.

Twice in the Fourth Gospel the curtain is drawn back on the content of remembrance. After Jesus raises his protest against the temple, he barks, "Destroy this temple, and in three days I will raise it up." His Jewish colleagues misunderstand and are, as a consequence, baffled, since the Herodian temple took forty-six years to build. John ventures, by way of an aside, "But he was speaking of the temple of his body. After he was raised from the dead, his disciples remembered that he had said this; and they believed the scripture and the word that Jesus had spoken" (John 2:19-22). This aside illuminates the process of teaching as reminding; such teaching is not mere memory work but recollection that brings deeper understanding.

Much later, Jesus enters Jerusalem on a young donkey, to the resounding praise of the crowd. As in the synoptic gospels, John sees this triumphal entrance as the fulfillment of Zechariah's words. However, unlike

---

52. Prediction is not at all the gist of the word *declare,* which John uses elsewhere of reporting or clarifying. The man healed at the pool "declared" to the Jews that Jesus had healed him (John 5:15). The Samaritan woman believed that the coming messiah would "declare all things to us," that is, make known all things that ought to be known (4:25).

the authors of the synoptic gospels, in a unique and fascinating aside, he explains how the disciples came to see this event in relation to Zechariah: "His disciples *did not understand* these things at first; but when Jesus was glorified, then *they remembered* that these things had been written of him and had been done to him" (John 12:16). The fingerprints of the paraclete are detectable in this aside because the association between understanding and remembrance is so like the connection drawn between teaching and reminding in the farewell discourse (14:26).[53]

The spirit's vocation, therefore, is to lead the disciples, in the aftermath of the glorification of Jesus in death and resurrection, into the truth of what they have already heard and experienced. In these two examples of the process of recollection, this entails the recollection as well of Israel's scriptures. An understanding of the temple saying leads the disciples to believe both *the scripture* and *the word* that Jesus spoke. Their comprehension of Jesus' entry on a colt hinges upon their remembrance that these things had been *written of him* and had been *done to him*. Both narrative asides draw a taut correlation between particular scriptures and a particular word or event in Jesus' life.

In a gospel that begins with an overture in which Jesus is the *logos,* in a gospel that is rife with an appreciation for knowledge, in a portrait of Jesus that is tinged with the hues of Wisdom personified, the paraclete, the holy spirit, the spirit of truth, teaches about Jesus by setting his words and actions in the context of Israelite scripture (John 14:26; 2:22; 12:16). With this observation, we are alerted to the belief that the study of sacred texts has a longstanding impact upon keenly virtuous individuals, imbues them with wisdom, fills them with a spirit of wisdom, with knowledge, with skill. This is the well from which Jesus draws so deeply in the Fourth Gospel, not least when he promises that the spirit of truth will be a teacher who reminds disciples, a coterie of select students, about the deepest meaning of what Jesus has already taught.

The Book of Acts

Luke's narrative of the early church contains a heavy dose of *Schadenfreude.* The story is populated by people who lay the sick on cots and mats

---

53. See also John 13:7, in which Jesus answers, "You do not know now what I am doing, but later you will understand." Later — once the paraclete, the spirit of truth, is given.

in the street in the hopes that Peter's shadow might fall on them (Acts 5:15), by a magician who thinks he can buy the power of healing (8:9-24), by trances and visions and divine voices on rooftops (10:9-23), by an angel who pokes a prisoner in the side (12:7), by people who are eager to believe that Zeus and Hermes have taken human form (14:8-18),[54] by four sisters with the gift of prophecy (21:10), and by a slave-girl who grasps the nub of the early church's message because she is a "belly-talker," possessed by a pythonic spirit deep within her (16:16-18). This is a world full of magic and wonder, which Luke barely repudiates. He does not close the door on this atmosphere of the extraordinary even when he describes the spoken word. Marvelous speech occurs during the Feast of Pentecost, when the house is full of a violent wind, when Jesus' followers have fiery tongues rest upon them, when they are filled with the holy spirit, and when they are charged, even falsely, with making a drunken spectacle of themselves. This band of believers, at least in the eyes of a good many of the spectators, appears to participate in the sort of fiery frenzy that characterized the Delphic priestess or the ribald devotees of Bacchus — so that Peter must disabuse the crowd of their impression that the band is drunk (Acts 2:14-15).

Throughout the book of Acts, however, spectacular events that border on magic take second place to the sanity of the inspired interpretation of scripture. The holy spirit amazes throngs of people because it catalyzes the impressive and entirely unexpected abilities of scriptural interpreters. The inspired interpretation of scripture, more than mission in a general sense or miracles or speaking in incomprehensible tongues, is the principal effect of the holy spirit in the book of Acts.

In fact, as we saw in chapter two, speaking in other tongues has clear content: the praiseworthy acts of God. Filled with the holy spirit and speaking with utter sobriety *(apophthengesthai),* the earliest followers of Jesus recite the praiseworthy acts of God, possibly from creation to the ascension of Jesus, in other languages. Peter's own speech at Pentecost follows suit. This speech, the first speech full of rhetorical flourish in the book of Acts (Acts 2:14-36), features a long and intricate list of scripture references. In addition to citations of Joel 2:28-32 (Hebrew 3:1-5), Psalm 15:8-11, and Psalm 109:1, this sermon is replete with numerous allusions to scriptural texts such as 1 Kings 2:10, Psalm 132:11, Isaiah 32:15, Isaiah 57:19, and Deuteronomy 32:5.

---

54. Acts 14:8-18 includes as well a priest of Zeus who brings animals to sacrifice.

A few chapters later, Luke cinches the relationship between the holy spirit and the inspired interpretation of scripture. After healing a disabled beggar and preaching about the resurrection of a wrongfully murdered messiah, Peter is arrested by the Sadducees. On the following day, a grand congress of Jerusalem leaders asks, "By what power or by what name did you do this?" (Acts 4:7). Before he responds, Peter is "filled with (the) holy spirit" (Acts 4:8). Inspired, Peter says surprisingly little. His apologia consists of two brief statements and a quotation from Psalm 118:22 sandwiched between them: "This Jesus is 'the stone that was rejected by you, the builders; it has become the cornerstone'" (Acts 4:11). The centerpiece of Peter's sermon is this psalm.

This quotation is extremely important for understanding the relationship between inspiration and the interpretation of scripture. Psalm 118:22 circulated widely in the early church; the letter of 1 Peter (2:1-10) even provides an instance in which Psalm 118:22 occurs alongside other scriptural texts — in what was probably a manual, of sorts, with key scriptural texts linked for mission work (1 Peter 2:7). Psalm 118:22, then, was not an isolated text that came off the top of Peter's head in a flash of inspiration. This text was clearly part and parcel of early church testimonies to Jesus rather than an inspired afterthought.

We need to stop and digest this insight. In this abbreviated speech, Luke combines a quintessential expression of inspiration, "filled with the holy spirit," with a scriptural text that had wide currency in the early church's memory bank. This little speech, perhaps more than any other portion of the New Testament, demonstrates clearly that inspiration, filling with the holy spirit, need not be spontaneous. As in the stories of Amasai, Jahaziel, and Simeon, the holy spirit brings out the *meaning* of ancient scriptures — texts known already to the speaker — for contemporary contexts. This sort of inspiration takes place when speakers are already familiar, through sustained study, with those scriptures.

The conclusion to this little speech solidifies the association of the holy spirit with the interpretation of scripture. The story ends in this way: "Now when they saw the boldness of Peter and John and realized that they were uneducated and ordinary men, they were amazed and recognized them as companions of Jesus" (Acts 4:13). What began with a statement about inspiration — Peter was filled with the holy spirit — concludes with the hearers' realization that Peter and company had been Jesus' companions. How so? Because Peter cites the same text Jesus cited in his parable of the wicked tenants, who murdered the owner's son when he came

INSPIRED

to collect rent. In all three synoptic gospels (Mark 12:10-11; Matt. 21:42; Luke 20:17), Jesus cites Psalm 118:22. Why then did the Jewish leaders realize that Peter had been with Jesus? He cited the same scripture as Jesus — and in the same way. In short, he learned this from Jesus.

Once again, the presence of the holy spirit and the study of scripture go hand in hand. The conclusion to Peter's speech takes this idea even a step farther: teachers can impart the knowledge of scripture that combusts in a moment of inspiration. Peter learned from Jesus this interpretation of Psalm 118:22, which went on to gain wide currency in the church, as in 1 Peter 2:7. That acquired knowledge did not keep Peter from being inspired. On the contrary, that knowledge was essential to delivering an inspired speech that amazed his well-educated and well-heeled audience.[55]

The Letter to the Hebrews

The book of Acts is chock-full of familiar figures, such as Peter, Barnabas, Paul, and Lydia. Not so the letter to the Hebrews, whose theology at times has more in common with Philo of Alexandria than Luke-Acts or the letters of Paul. Pneumatology, too, is something of an aberration in this anonymous letter — and that is why the letter is so fascinating. It offers distinctive perspectives on the holy spirit.

The letter contains a total of seven references to the spirit (an interesting number in its own right). Of these seven, three references to the spirit address the enormity of salvation and the egregious error of turning aside from salvation, or even just letting it slip a bit (Heb. 2:4; 6:4; 10:29). The seventh and final reference is to the enigmatic "eternal spirit" (9:18). As captivating as these four references are, we need to set them aside in order to explore three other references to the spirit in the letter to the Hebrews, which lead in another direction: to the ability of the spirit to merge past and present in what amounts to a fresh take on the inspired interpretation of scripture. In the first instance, the holy spirit is the source of Psalm 95:7-11:

Therefore, as the holy spirit says,
"Today if you hear his voice,

55. For a detailed analysis of many other examples of this form of inspiration in the book of Acts, see my *Filled with the Spirit*, pp. 347-63.

154

do not harden your hearts as in the rebellion,
as on the day of testing in the wilderness. . . ." (Heb. 3:7-8)

In the second mention, the holy spirit explains the practice of Israel's high priest:

> Such preparations having been made, the priests go continually into the first tent to carry out their ritual duties; but only the high priest goes into the second, and he but once a year, and not without taking the blood that he offers for himself and for the sins committed unintentionally by the people. By this the holy spirit indicates that the way into the sanctuary has not yet been disclosed as long as the first tent is still standing. This is a symbol of the present time. . . . (Heb. 9:6-9)

The third of these references consists of quotations of Jeremiah 31:33 and 31:34.

> And the holy spirit also testifies to us, for after saying, "This is the covenant that I will make with them after those days, says the Lord: I will put my laws in their hearts, and I will write them on their minds," he also adds, "I will remember their sins and their lawless deeds no more." (Heb. 10:15-17)

All three references look both similar and straightforward. The holy spirit, plain and simple, inspired the production of the Jewish Bible — in this case, the Septuagint, which functioned as the early church's Old Testament. The spirit inspired Psalm 95 (Heb. 3:7-8), the regulations for the priests and high priest in Exodus and Leviticus (Heb. 9:6-9), and Jeremiah 31 (Heb. 10:15-17).[56]

This first impression, however, is misleading. Something other than the inspiration of scripture is going on in the letter to the Hebrews, where the focus lies less on the inspiration of the original text of the Jewish Bible and more on the inspired *extension* of these texts to the recipients of this letter. In brief, the holy spirit does not in Hebrews inspire the production of scripture; the holy spirit inspires the *application* of scripture.

---

56. This function of the spirit resembles Acts 28:25, in which Paul prefaces a citation of Isaiah 6:9-10 with the words "The holy spirit was right in saying to your ancestors through the prophet Isaiah. . . ." (Then follows a quotation of Isaiah 6:9-10.)

THE HERE AND NOW

The first indication that something other than mere citation is going on lies in the tense of the verbs that describe the spirit's activity. The tense is always present, rather than past, pointing to inspiration during the time when the letter is written rather than the time when the psalmist David or Moses or Jeremiah wrote. The author of the letter does not argue that the holy spirit *spoke* Psalm 95 but that the holy spirit *says* it. The author does not say the holy spirit *indicated* something about the behavior of the high priest but that the holy spirit *indicates*. The author does not say that the holy spirit *testified* but that the holy spirit *testifies* "to us." In short, the holy spirit in Hebrews is not associated with the inspiration of scripture when it was composed but with the inspired interpretation of scripture in the context of a living community.

CITATIONS WITH A TWIST

The second indication of the holy spirit's role as the interpreter of scripture arises from a detailed analysis of the quotations themselves. When the holy spirit cites scripture, the text is tweaked in order to suit better the situation of the letter's readers. Compare, for example, Psalm 95 (LXX 94) and its form in Hebrews:

LXX Psalm 94:9-10	Hebrews 3:9
Where your fathers tried me;	where your ancestors put me to the test,
they put me to the proof and saw my works.	though they had seen my works
For forty years	*for forty years.*
I loathed that generation.	Therefore I was angry with that generation.

In the Septuagint, forty years is the length of God's loathing Israel. In Hebrews, forty years is the length of Israel's testing God. This is a substantial difference. The tweaking of the text heightens both the grace of God's provision and the prolonged intensity of Israel's rebellion; it also lessens the emphasis upon God's protracted anger. This difference is not due to the author's having before him a different form or variant reading of Psalm 95 from the reading in the Septuagint (or the Hebrew text on which it is based). On the contrary, the author is fully aware of the original text of Psalm 95:9-10; he or she preserves it when writing later, "But with whom was God angry forty years?" (Heb. 3:17). Here, as in the Septuagint, "forty years" applies to God rather than, as in Hebrews 3:9, to God's people. This question, then, demonstrates that the author is familiar with Psalm 95

(LXX 94) as it now stands, but in Hebrews 3:9 the holy spirit speaks a modified version that serves a key purpose of the letter just a bit better than the original by underscoring how awful it is to become hardened toward God over a span of years. This protracted resistance, cautions the author, is the stuff that leads to irreversible unbelief.

The inspired interpretation of scripture occurs again in Hebrews 10:16, where the holy spirit tweaks Jeremiah 31:33-34. Here, too, the change does not arise because the author of the letter has a text of Jeremiah in front of him that differs from the ones we possess. We know this because he has already quoted Jeremiah 31:31-34 at length *without* these modifications:

Jeremiah 31:33, 34 (LXX 38:31, 34)	Hebrews 8:10-12	Hebrews 10:16-17
Because this is the covenant	This is the covenant	This is the covenant
that I will make	that I will make	that I will make
with the house of Israel	with the house of Israel	*with them*
after those days,	after those days,	after those days,
quoth the Lord . . .	says the Lord . . .	says the Lord . . .
because I will be gracious	For I will be merciful	
regarding their injustices,	toward their iniquities,	
and remember	and I will remember	I will remember
their sins	their sins	their sins
		and their lawless deeds
no more	no more	no more

When, earlier, in chapter 8, the author of the letter cites the words of Jeremiah, the quotation is similar to the text of Jeremiah as we know it. When, later in the letter, the author attributes these words to the holy spirit and regards this as a present testimony to his hearers ("the holy spirit also testifies to us . . ."), the words are bent to accommodate the situation of the letter's recipients. The covenant is no longer with the house of Israel, as in the Septuagint and chapter 8 of Hebrews. Instead, the more generic words, "with them," supplant "the house of Israel" and allow the text of Jeremiah to apply directly to the readers of the letter, who can be counted among "them" even if they do not belong to the house of Israel in Jeremiah's day. The holy spirit, according to the author, also adds "and their lawless deeds" to Jeremiah 31:34. The addition of these words may signal an effort to accentuate concrete sinful activity in order to underscore the scope and depth of divine forgiveness (Heb. 10:17). Whatever the reason for the addition, this is another instance of inspired tweaking — a modification of the original text by the holy spirit to heighten its relevance for the recipients of the letter.

The holy spirit, in other words, does not "testify to us" because the spirit at some time in the past inspired scripture. The spirit does not "testify to us" just through what David or Moses or Jeremiah wrote. Something different from the initial inspiration of scripture is taking place here. The holy spirit testifies to the recipients of the letter by *interpreting* scripture through tweaking ancient texts and bending them to the needs of the letter's recipients.

HOMILETICAL EXPANSION
Another arresting feature of the inspired interpretation of scripture in the letter to the Hebrews is the sermonic thrust of these scriptural citations and examples. In three instances, the spirit is the source of the homiletical expansion of scripture.

Hebrews 3:7-8. In the first instance of inspiration, the author of the letter introduces a modified citation of Psalm 95 (LXX 94) with a clear formula: "Therefore, as the holy spirit says" (Heb. 3:7). Following the citation, however, the author offers no signal that the quoted psalm is over, that inspiration has come to a close. On the contrary, the author continues, "Take care, brothers and sisters, that none of you may have an evil, unbelieving heart that turns away from the living God" (3:12). This exhortation follows directly from the scriptural text without any indication that the text is over and the application about to begin. The shift from text to application, in other words, is seamless. Further, the sermon continues as the author returns to the same text several more times in the course of a single section of the letter, citing it on each occasion:

- He or she quotes Psalm 95:7-8 in Hebrews 3:15, followed by sermonic reflection on sin and rebellion during the wilderness wanderings under the leadership of Moses;
- He or she quotes Psalm 95:11 in Hebrews 4:3, followed by a quotation of Genesis 2:4 and still another of Psalm 95:11, all of them a sermonic reflection upon the conception of rest;
- He or she quotes Psalm 95:7-8 yet again, in Hebrews 4:7, with further sermonic reflection upon the meaning of "today" and "rest" in rela-

tion to sabbath rest (Gen. 2:4) and the peaceful rest of entry into the promised land under the leadership of Joshua.

The simple words "as the holy spirit says" in Hebrews 3:7 do not, therefore, simply introduce the quotation of a psalm. They introduce a psalm and its protracted interpretation — interpretation that entails numerous quotations of the psalm, coupled with other scriptural texts, such as Genesis 2:4. Inspiration extends well beyond the initial quotation to a written sermon that returns repeatedly to this text and ties it into the tapestry of scripture — all of this with a single aim: "Let us therefore make every effort to enter that rest, so that no one may fall through such disobedience as theirs" (Heb. 4:11). This word of encouragement is no less a product of the holy spirit than the text of Psalm 95.

Hebrews 9:6-9. The vocation of the holy spirit as the interpreter of scripture bubbles to the surface again when, after describing how the high priest brought blood into the second tent annually, the author writes, "By this the holy spirit indicates that the way into the sanctuary has not yet been disclosed as long as the first tent is still standing" (Heb. 9:8). This interpretation is barely traceable to the high priest's actual annual activity, as it is outlined in Torah. In fact, contrary to what the author says, the first tent did continue to stand when the high priest entered the second. How can the author argue from this that the way into the second tent cannot be disclosed while the first tent still stands? He or she cannot — except by inspiration. In fact, the Greek verb *dēloun,* which is translated "indicates," could just as easily be translated "reveals" — what the word communicates in 1 Corinthians 3:13 and 12:27, as well as in 1 Peter 1:1 and 14. The holy spirit here reveals the true meaning of the high priest's actions; this meaning goes well beyond the actions themselves.

The author apparently recognizes that this interpretation outstrips the literal sense of the priest's activity, so he or she, in the next line, characterizes this interpretation as a parable or symbol: "This is a parable of the present time, during which gifts and sacrifices are offered that cannot perfect the conscience of the worshiper . . ." (Heb. 9:9). The author has now extended the interpretative reach, by way of parable, well beyond the clear sense of the priest's actions. Yet this is no mere parable or fable. The priest's activities lead to Christ: "But when Christ came as a high priest of the good things that have come, then through the greater and perfect tent (not made with hands, that is, not of this creation), he entered once for all into the holy place, not with the blood of goats and calves, but with his own blood, thus obtaining eternal redemption" (Heb. 9:11-12).

This is a spellbinding move from the literal sense of the text to its christological significance. Inspiration, the author believes, has led him or her through several levels of meaning. The tents can be understood *temporally* to symbolize the tent that cannot be revealed as long as its predecessor is left standing, *anthropologically* to symbolize the inability of sacrifices and offerings to assuage human consciences, *cosmically* or spatially to symbolize the eternal or heavenly tent made without hands, and *christologically* to symbolize the willing sacrifice of Christ. It is little wonder that the author attributes this layering of symbolic interpretations — what he or she calls parables — to the holy spirit (as in Heb. 11:19).[57]

Hebrews 10:15-18. The scenario is no less profound in Hebrews 10:15-18, the third and final instance of the interpretation of scripture, which transpires in several steps. (1) The author refers first to the holy spirit. (2) A transitional phrase, "for after saying," introduces a scriptural citation. (3) A slightly modified citation of Jeremiah 31:33 follows. (4) In several ancient witnesses, the holy spirit (according to the author) is said to speak something else; this is indicated by the words "then says." (5) The first part of Jeremiah 31:34 is omitted. (6) The end of Jeremiah 31:34 is cited. (7) An inference closes the section. The result of this flurry of activity is fascinating:

1	Introductory statement	And the holy spirit also testifies to us,
2	Citation formula	for after saying,
3	Citation of first text: Jeremiah 31:33	This is the covenant that I will make with them after those days, says the Lord: I will put my laws in their hearts, and I will write them on their minds.
4	Connective formula	[the holy spirit] then says

---

57. Recall, according to an earlier discussion in this chapter, that Philo Judaeus does not lay claim to inspiration when he discusses the literal sense of scripture. Philo appeals especially to inspiration when he interprets scripture allegorically, in ways that take the reader far beyond the natural sense of the text. To arrive at this level of meaning, at which Philo is at his most creative, requires inspiration. Something similar seems to characterize inspiration in the letter to the Hebrews.

5	Omission of Jeremiah 31:34a	and I will become a god to them, and they shall become a people to me. And they shall not teach, each his fellow citizen, and each his brother, saying, "Know the Lord, because they shall all know me, from their small even to their great . . ."
6	Citation of second text: Jeremiah 31:34b	I will remember their sins and their lawless deeds no more.
7	Concluding statement	Where there is forgiveness of these, there is no longer any offering for sin.

We noticed already that the holy spirit modifies the text of Jeremiah 31:33-34, especially by changing "the house of Israel" to "them" in order to encompass the readers of his day. Now we see, from the author's perspective, that the holy spirit testifies by citing a single prophetic text while omitting a sizeable, central portion of that text. The holy spirit is a conscious and engaged interpreter of scripture, selecting some passages, tweaking them, and omitting others.

Yet there is more. Both quotations are followed by the crisp conclusion "Where there is forgiveness of these, there is no longer any offering for sin" (Heb. 10:18). As we have come to expect, there is no seam between the citation and extension of the scriptural text to the community — no formula to signal the end of an inspired prophetic text and the beginning of uninspired exhortation. Without the quotation marks or indentations that distinguish scriptural citations in modern Bibles, ancient readers of this letter would likely not have known that the scriptural text had concluded and its extension to the recipients of the letter begun.

This final instance of the inspired interpretation of scripture in the letter to the Hebrews follows the pattern of both Hebrews 3–4 and Hebrews 9. The conclusion — the extension of the text to include the community that reads or hears this letter — is also the testimony of the spirit, part and parcel of what the holy spirit "testifies to us."

SUMMARY OF HEBREWS

The holy spirit is the *interpreter* of scripture in the letter to the Hebrews. Three elements of the letter confirm this: the present tense, modifications and omissions of scripture (even when the author elsewhere cites the original version, where the holy spirit is not mentioned), and the extension of scriptural texts to the community.

The holy spirit communicates in the *present:* the holy spirit says, indicates or reveals, and testifies. The holy spirit *modifies* scripture to accentuate its relevance for the readers of the letter. The holy spirit *extends* the meaning of scripture seamlessly into the world of the letter's recipients with fresh meaning that may go well beyond the plain sense of scripture.

The Letters of Paul

Pinning Paul down on most topics is a challenge, even where he offers explicit instructions or advice. Pinning him down where he writes more obliquely is nigh near impossible. Paul never once, for example, claims to be an inspired interpreter of scripture. He is not like Philo, who floats on the winds of knowledge when he peers into the mysteries of Moses. He is not like Josephus, who traces his traitorous tack to nightly dreams and an inspired interpretation of ancient oracles. He is not like the hymn writer, who has the ability to solve mysteries because he has received God's spirit. Paul makes no such claims.

Although he makes no explicit claims to the inspired interpretation of scripture, two aspects of his letters rise to the surface. His letters are peppered, permeated by scripture. And he traces the entirety of his apostolic ministry to the holy spirit. He may not tie these at the hip in any sort of explicit way, but his letters are shaped by the presence of scripture and the conviction that the holy spirit inspires, not just his ministry, but the entire work of the body of Christ.

PAUL THE PREACHER OF THE CROSS

In the first chapter, I noted briefly that the principal lesson of 1 Corinthians 2 has to do with the *content* of Paul's message — not just the *demeanor* of the messenger or the *experience* of the hearers: "For I decided to know nothing among you except Jesus Christ, and him crucified" (1 Cor. 2:2). This point about content deserves a bit more elaboration if we are to understand Paul's vocation as a preacher whose sermons arose in good measure from the inspired interpretation of scripture.

At first blush, Paul seems to be concerned primarily with his demeanor. He came to Corinth, he recalls, without rhetorical polish and pedantry and "in weakness and in fear and in much trembling" (1 Cor. 2:3). Yet this diminished demeanor contributed to the gospel message because the message was about apparent weakness: "For I decided to know nothing among you except Jesus Christ, and him crucified" (2:2). From where does this message come? From the spirit, the source of the sermon's *content;* it is the *message* of the cross that "God has revealed to us through the spirit" (2:10). The rulers of this age cannot grasp the cross, which lies at the heart of God, where the spirit searches, from which truest wisdom arises (2:11). The spirit, which "comprehends what is truly God's," transforms the cross into a powerful message (2:11).

The deportment of the messenger or the miracles accompanying Paul's speeches — if that is what "a demonstration of the spirit and of power" means (1 Cor. 2:4) — are not alone what the rulers and rhetoricians of this age cannot apprehend. They simply cannot grasp that God's power is evident in the weakness of the cross. They cannot accept the *central content* of the gospel. Yet that is what the spirit reveals. The spirit may enliven a preacher and inspire miracles, but the spirit's primary work is to shine a light upon the central content of the gospel: Christ crucified.[58]

To lose sight of this content in the awesome presence of powerful miracles or the compelling conviction that can accompany the sermons and speeches of a flamboyant and capable communicator is altogether too easy. Where miracles take place, where a speaker sways crowds, the actual content of preaching may slip into a secondary status. Yet to allow an overpowering *experience* of the spirit to eclipse the importance of *cross-centered content* is to truncate the work of God's spirit.

That content, of course, has to do with the cross — with Jesus. That content also takes Paul to the scriptures. This is not a difficult step to make, because the gospel of the cross that Paul preached to the Corinthians stands, in the way he frames it later in the letter, on the shoulders of scripture:

> Now I should remind you, brothers and sisters, of the good news that I *proclaimed* to you, which you in turn received, in which also you stand, through which also you are being saved, if you hold firmly to the message that I proclaimed to you — unless you have come to believe in vain. For I handed on to you as of first importance what I in turn had received: that Christ died for our sins *in accordance with the scriptures,* and that he was buried, and that he was raised on the third day *in ac-*

58. For a discussion of teaching and revelation, see Gordon D. Fee, *God's Empowering Presence: The Holy Spirit in the Letters of Paul* (Peabody, MA: Hendrickson, 1994), pp. 98-99.

cordance with the scriptures, and that he appeared to Cephas, then to the twelve. (1 Cor. 15:1-5)

There is, therefore, a clear connection between the content of Paul's preaching, which he attributes with robust conviction to the spirit (2:6-16), and the scriptures that comprise the bedrock of this preaching (15:3-4).

PAUL THE REVEALER OF MYSTERIES
The wisdom he speaks, Paul urges the recalcitrant Corinthians, is "God's wisdom, secret and hidden," only now "revealed to us through the spirit; for the spirit of God searches everything, even the depths of God" (1 Cor. 2:7, 10). Paul the preacher, in other words, receives the meaning of mysteries from the spirit. This is not an empty claim. His letters contain examples of mysteries once hidden, now revealed. He concludes his letter to the Romans with a closing reference to the validity of *my* gospel, which is nothing less than "the proclamation of Jesus Christ" depicted as the revelation of a mystery found in the prophetic writings of scripture:

> Now to God who is able to strengthen you according to my gospel and the proclamation of Jesus Christ, according to the revelation of the mystery that was kept secret for long ages but is now disclosed, and through the prophetic writings is made known to all the Gentiles, according to the command of the eternal God, to bring about the obedience of faith — to the only wise God, through Jesus Christ, to whom be the glory for ever! Amen. (Rom. 16:25-27)

Earlier in his letter to the Romans, in a portion replete with citations and allusions to scripture, he unlocks the mystery of Israel's temporary resistance to the gospel with a catena of scriptural quotes about Israel's temporary hardness:

> So that you may not claim to be wiser than you are, brothers and sisters, I want you to understand this mystery: a hardening has come upon part of Israel, until the full number of the Gentiles has come in. And so all Israel will be saved; as it is written,
>
> > "Out of Zion will come the Deliverer;
> > he will banish ungodliness from Jacob."

164

"And this is my covenant with them,
when I take away their sins." (Rom. 11:25-27)[59]

Late in his letter to the Corinthians, at the conclusion to an inventive interpretation of the creation of Adam, Paul divulges still another mystery:

> Listen, I will tell you a mystery! We will not all die, but we will all be changed, in a moment, in the twinkling of an eye, at the last trumpet. For the trumpet will sound, and the dead will be raised imperishable, and we will be changed. (1 Cor. 15:51-52)

This particular revelation does not float freely. Paul traces his conviction that mortality must be swallowed up by immortality to scripture — this time a combination of Isaiah 25:8 and Hosea 13:14:

> When this perishable body puts on imperishability, and this mortal body puts on immortality, then the saying that is written will be fulfilled:
>
> "Death has been swallowed up in victory."
> "Where, O death, is your victory?
> Where, O death, is your sting?" (1 Cor. 15:54-55)

The method Paul adopts here is strikingly similar to the method of expansion in the letter to the Hebrews. Paul continues, without any signal that he has completed his quotation, with an interpretation that grows genetically out of scripture: "The sting of death is sin, and the power of sin is the law. But thanks be to God, who gives us the victory through our Lord Jesus Christ" (1 Cor. 15:56-57). Paul takes the word *sting* from scripture and moves immediately to a commentary on it, in which he associates this sting with sin, and sin with Torah. Readers and hearers unfamiliar with the details of scripture would hardly recognize that Paul has moved from citation to interpretation to application.

Paul refers to the spirit in none of these revelations, but we know that the baseline of his proclamation, the foundation of his gospel, according to discussions such as we find in 1 Corinthians 2:6-16, is none other than the spirit God gives: "these things God has revealed to us through the spirit" (2:10).

Nor must it be forgotten that Paul understands the revelation of mys-

---

59. See Isaiah 59:20-21, 27:9; Psalm 14:7; also Jeremiah 31:33-34.

teries to be a work of the spirit in his discussion of spiritual gifts (1 Cor. 13:2; 14:30). At the center of his discussion of *charismata,* he rhapsodizes, "if I have prophetic powers, and understand all mysteries and all knowledge" (13:2). In more prosaic directives about how to exercise *charismata* in the context of worship, he advises, "Let two or three prophets speak, and let the others weigh what is said. If a revelation is made to someone else sitting nearby, let the first person be silent" (14:29-30).

Paul was not the sole claimant to a knowledge of mysteries in his era. Ben Sira's ideal scribe "is concerned with prophecies . . . penetrates the subtleties of parables . . . seeks out the hidden meanings of proverbs and is at home with the obscurities of parables" (Sir. 39:1-3). This description crescendoes when Ben Sira writes, "if the great Lord is willing, he will be filled with (a) spirit of understanding" (39:6) and "will direct his counsel and knowledge, as he meditates on his mysteries" (39:7). This description of the inspired scribe reveals a direct link between filling with (a) spirit of understanding and meditation on the mysteries that only a highly trained and inspired scribe is able to unlock.

Paul and Ben Sira exhibit a family likeness to the author of hymns found among the Dead Sea Scrolls, who claims that God gives him a peculiar capacity to understand God's secrets and mysteries.

> And I, the Instructor, have known you, my God,
> through the spirit which you gave (in)to me,
> and I have listened loyally to your wonderful secret
> through your holy spirit.
> You have opened within me
> knowledge of the mystery of your wisdom,
> the source of your power. . . . (1QH 20.11-12)[60]

Ben Sira, the hymn writer at Qumran, and Paul connect the dots: Israel's prophetic literature, the revelation of obscure mysteries, and the spirit. Differences divide them, of course. Ben Sira is a traditional teacher whose revelations raise the status of scribes among the people of Jerusalem. The hymn writer's revelations are the scaffolding of harsh judgments toward outsiders who do not belong to his isolated community on the shores of the Dead Sea. Paul's revelations serve a movement composed of Jew and Gentile that takes Israel's prophetic literature to coastlines far from the

---

60. See the more detailed discussion of this text earlier in this chapter.

Dead Sea. Yet they are united in the conviction that the spirit unlocks inscrutable scriptural mysteries.

PAUL THE TEACHER

According to the book of Acts, after Saul's encounter with the risen Jesus while en route to Damascus, a wary Ananias lays his hands upon him and says, "Brother Saul, the Lord Jesus, who appeared to you on your way here, has sent me so that you may regain your sight and be filled with the holy spirit" (Acts 9:17). As soon as Saul can see, he is baptized, eats some food, and regains his strength. The impact of the holy spirit is apparent immediately: "For several days he was with the disciples in Damascus, and immediately he began to proclaim Jesus in the synagogues, saying, 'He is the Son of God' " (9:19-20). This proclamation consists of more than enthusiastically expressed convictions. It is not even a testimony to Saul's amazing experience on the road to Damascus, though we might be pardoned for expecting precisely that. Instead, "Saul became increasingly more powerful and confounded the Jews who lived in Damascus *by proving* that Jesus was the Messiah" (9:22). Saul's preaching entails arguments that demonstrate, to the amazement of his hostile Jewish hearers, the messiahship of Jesus. And how does he do this? By appeal to the scriptures, of course, which is how such preaching is always accomplished in the book of Acts. Even the verb *to prove* (*symbibazein* in Greek) connotes gathering up or bringing together — in this case, marshaling arguments from the Jewish scriptures.[61] Saul's compelling and confounding proclamation, like Peter's and the church's in Jerusalem, consists principally of scriptural interpretation inspired by the holy spirit.

This little story may provide entrée, even oblique entrée through the lens of another author altogether, to the Paul who penned some notable occasional letters. These letters are chock-full of scripture, and though we might agree with one scholar's assessment, that "whatever the passage from the Old Testament originally meant, it certainly was not this!" we are forced to admit that when Paul taught, he typically taught out of scripture.[62] Quotations and allusions pepper the pages of his letters, and

61. See Joseph Fitzmyer, *The Acts of the Apostles,* Anchor Bible 31 (Garden City, NY: Doubleday, 1998), p. 436; F. F. Bruce, *The Acts of the Apostles,* 2nd ed. (London: Tyndale, 1952), p. 204; Robert W. Wall, "The Acts of the Apostles: Introduction, Commentary, and Reflections," in *The New Interpreter's Bible* 10 (Nashville: Abingdon, 2002), p. 153.

62. Morna Hooker, "Beyond the Things That Are Written? St Paul's Use of Scripture," *New Testament Studies* 27 (1981): 295.

brief snippets are actually windows to much larger scriptural realities. As Francis Watson notes, Paul is much less preoccupied by dogmatic assertions, such as "Paul and the law" or "Paul and the spirit," than he is with the actual words on the pages of Torah. "Paul's 'view of the law' is nothing other than his reading of Exodus, Leviticus, Numbers and Deuteronomy. He speaks of the law not as a propounder of dogmatic assertions but as an interpreter of texts."[63] The payoff of Paul's commitment to scripture is that "in each case, the individual text plays a representative role, standing for a broad complex of scriptural material relating to the giving of the law, to its positive goal, or to its negative impact."[64] Further payoff of the realization that Paul is a teacher of *texts* first, ideas second, is that he takes these texts as a whole seriously. Because his interpretations sometimes seem odd to us, puzzling, bemusing, it has been rather too easy to accuse Paul of manipulating scripture, of writing letters the way many students write papers: by cutting and pasting with disregard for original contexts. Paul's interpretation of scripture is nothing like this. Close readings reveal that Paul reads more deeply, not less, more attentively, not less, more carefully, not less. To put the case somewhat formally but accurately: "From a Pauline perspective, it is of the nature of the Christ-event to make itself known, and to do so by way of scriptural texts and a proclamation that is nothing other than the authoritative exegesis of these texts. If it is true that for Paul 'the scripture must be read in the light of Christ,' it is equally true that Christ must be read in the light of the scripture."[65]

Although there are relatively few descriptions that help us to pinpoint precisely the responsibility of teachers in the churches associated with Paul, they may be relevant nonetheless. On the one hand, a teacher in the early church was responsible for passing along the church's established traditions, including the words and actions of Jesus. Paul commends the Corinthians because they remember him "in everything and maintain the traditions just as I handed them on to you" (1 Cor. 11:2). He introduces the tradition of a holy meal with the words "For I received from the Lord what I also handed on to you. . . ." Often, it seems, such tradition included scriptural support, as in Paul's teaching about the resurrection: "For I handed on to you as of first importance what I in turn had received: that

63. Francis Watson, *Paul and the Hermeneutics of Faith* (London: T. & T. Clark, 2004), p. 275.
64. Watson, *Hermeneutics of Faith,* p. 276.
65. Watson, *Hermeneutics of Faith,* p. 298.

Christ died for our sins in accordance with the scriptures, and that he was buried, and that he was raised on the third day in accordance with the scriptures, and that he appeared to Cephas, then to the twelve . . ." (15:3-5). The teacher, then, was responsible for handing down traditions intact. On the other hand, teaching was a charismatic gift. Paul includes teaching alongside other charismatic experiences, such as revelation, knowledge, and prophecy (14:6; see Rom. 12:7).[66] In the church at Antioch, where the holy spirit authorized Paul and Barnabas's first mission, teachers and prophets provided tandem leadership (Acts 13:1-3). For all of the study that was demanded of learning the scriptures and mastering the traditions, teachers in the early church were not considered a dispirited band; they, like prophets at their side, were able to teach because they had received a gift, a *charisma*.

This model of teaching as a combination of charisma and knowledge fuels the urgency of commands written to a youthful leader in the Pastoral letters: "These are the things you must insist on and teach. Let no one despise your youth, but set believers an example in speech and conduct, in love, in faith, in purity. Until I arrive, give attention to the [public] reading [of scripture], to encouragement, to teaching. Do not neglect the gift that is in you, which was given to you through prophecy with the laying on of hands by the [council of] elders" (1 Tim. 4:11-14). This is quite a coalescence of virtue, diligence, charisma, the study of scripture, and public responsibility. The association of reading, encouragement, and teaching ought to be understood in light of a story about Paul that takes place in the Jewish synagogue in Antioch of Pisidia. After the Torah and prophets are read, the synagogue officials ask, "Brothers, if you have any word of exhortation [*encouragement*] for the people, give it" (Acts 13:15). Paul responds to this invitation by standing to deliver a lengthy speech, in which he recounts Israelite history in detail, including the recent history of Jesus, replete with citations of the Jewish scriptures (13:16-41). The exodus from Egypt, the destruction of the Canaanites, judges, Samuel, Saul, David, plus quotations of the psalms (2:7 and 16:10) and prophets (Isa. 55:3 and Hab. 1:5 [Greek]) — all of these lead Paul straight to Jesus, David's posterity, whom he brings to the attention of his audience, "descendants of Abraham's family, and others who fear God" (Acts 13:26). His "word

66. See James D. G. Dunn, *Jesus and the Spirit: A Study of the Religious and Charismatic Experience of Jesus and the First Christians as Reflected in the New Testament* (Grand Rapids: Eerdmans, 1997), p. 237.

of encouragement" is the interpretation of scripture, which finds its climax in Jesus. When, therefore, Timothy is told to attend to reading, encouragement, and teaching, he is being prepared for the arduous work of immersing himself in the Jewish scriptures. For this, Timothy needs two things. First, he needs the gift that is in him through prophetic action.[67] That is, he needs *charisma*. And second, he requires the scriptures themselves, which are suited perfectly to the task of teaching, for they are themselves God-breathed, "inspired by God" to be "useful for teaching, for reproof, for correction, and for training in what is righteousness, so that everyone who belongs to God may be proficient, equipped for every good work" (2 Tim. 3:16-17). The scriptures he is ordered to study supply what he needs, if he also nurtures the gift that is his through prophecy and the laying on of hands.[68]

Charisma and study. Both were indispensable to the teachers of the early church, among whom Paul counted himself. "In Paul's understanding 'teaching' included both a recognition of traditional material as authoritative and an appreciation of the need for it to be interpreted and applied charismatically to the ever changing needs and situations of the believing communities."[69] Teachers, in brief, were, among other things, the inspired interpreters of scripture. And Paul was nothing if not a teacher.

PAUL THE INTERPRETER OF SCRIPTURE

How Paul taught is an open book — or an open letter, at least: revelations of mysteries, the handing down of traditions, the occasional word of Jesus, and myriad interpretations of scripture. Not surprisingly, several fresh interpretations in his letters may be candidates for pinpointing his claim to being an inspired interpreter of scripture.

Paul's interpretation of the exodus, for example, is novel: the Israelites "all were baptized into Moses in the cloud and in the sea, and all ate the same spiritual food, and all drank the same spiritual drink. For they drank from the spiritual rock that followed them, and the rock was Christ"

---

67. See also 2 Timothy 1:13-14.

68. I recognize that the authorship of the Pastoral letters is debated. My analysis here accepts them as a valuable contribution to our understanding of practices in the early church, whether or not they are authentic Pauline letters.

69. Dunn, *Jesus and the Spirit*, p. 238. Traditions for teaching, according to Dunn (p. 237), included "OT writings, tradition of Jesus' sayings, the gospel which they initially received (cf. I Cor. 11.2, 23; 15.3; II Thess. 2.15, 3.6)."

(1 Cor. 10:2-4). A communal baptism into Moses, spiritual food and drink, and a spiritual rock — Jesus himself — who follows them around, hardly arise from the surface of Exodus 16–18 and Numbers 11–14. Does Paul offer such a radical interpretation of Torah because he thinks he is inspired? He does not say.

This is not the only novelty in his cache of interpretations. Paul interprets Hagar and Sarah allegorically as the earthly and heavenly Jerusalems (Gal. 4:24). Paul is like Philo, discerning a level of meaning — for both, this is the allegorical level — that takes the reader beyond the literal meaning of scripture. Philo is clear about how he discovers the allegorical level of meaning: the divine spirit speaks to him, teaching him or driving him into ecstasy or lifting him on the winds of knowledge. Paul is more circumspect. Does he offer an allegorical interpretation of Torah because he thinks he is inspired? He does not say.

Paul's letter to the Romans contains other candidates for inspired interpretation. His lengthy interpretation of the words "Abraham believed God, and it was reckoned to him as righteousness" (4:3) leads him well beyond those few words of scripture to the psalms and to interpretations that are, once again, barely transparent. His prodigious, if idiosyncratic, effort to explore and explain the fate of Israel is rife with scripture from start to finish (Romans 9–11). Does Paul put this impressive collection of scriptural texts on display because he thinks he is inspired? He does not say.

There may be one text in which Paul does lay claim, in a muted way, to inspiration. This text opens a window, not only to Paul's self-consciousness, but also to his methods of interpretation. In his second letter to the Corinthians, Paul draws several contrasts, one of which is between the ministry of Moses, encapsulated in the ten commandments written on stone tablets, and his own ministry, encapsulated in the work of the spirit written on the tablets of human hearts (2 Cor. 3:1-3). To develop this contrast, Paul interprets, among other texts, Exodus 34:29-35, in which Moses has to wear a veil so that the Israelites do not see the glory on his face that resulted from his being in the presence of God.

The story goes like this: Moses descended from the mountain (a second time) with stone tablets in hand. To shield the Israelites from God's glory, which shone on his face, he wore a veil after he received the commandments. Whenever he went to meet God, he took the veil off in God's presence; whenever he returned to Israel, he put the veil on again. Paul takes something else surprising from this basic storyline:

Since, then, we have such a hope, we act with great boldness, not like Moses, who put a veil over his face to keep the people of Israel from gazing at the end of the glory that was being set aside. But their minds were hardened. Indeed, to this very day, when they hear the reading of the old covenant, that same veil is still there, since only in Christ is it set aside. Indeed, to this very day whenever Moses is read, a veil lies over their minds; but when one turns to the Lord, the veil is removed. Now the Lord is the spirit, and where the spirit of the Lord is, there is freedom. And all of us, with unveiled faces, seeing the glory of the Lord as though reflected in a mirror, are being transformed into the same image from one degree of glory to another; for this comes from the Lord, the spirit. (2 Cor. 3:12-18)

One modern reader has noted that 2 Corinthians 3 "is full of problems, ambiguities and pitfalls."[70] She is right. Unfortunately, discussions such as we find in 2 Corinthians 3 lead too many modern readers to assume that Paul's "engagement with scripture amounts to little more than an *ad hoc* citation of isolated texts, pressed into the service of whatever argument he happens to be pursuing at the time — usually in defiance of their plain sense."[71]

Several characteristics of Paul's argument do collude to give the impression that he is a cavalier interpreter who has little regard for scripture itself because he is preoccupied with his own agenda.[72] First, several times Paul changes the wording of scripture. For instance, it is not Moses who turns to the Lord, as in Exodus 34:34, but *anyone* can turn to the Lord in 2 Corinthians 3:16. Second, Paul collapses fragments of texts with apparent disregard for their contexts. The contrast of stone tablets and the tablets of human hearts, written with the spirit, reflects Ezekiel's contrast of hearts of stone and flesh and the promise to give Israel a new heart

---

70. Hooker, "Beyond the Things That Are Written?" p. 296. For a coherent analysis of 2 Corinthians 3:7-14, see Scott J. Hafemann, "The Glory and Veil of Moses in 2 Cor 3:7-14: An Example of Paul's Contextual Exegesis of the OT — A Proposal," *Horizons in Biblical Theology* 14 (1992): 31-49. Hafemann (31) begins by quoting Hooker's line, cited above, "whatever the passage from the OT originally meant, it certainly was not this!" in order to wrest some coherence in Paul's thought from its apparent incoherence.

71. Watson, *Hermeneutics of Faith*, p. 273.

72. On Paul's free association of ideas, which leads from letters of recommendation to the ministry of Moses, see the lucid analysis of Joseph Fitzmyer, "Glory Reflected on the Face of Christ (2 Cor 3:7–4:6) and a Palestinian Jewish Motif," *Theological Studies* 42 (1981): 634-39.

and a new spirit (Ezek. 11:19-20). The citation, just slightly later, "Let light shine out of darkness," alludes to the first lines of Torah: Genesis 1:3 (2 Cor. 4:6). Third, Paul may be following Jewish interpretative agendas rather than looking for the meaning of scripture itself. The illumination of Moses' face, for instance, may reflect a Jewish tradition of facial illumination in the Dead Sea Scrolls. The hymn writer thanks God that "through me you have enlightened the face of the Many; you have increased them, so that they are uncountable, for you have shown me your wondrous mysteries" (1QH 12.27). Fourth, Paul is obviously responding to problems and issues at Corinth, leading him to obfuscation rather than interpretation. One modern reader attributes Paul's turgid use of Exodus 34 to the need to respond to a Corinthian misinterpretation that takes its cue from the writings of Philo, according to whom Moses' preparation for his ascent was intensely ascetic; the Corinthians were adopting a similar form of asceticism, of which Paul must disabuse them.[73]

Despite the problems, ambiguities, and pitfalls that characterize Paul's interpretation of scripture, some modern readers have been challenged, rather than deterred, to discover the motivation and method in Paul's interpretation of Exodus 34. Take, for example, the question of how Paul could characterize the ten commandments as a ministry of death. This seems like a horrible mischaracterization that bolsters Paul's ministry at the expense of Moses'. Yet Francis Watson has shown that this may arise from Paul's taking Moses' two ascents together. The second, in Exodus 34, brought glory to rest on Moses' face; the first, in Exodus 32, resulted in the death of three thousand Israelites, who had been cavorting while Moses was on the mountain. The stones, which shattered when Moses threw them to the ground, led in this initial episode to actual death.[74]

Paul's reading of scripture, then, may be more carefully constructed than the smattering of fragments in his letters suggest. Whether he is composing allegory, collecting excerpts into a single scriptural testimony, or interpreting a single text, such as Exodus 34, he tends to take scripture beyond its obvious meaning — or what would be obvious to us. If he were Ben Sira or Philo or Josephus or the hymn writer of the Dead Sea Scrolls, he might be prone to attribute the unlocking of mysteries or the composition of allegories to the holy spirit. This Paul does not do.

---

73. David L. Balch, "Backgrounds of I Cor VII: Sayings of the Lord in Q; Moses as an Ascetic *theios anēr* in II Cor. III," *New Testament Studies* 18 (1972): 358-62.

74. Watson, *Hermeneutics of Faith*, pp. 288-89.

He does, however, offer us a veiled clue to his experience of inspiration in his freehand interpretation of Moses' veil, so his interpretative movements repay careful scrutiny. In the scriptural story, the veil lies only over Moses' face. In Paul's interpretation, Moses is not the only one who wears a veil. The succession of Paul's thought goes like this:

(1) *A veil covers Moses' face (3:12-13):* "Since, then, we have such a hope, we act with great boldness, not like Moses, who put a veil over his face to keep the people of Israel from gazing at the end of the glory that was being set aside."
(2) *A veil covers the reading of [this portion of] the old covenant (3:14):* "But their minds were hardened. Indeed, to this very day, when they hear the reading of the old covenant, that same veil is still there. . . ."
(3) *A veil covers the hearts of readers who are not "in Christ" (3:15):* "Indeed, to this very day whenever Moses is read, a veil lies over their minds."
(4) *The veil is removed from the faces of those who turn to Christ (3:16-17):* "but when one turns to the Lord, the veil is removed. Now the Lord is the spirit, and where the spirit of the Lord is, there is freedom."
(5) *A veil covers the gospel for those who are perishing, unbelievers whose minds the god of this world has blinded (4:3-4):* "And even if our gospel is veiled, it is veiled to those who are perishing. In their case the god of this world has blinded the minds of the unbelievers, to keep them from seeing the light of the gospel of the glory of Christ, who is the image of God."

In this string of interpretations, the veil shifts from Moses (#1), to the public reading of the old covenant (#2), to the hearts of readers who are not in Christ (#3), to believers in Christ whose veils are removed (#4), to the gospel itself (#5). In many respects numbers one and five are similar: those outside cannot see something good, something possessed of the glory of God. More germane for grasping whether Paul understands himself as an inspired interpreter of scripture are numbers two, three, and four. Numbers two and three parallel one another and therefore make one and the same point: those who are not "in Christ" cannot read the old covenant correctly. Number four explains why: only those who turn to Christ can read Exodus 34 correctly.

Stop here for a moment to gaze at Paul's interpretation rather than slipping immediately into the magnificence of verse eighteen, with its spotlight on dazzling transformation from glory into glory. It is tempting to focus on what bedazzles in 2 Corinthians 3:18 — transformation from glory into glory, which comes from the Lord, the spirit — but that will arise soon enough. For now, it is crucial to recognize that Paul is talking about *reading* — and reading right. If he is interested in experience, it is a single sort of experience: *the experience of reading Torah,* of interpreting Moses. "Paul's explanation of the veil intends to speak not just of Moses' person but also and above all of the text, with which Moses is so closely associated throughout this passage (cf. vv. 7, 15). The story of Moses' veil is the text speaking of itself: we have here a self-referential parable or allegory of the Torah."[75]

Paul is, then, concerned in 2 Corinthians 3 with how people read Moses. This is what the veil signifies. "Paul's understanding of Moses' veil is ultimately concerned not with matters of history or biography but with 'Moses' as a text that is read, and with 'the sons of Israel' as the (non-Christian) Jewish community of the present, gathered each Sabbath to hear it being read. This shift from past to present occurs in verses 14-15, where it is underlined by the repeated use of the phrase, 'to this day.' "[76] Reading. Texts. Readers — Paul included. This is the topic of 2 Corinthians 3.

If the second and third references to the veil are about reading — or not reading — Moses right, then the fourth reference to the veil should also be about reading Moses, the text, correctly. Paul gives no signal that he has shifted his attention from reading to some other topic, some other experience, some grand phase of *Heilsgeschichte.* His question is more modest but not, for that reason, less significant: If the heirs of the Israelites do not read Moses right, then who does? Those who turn to the Lord, who is the spirit. Those who are "in Christ." *The principal purpose of the spirit is to inspire the correct interpretation of scripture* — in this case, Exodus 34.

At its base, therefore, Paul's discussion is about how the spirit leads believers to read Moses. Yet this is not all it is about. It is also about Paul's apostleship, though we must be careful not to detach his apostleship from his interpretation of scripture. Paul is at pains throughout his letters to ground his gospel, his proclamation, his apostolic calling in a particular reading of scripture. The tradition he handed to the Corinthians, we can

---

75. Watson, *Hermeneutics of Faith,* p. 295.
76. Watson, *Hermeneutics of Faith,* p. 295.

recall, is principally about the crucifixion of Jesus "according to the scriptures" and his resurrection "according to the scriptures" (1 Corinthians 15). His apostolic calling, on which he expends so much energy in the early chapters of 2 Corinthians, is once again not just a matter of personal conviction; the boldness, the inspiration, the life-giving quality of Paul's gospel is deeply rooted in how he reads the glory of Exodus 34, the promise of Ezekiel 11, and the explosion of light in Genesis 1.

And how does he read Exodus 34? In the light of Christ, Paul reads Torah as one who has turned to the Lord, the spirit. From this vantage point, which Israel's heirs do not share, Paul sees what they do not. Ultimately, the spirit prompts a different sort of reading, a different interpretation of scripture, a different perspective on Moses. As an inspired reader, Paul sees that the story of Moses is actually a story about how Moses' heirs read the story wrongly because they fail, "to this day," to recognize the presence of a new covenant, which renders the old covenant obsolete. This is not just a story about how Moses turned — past tense — to the Lord but also an agenda for how anyone can turn — present tense — to the Lord, the spirit, and have the veil lifted and, without a veil, read Moses right.

Though Paul spreads the spirit to a variety of other spheres, from miracles in Galatians 3 to charismatic gifts in 1 Corinthians 12–14, here in 2 Corinthians 3 he draws a clear and unavoidable contrast between those who read Moses without the spirit and those who read him with the spirit. To validate his own reading of scripture, he plays what might seem to be loose and free with Torah; he shifts the locus of the veil, changes past verb tenses to present, and situates the discussion in terms familiar from Ezekiel's contrast between stony hearts and new spirits. These are not minute interpretative moves. Yet Paul can do this, can introduce apparent innovations and changes, at least to his own satisfaction, because he is an inspired interpreter of scripture, because he has turned to the Lord, the spirit.

All of this is complicated, and it becomes even more inscrutable in what follows: "And all of us, with unveiled faces, seeing the glory of the Lord as though reflected in a mirror, are being transformed into the same image from one degree of glory to another; for this comes from the Lord, the spirit" (2 Cor. 3:18). Modern interpreters have tripped over the image of the mirror, yet this mirror may provide the key to understanding Paul as an inspired interpreter of scripture. What can the mirror possibly mean?

We begin with what the mirror does *not* mean. When Paul says that believers "with unveiled faces" see "the glory of the Lord as though reflected in a mirror," he is not painting in broad strokes a picture of the Christian experience. His strokes are subtler and his topic more slender. He is talking about one indispensable, pivotal experience of faith: reading the story of Moses right, which, of course, is all about glory. Believers in Christ are transformed from glory into glory because they are able to read the text of Moses, a text about God's glory, right — or in the right direction — from back to front. They cannot read it this way — the mirror way — if they read it, as it is read in the synagogue, from beginning to end. But that is not how believers are transformed; they are transformed when they read the mirror-image of the text. And the mirror provides the reverse image of how to read scripture. The mirror gives believers the ability to read the whole story from Christ backwards. In fact, an experience of Christ drives readers relentlessly, voraciously back to the story of Moses, though with an entirely new perspective.

The image of the mirror illuminates what Paul is saying in this highly inventive discussion of reading Moses. In a mirror world, left is right and right is left. Paul gazes into scripture, where he sees the opposite of how scripture is normally read in his day. His colleagues in the synagogue read the normal way, from front to back rather than back to front, from beginning to end rather than end to beginning, but this way of reading causes them to miss the central point of inspiration: the new covenant eclipses the old, the spirit supplants stone, boldness replaces hiddenness, open-ended glory unseats veiled glory. They fail to see that they, like their Israelite ancestors, are missing out on the glory of God; it is veiled to them.

Paul, an interpreter of scripture whom the Lord the spirit inspires, reads from end to beginning. By playing on what Israel's heirs do incorrectly, he comes to terms with what he and those in his apostolic band do correctly: read scriptures as they ought to be read because Paul's people inhabit the realm of the spirit and know the end of the story. I suppose we could quip that Paul has cheated: he has read the last part first, and knowing the end has changed the way he reads the story from the first part to the last, from glory into glory.

The Significance of the Inspired Interpretation of Scripture

This chapter is the natural outgrowth of the prior two. In our study of the spirit and the cultivation of virtue, we noticed that in scripture the spirit-breath is the locus of wisdom, knowledge, and virtue. In our effort to put ecstasy in its place, we determined that ecstasy (or experiences akin to ecstasy) throughout scripture — as opposed to much that we discover in the literature of the Greco-Roman world — is tied at the hip to serious reflection. In the chapter we are now about to complete, we have drawn the circle tighter to a single sort of inspiration: the work of the holy spirit in the effort to understand scriptural texts. I have tried to trace, with a few examples, the contours of the inspired interpretation of scripture in the worlds of Israel, Judaism, and early Christianity. This chapter, like the first two, is also significant for the contemporary study of scripture, with implications for: (1) how Christians assess the value of the Jewish Bible or Old Testament; (2) how Christians can appreciate the role of the community for inspired interpretation; and (3) how preparation paves the way for inspiration.

How to Assess the Value of the Jewish Scriptures

I will begin with a story. I dated a girl in high school who had been baptized as an infant. Because I belonged to a church that believed in adult baptism, I went in resplendent naïveté to her pastor about the possibility of her being baptized. (I realize there is a great deal wrong with this picture, not least, why my girlfriend is not in it.) It was nearly forty years ago, but I remember the conversation as if it were yesterday. The pastor was stern and angry. In less than thirty minutes, he told me that the God of the Old Testament is most decidedly not the God of the New, that the Bible has contradictions, and that in no way would he accede to my girlfriend's rebaptism.

I have read my share of theology since then, and I know now the theological sources of his dichotomies. I can see that he supposed, not altogether incorrectly, that my views on baptism came from a particular way of reading the Bible. So he attempted to pull the rug of biblical authority out from under me.

On further reflection, I realize that he was no less misguided than I — and more egregiously so. I, a barely educated public high school student in love with a blonde-haired, blue-eyed girl, was overly zealous about her need for a baptism in my tradition. He, a seminary-educated pastor, was wrong about the whole of scripture.

The New Testament authors did not draw this sort of radical dichotomy between the testaments, between two gods, between (as the master of Trinity College says in the film *Chariots of Fire*) two distinct mountains. In fact, a paradigm of inspiration, the story of Pentecost, draws a direct line through the Jewish scriptures to Jesus and the experience of the church. The "praiseworthy acts of God," which they recited at Pentecost, is shorthand for that single, remarkable trajectory, which leads the psalmist, for example, from creation to exodus to monarchy, and beyond.[77] The earliest followers of Jesus drew no line in the sand, no gossamer veil separating the God of the Old Testament from the God of the New. Filled with the spirit, proclaiming with clarity *(apophthengesthai)*, Jesus' earliest followers recounted the praiseworthy acts of God in an array of dialects. Peter, with equal clarity, began his inspired speech with an explanation from the prophet Joel and concluded it with an invitation rooted in Isaiah 57.

When an inspired Simeon spoke to Jesus' parents (Luke 2:28-32), he resurrected the words of Isaiah 40 and 42. When Jesus promised that the holy spirit, the paraclete, would teach the disciples by reminding them and guiding them in (into) all the truth (John 16:13), where did the promise lead them? To their scriptures — despite an enormous antipathy in the Fourth Gospel between Jesus and "the Jews." Jesus' words about the destruction of the temple came into focus when "his disciples remembered that it was written, 'Zeal for your house will consume me' " (John 2:17; Ps. 69:9). Toward the end of the story, Jesus' "disciples did not understand" his entry to Jerusalem and the words of Zechariah, "Do not be afraid, daughter of Zion. Look, your king is coming, sitting on a donkey's colt" (John 12:15; Zech. 9:9). Only later, according to the promise of the paraclete, "when Jesus was glorified, then they remembered that these things had been written of him and had been done to him" (John 12:16). Inspired recollection leads the disciples of Jesus to texts we might consider arcane or odd; to the author of the Fourth Gospel, their ability to interpret the words and actions of Jesus in light of these texts is nothing short of inspired.

The Jewish authors of the New Testament did divide from other Jews over the person of Christ, and this division led, of course, to a distinction between Israel and the so-called new Israel. This division is marked by

---

77. For example, Psalms 104-6.

a different way of reading scripture: from Christ to Moses, from end to beginning. Yet this way of reading does not draw the apostle Paul or any other New Testament interpreter away from scripture. On the contrary, when Paul defends his apostolic work or explains the resurrection of the body or clarifies the nature of faith, he turns invariably to the Jewish scriptures. The bottom line for Paul's thinking is the Jewish Bible — the heart of Torah, in fact — the person of Moses as he descended from Sinai to join his headstrong community. Even when he distinguishes himself from other readers in the synagogue, therefore, Paul appeals to their — to *his* as well — scripture. The spirit that transforms him from glory to glory does not transport him to another set of scriptures; the spirit inspires him to read Moses right, or from left to right. Same God. Same Bible. Same spirit.

How to Appreciate the Role of the Community for Inspired Interpretation

Often interpreters of scripture who claimed to be inspired were leaders in their communities. Ezra was a leading scribe in the period of Jewish reconstruction following the return from exile. Ben Sira led his own scribal academy in Jerusalem. Philo was so preeminent a citizen of Alexandria that he participated in an embassy to the emperor Gaius. The author of the Hymns in the Dead Sea Scrolls stands somewhat alone in his claim to inspiration and has often been identified with the founder of the community, the Teacher of Righteousness.[78]

Notwithstanding this impression of the lone interpreter, the community stands silently in the background of their interpretative strategies. Ezra, for example, was not alone; prior to the prayer in which he joins the gift of Torah with the gift of God's good spirit (Neh. 9:20), he stands shoulder to shoulder with other interpreters. Ezra blessed the LORD, and the people, men and women, responded. After the people lifted their hands and bowed to the ground, the story continues: "Also Jeshua, Bani, Sherebiah, Jamin, Akkub, Shabbethai, Hodiah, Maaseiah, Kelita, Azaria, Jozabad, Hana, Pelaiah, the Levites, helped the people to understand the

---

78. Though recently see the fine study of Angela Kim Harkins, *Reading with an "I" to the Heavens: Looking through the Qumran Hodayot through the Lens of Visionary Traditions*, Ekstasis 3 (Berlin: Walter de Gruyter, 2012), pp. 8-24, in which Harkins argues that the hymns are not the product of the Teacher of Righteousness but a model to lead readers to a deeper experience of prayer.

law, while the people remained in their places. So they read from the book, from the law of God, with interpretation. They gave the sense, so that the people understood the reading" (8:6-8). Recall that the verb translated as "gave the sense" is translated as "instruct" in Ezra's prayer: "You gave your good spirit to instruct them" (9:20). Inspired instruction in Torah — the interpretation that is tied to the gift of the good spirit in the prayer that follows — was a communal event.

Nor does Philo stand alone; his approach to scripture, particularly his allegorical interpretation of scripture and the heavy dose of Greco-Roman culture he imports into the writings of Moses, belongs to a line of Alexandrian interpreters. Although we lack the space to undertake a thorough study of Alexandrian interpretation, a comparison of Philo's commentaries with other Alexandrian texts, such as Aristobulus, the Letter of Aristeas, 4 Maccabees, and Wisdom of Solomon, reveals notable affinities with one another and points to a coherent interpretative tradition in Alexandria.[79] Therefore, while Philo's claims to inspiration suggest a deep sense of isolation — wafted alone on the winds of knowledge or listening to the familiar secret tenant or entering the frenzy of corybantic dance — what he actually produces represents the presumptions and perspectives of an established community.

When Peter stands at Pentecost, he too represents an established interpretative pattern. While his ability to leapfrog from Jewish scripture to the events of his own day mirrors the *pesher* method of interpretation so prevalent in the Dead Sea Scrolls, the highly Christ-centered content of his interpretation reflects the influence of the community with whom he stands shoulder to shoulder. Luke even describes the communal context of his sermon: a group of one hundred twenty people, including the reconstituted twelve, gathered in an upper room and engaged in unified prayer. The interpretation of scripture, in other words, can focus on an individual's inspiration without cutting him or her off from a community that provides both the methods and content of interpretation.

WHEN PETER SPEAKS LATER before the Sanhedrin, which he amazes, his hearers grasp his boldness, realize that he and John with him are unlet-

---

79. On the Alexandrian tradition, see David Dawson, *Allegorical Readers and Cultural Revision in Ancient Alexandria* (Berkeley: University of California Press, 1992). For a reliable introduction to Jewish Alexandrian literature, see George W. Nickelsburg, *Jewish Literature between the Bible and the Mishnah*, 2nd ed. (Minneapolis: Fortress, 2005), pp. 191-229.

tered men, and recognize — here is the key — that they were companions of Jesus (Acts 4:13). First, of course, because, according to all three synoptic gospels, Jesus had cited Psalm 118:22 in his parable of the wicked tenants. And second, because Psalm 118:22 was a popular section of Jewish scripture adopted by the early church. In 1 Peter 2:7, this text occurs alongside several other scriptural snippets in testimony to Jesus Christ. When the holy spirit fills Peter, then, the words that arise in testimony to Jesus are ones that he — and the community of which he is a part, starting with Jesus — has committed to memory.

The apostle Paul frequently cites the traditions of the church (1 Cor. 15:3-8), and he commends his readers for adhering to them (11:2). Even his inventive interpretation of Moses' veil probably mirrors Jewish strategies of interpretation; an array of reputable scholars has pointed to Jewish motifs to which Paul's interpretation bears a strong family resemblance.[80] There is a measure of irony here: Paul, while criticizing how Moses is read in the synagogue, interprets the story of Moses with the tools and methods he has garnered from the ongoing life of the synagogue. Once again, then, inspiration, even in apparently idiosyncratic and combative interpretations, does not necessarily entail isolation. Inspiration can take place in the context of a living community, a community's traditions, even a community that presumably comprises one's ideological opponents.

How Preparation Paves the Way for Inspiration

We have seen throughout this book that inspiration is tied closely to human endeavor. This realization crystallizes with the inspired interpretation of scripture. Ezra and his colleagues needed to study even while they taught, so "the heads of ancestral houses of all the people, with the priests and the Levites, came together to the scribe Ezra in order to study the words of the law" (Neh. 8:13). While they studied, "they found it written in the law" that the Israelites should live in booths, so they made this provision and command known. Study and teaching, learning and interpretation, went hand in hand.

Ben Sira offers a catalogue of activities that are required before the

---

80. See Fitzmyer, "Glory Reflected"; Balch, "Backgrounds"; and A. T. Hanson, "The Midrash in II Corinthians 3: A Reconsideration," *Journal for the Study of the New Testament* 9 (1980): 2-28.

scribe is "filled with (a) spirit of understanding" and "will pour forth words of wisdom of his own" (Sir. 39:6). In general, the scribe must first be a pupil, whose foot wears out his mentor's doorstep (Sir. 6:32-37). He must scrutinize ancient wisdom, prophecies, sayings of the famous, and riddles or parables (39:1-3). He must sharpen his insight in foreign courts (39:4). He must rise early to pray (39:5). Then, and only then, "if the great Lord is willing, he will be filled with (a) spirit of understanding" (39:6). Intense apprenticeship, travel, study, and prayer — and a lifetime full of them — are essential ingredients in the formation of an inspired scribe.

We see a different lifetime of learning in the figures of Simeon and Anna. For them, preparation takes the form principally of earnest longing for what Luke calls the consolation of Israel — an expectation rooted in the hope of Isaiah 40. Both figures are steeped in the vision of Isaiah 40–55. When he sees the baby Jesus in the temple, words replete with the language of Isaiah 40–55 tumble from the mouth of Simeon, whose inspiration Luke describes three times in relation to the spirit. Luke describes Anna as an eighty-four-year-old widow who "never left the temple, but worshiped there with fasting and prayer night and day" (Luke 2:37). When Jesus is brought to the temple, Anna begins to praise God and "to speak about the child to all who were looking for the redemption of Jerusalem" (2:38). The words "redemption of Jerusalem" are akin to the words describing Simeon's hope for the "consolation of Israel." Anna, like Simeon, sees Jesus because she is well prepared: prayerful, devoted to fasting, and saturated by the vision of Isaiah.

Peter and Paul in the book of Acts make up a fascinating contrast. Peter's sermon in the presence of the Sanhedrin, in which he quotes Psalm 118:22 (Acts 4:11), reveals the informality of his education at the feet of Jesus. Lacking formal education, Peter nonetheless amazed his cultured despisers. Paul's preparation is of a different nature. As soon as Paul is filled with the spirit, he begins to muster the scriptural texts in which he is so well schooled — only now he does this to demonstrate that Jesus was the messiah (Acts 9:22). Two people. Two inspired people. Two different forms of preparation, but both well prepared by interpretative communities and both well equipped to receive the holy spirit and to speak confidently about Jesus.

Let me conclude briefly by reflecting on Maria Woodworth-Etter, whose fascinating story appeared on the front page of the *The New York Times* and the first page of this chapter. The intriguing trance evangelist would "take a text and trust God to lead me in his own way."[81] We might wish that inspiration, as in Woodworth-Etter's claim, would supplant close inspection of the text, that the holy spirit might do the hard work of sermon preparation. We have seen, however, that this is not a biblical model of inspiration. In the first chapter, we noted that virtue emerges from a lifetime in which people cultivate the spirit-breath within them. In the second chapter, we saw that preparation is required to put ecstasy in its place and that the work of inspiration becomes even more arduous after the spirit speaks a word of revelation. In this third chapter, we have seen that assiduous preparation sets the stage for inspiration. There is no shortcut to effective preaching and teaching. Inspired speakers, at least from a biblical perspective, do not offer compelling speeches and gripping sermons because the holy spirit inspires them on the spot, in utter spontaneity, void of preparation, unmoored from a community. Tangling with the text is tough going — even, or perhaps especially, when preachers or teachers are inspired. The holy spirit fills them because they are already prepared, well studied, alert. With this insight, if you are able to recall, we return to the worlds of Joseph, Bezalel, Daniel, Simeon, and Anna — whose ardor and arduous labor led to sparkling inspired moments in the history of an ancient faith tradition.

81. Woodworth, *Life and Experience*, p. 45.

An Agenda for the Future of Pneumatology

I have probed the spirit's expansiveness in this book, not by unleashing the spirit from constraints, but by connecting it to qualities that are prized as they wend their way through Israelite literature, Jewish literature, and the New Testament. Those elements are virtue and learning.

There is not much mystery in this choice of virtue and learning. As I said in the early pages of this book, I am deeply concerned about the divide in the church between Christians who are drawn to ecstatic experiences and those who are rooted in staid and stable experiences.[1] I worry that Pentecostals, especially those in the Global South, may be drawn to the transport of ecstatic experiences without the counterbalance of virtue and learning. I worry too that Christians in historic Protestant, Catholic, and Orthodox traditions may lose the penchant for ecstatic experiences as they pursue virtue and learning in a sort of spiritless void. I know this dichotomy, like most dichotomies, can lend itself to caricature. Yet I think it holds, and holds a peculiar danger to the church, especially as so many Christians in the Global North sit in mainline pews while so many in the Global South dance to the rhythm of ecstasy.

In order to make my case, I have turned squarely to scripture, which Christians of all stripes hold as an authority of one sort or another. This is the sole platform on which we — the global *we* of the church catholic — can agree (again, to varying degrees) to build our future. We do not need a theology of scripture, or even a theology of inspiration, to adopt this foundation. Simply from a historical point of view, the Bible is the single

---

1. This is why I named a grant I received from the Louisville Institute in 2008, *For Snake-handlers and Sacramentalists: An Essential Introduction to the Holy Spirit.*

resource in a confessionally divided world on which Christians are able effectively to develop an agenda for the future of pneumatology. The fact that Christians share Torah, prophets, and writings with adherents of the Jewish faith makes the use of this foundation even more appealing.[2] I have resisted, therefore, the temptation to engage other theologians because my readers share a single, if variegated, commitment to scripture. Only now, at this late moment of the book, with scriptural underpinnings squarely in place, will I turn to Christian theologians such as Karl Barth, Jürgen Moltmann, Wolfhart Pannenberg, Karl Rahner, and Frank Macchia.[3]

This book may be about pneumatology, but its significance ranges far wider. While I have charted the significance of this study at the end of each chapter, in this conclusion I take the edges of that significance to even farther reaches of our lives, reaches that can be loosely identified as theology, hermeneutics, culture, and ecclesiology. I intend to: (1) develop a pneumatology of creation, in which the spirit is present outside the community of Christian faith (theology); (2) demonstrate the significance of starting-points for interpreting the Bible (hermeneutics); (3) show the indispensable connection between the Bible, particularly the New Testament, and the world that shaped it (culture); and (4) develop a model of inspiration that has the potential to provide a unified future for the church (ecclesiology).

(1) A Pneumatology of Creation

As a young Christian, I learned that the holy spirit filled me when I was baptized by immersion with water once I had professed my faith. I learned this again and again and in no uncertain terms. And I learned this with substantial biblical backing. Peter instructs the throngs who have seen the inspired events of Pentecost, "Repent, and be baptized every one of you in the name of Jesus Christ so that your sins may be forgiven; and you will receive the gift of the holy spirit" (Acts 2:38). I memorized as well a snippet of the letter to Titus: "But when the goodness and loving kind-

2. I am, of course, aware of the differences between *Tanak* and the Christian Old Testament, due in part to the subsequent adoption of the Septuagint and Vulgate. Still, these differences pale in light of millennia of shared, if disparate, use.

3. See also the pioneering work of Elizabeth A. Johnson, *She Who Is: The Mystery of God in Feminist Theological Discourse* (New York: Crossroad, 1992), pp. 124-49.

ness of God our Savior appeared, he saved us, not because of any works of righteousness that we had done, but according to his mercy, through the water of rebirth and renewal by the holy spirit. This spirit he poured out on us richly through Jesus Christ our Savior" (Titus 3:4-6). Like so many Christians, I learned what my church taught me. And what they taught me was good — just not the whole story.

I did not learn that the holy spirit was active in the ongoing experience of sanctification. This insight I garnered later, when I embraced the Wesleyan spirit — or more honestly put, when I embraced a Wesleyan woman, whom I married. Nor did I learn that the holy spirit was present in creation — in what I would like here to call a pneumatology of creation. That insight I encountered only as I wrote *Filled with the Spirit*, in which I tried to demonstrate exegetically that God's spirit-breath exists in all people, not just in Christians who have repented or been reborn and renewed by the holy spirit in baptism. If we begin our exegesis with the New Testament, I discovered, we may miss this strand of scripture altogether, according to which the spirit that people receive from birth is no less divine or holy than the spirit they receive through sacraments or charismatic endowments.

The first move God makes in the entire sweep of scripture, in fact, entails the stirring of the *ruach:* "the earth was a formless void and darkness covered the face of the deep, while a *ruach* of God swept over the face of the waters" (Gen. 1:2). Translations are not much help in figuring out what exactly this *ruach* is. One reads, "a wind from God swept over the face of the water" (NRSV), another, "God's wind swept over the waters" (CEB), and still others, "the Spirit of God was hovering over the waters" (NIV) or "God's Spirit brooded like a bird above the watery abyss" *(The Message)*. The Hebrew word *ruach* does mean wind — "a wind from God swept over the face of the waters." The water's untamed waves are stirred by wind, God's wind, so something good, something beautiful, must be yet to come. But the Hebrew word also means breath that produces words, as in the opening poem of the Bible, where God's powerful words divide darkness from light, sea from land, day from night (Gen. 1:1–2:4). The refrain "And God said" gives structure and stability to creation, as life-ordering words are formed by spirit-breath rolling over God's tongue. Yet even wind and breath do not exhaust the mystery of God's spirit. The verb *hover* or *sweep*, which offers the first glimpse of the spirit's power in the Bible, occurs only once elsewhere in the Old Testament, when God is an eagle that "stirs up its nest, and hovers over its young; as it spreads its wings, takes them up, and bears them aloft on its pinions" (Deut. 32:11-12). This is tender care, powerful pinions grasping Israel's neck to "set it atop the heights of the land" (32:13). The spirit of God, at the birth of creation, hovers over an expectant earth, broods like a bird over the watery abyss — an eagle-like spirit poised with powerful wings over a fledgling creation. Order is on the horizon. Chaos is about to slip into nothingness.

To ground pneumatology in the work of salvation without casting a protracted glance at creation is to truncate the breadth of the spirit. Creation, after all, is where the grand drama begins. The act of creation identifies humankind as *imago dei* (Gen. 1:26-28), a reflection, perhaps even a surrogate for God in the created world, through which God stakes a claim to order amidst chaos: "let us make humankind in our image, according to our likeness." The act of creation reveals the playful participation of Sophia, God's partner, who offers human beings the chance to learn, to nurture virtue, to "lay aside immaturity, and live, and walk in the way of insight" (Prov. 9:6). And the act of creation is the moment, too, when God nuzzles up to the molded earth and breathes life into it (Gen. 2:7).

All of this, of course, comes to fruition in salvation, but we miss the full weight and worth of that salvation if we understand it without the foreground of creation's expansive scope. *Imago dei. Inbreathing. Sophia.* At the dawn of creation, human beings reflect, receive, and are equipped with what they are intended, in the fullness of salvation, the fullness of time, to be.

Spirit versus spirit

The dire drama of Genesis 3, however, disrupts the idyllic cosmos of the opening poem and the first story of Torah, which sets the primeval pair in paradise. Sin erupts from the snake's handling of the primeval pair, and sin spreads as the woman hands the fruit to the man, who is with her. In light of this disruption, it would be a hermeneutical miscalculation to isolate the strand in scripture that sees the spirit of God within as the uninterrupted source of virtue and learning.

The exegetical insights of this book, therefore, cannot be reduced to a newly formulated iteration of nineteenth-century German Idealism. The human spirit is not merely the unbroken path to moral perfection. The human spirit is marred, charred — even, to quote the psalmist, *broken.* Were it not marred, Daniel would hardly need to forgo rich foods and fine wines in order to distinguish himself from other royal refugees. Were it not charred, a holy spirit would hardly require the discipline and teaching that the sage who composed the Wisdom of Solomon imputes to it. Were it not broken, the divine spirit within humans would naturally join to the pure aether-oriented mind rather than the fleshy, earthy soul of Philo Judaeus's anthropology. Were it not impure, the wisdom teacher of the Dead Sea Scrolls would not have to warn his people not to barter their holy spirits for lucre. Were it not sinful, Paul would not have to distinguish between the *psykikoi,* psychic or earthy people, and the *pneumatikoi,* people of the spirit, both of whom inhabited the fractured corners of the church in Corinth.

There is no room ultimately for the optimism, even arrogance, of late nineteenth-century German Idealism, proponents of which drew too cozy a relationship between the divine spirit and the human spirit. Geist (spirit or mind), understood along the lines of German Idealism, came to be identified with the moral sphere of human potential. This understanding of spirit seeped into New Testament scholarship. One of the nineteenth century's most eminent New Testament scholars, F. C. Baur, discussed the divine spirit under the rubric "Principle of the Christian Consciousness,"[4] which he described further as "a truly spiritual consciousness, a relation of spirit to spirit, where the absolute spirit of God, in becoming the principle of the Christian consciousness, opens itself up to the consciousness of man."[5] From this perspective, justification occurs when a human being "has received the spirit into himself as the principle of his Christian consciousness and life."[6] I need not belabor the point that this is hardly Pauline theology at its best; it is certainly suspect exegesis that imports a dominant (and discordant) ideological perspective — German Idealism — into the letters of Paul.

When in the 1880s an intrepid twenty-six-year-old scholar by the name of Hermann Gunkel confronted the virtual identification of the divine spirit with the human spirit, his innovative ideas were met with enormous resistance by some of Germany's intellectual luminaries. Gunkel played the iconoclast and claimed to discover "what the apostolic age had in mind by the term *Spirit.* It is the supernatural power

---

4. F. C. Baur, *Paul the Apostle of Jesus Christ, His Life and Work, His Epistles and His Doctrine* (London and Edinburgh: Williams & Norgate, 1875).

5. Baur, *Paul the Apostle,* p. 128.

6. Baur, *Paul the Apostle,* p. 140.

of God which works miracles in and through the person."[7] Gunkel disavowed any relationship between spirit and Spirit. "The relationship between divine and human activity," he wrote, "is that of mutually exclusive opposition. The activity of the Spirit is thus not an intensifying of what is native to all. It is rather the absolutely supernatural and hence divine."[8] This is hardly the conceptual framework adopted by F. C. Baur, but it is certainly a more legitimate reading of the New Testament than Baur's, with its insertion, intrusion really, of German Idealism into the theology of the apostle Paul.

Along a parallel vein to Gunkel, theologian Karl Barth recognized the danger of German Idealism. In 1929, Barth delivered the lecture "The Holy Spirit and Christian Life" at a crucial juncture in history that illuminated the brokenness of the spirit: just a decade after the troops had returned from the First World War and a scant decade prior to the start of the Second World War. In this ominous atmosphere, Barth had little patience for the optimism of German Idealism. He set in place, therefore, a rigid dichotomy between divine revelation and human experience. The lecture's opening words proved to be a line in the sand. "Augustine knew," Barth began, "what later idealistic theologians no longer rightly understood, that God's life, as it is named in the Bible as Spirit, Holy Spirit, is not identical with what we know of as our own created spirits, or our own

---

7. Hermann Gunkel, *The Influence of the Holy Spirit: The Popular View of the Apostolic Age and the Teaching of the Apostle Paul*, 3rd ed. (Philadelphia: Fortress, 1979; paperback edition, 2008), p. 35.

8. Gunkel, *Influence of the Holy Spirit*, p. 34. The "most striking and characteristic" effect of the spirit in the early church was *glossolalia* (30). Despite this portrayal of early Christianity, Gunkel himself was more of a German Idealist than an adherent of first-century Christianity, as he understood it; toward the end of *The Influence of the Holy Spirit*, he writes (p. 96), "The gifts of the Spirit in the apostolic age have vanished, though in isolated Christian circles something similar may perhaps be observed to this day. But we can also do without these miraculous gifts. For even now we daily perceive other activities of the Spirit in our life. Even for us, the Christian is a miracle of God." He also expressed in poetry as well his personal belief that there is no breach between the divine and human spirits:

> From all the commerce of earthly spirits [Aus allem Handeln irdischer Geister]
> Is woven a gown of the eternal Lord [Webt sich ein Kleid der ewige Meister].

See Werner Klatt, *Hermann Gunkel: Zu seiner Theologie der Religionsgeschichte und zur Entstehung der formgeschichtlichen Methode*, Forschungen zur Religion und Literatur des Alten und Neuen Testaments 100 (Göttingen: Vandenhoeck & Ruprecht, 1969), p. 33.

inner life."[9] Nothing in human beings makes them capable of knowing what they can know only by revelation. Barth proceeds:

> there can be continuity between God and humans (a true analogy of being), by virtue of the fact that He, the uncreated Spirit, can be revealed to the created spirits.
>
> Not that the revelation is given to the creature as such, on the contrary it belongs only to the Creator, though it comes in a *manner suitable* to the creature. It cannot, then, be understood as an original giftedness of the creature, on the contrary, only as a second wonder of God's love, as an inconceivable, undeserved, divine blessing.[10]

A human being, Barth argues, does not receive revelation because his or her spirit is possessed of a divine character or a peculiar suitability. Revelation comes to people with an utter lack of giftedness.[11]

In the light of that age, that day, the rigidity of Barth's dichotomy may not only have been defensible but indispensable. The spirit of nations was swelling with unprecedented greed, and Barth may well have been right to reject altogether the alleged loftiness of the human spirit that rests with — and within — humans from birth.[12]

---

9. Karl Barth, *The Holy Spirit and the Christian Life*, trans. Michael Raburn (2002), p. 5.

10. Barth, *Holy Spirit and the Christian Life*, pp. 8-9. Frank D. Macchia (*Justified in the Spirit: Creation, Redemption, and the Triune God* [Grand Rapids: Eerdmans, 2010], p. 34) points out that Barth, in his *Church Dogmatics* III/2: *The Doctrine of Creation* (Edinburgh: T. & T. Clark, 1960), pp. 362-63, did later come to see the spirit of God in the creation itself: "The whole man is of the Spirit, since the Spirit is the principle and power of the life of the whole man.... Every moment that he may breathe and live he has in this very fact a witness that God turns to him in His free grace as Creator."

11. For a critique of this lecture, see Jürgen Moltmann, *The Spirit of Life: A Universal Affirmation* (Minneapolis: Fortress, 1992), pp. 6-7.

12. Unfortunately, scholars of later decades promulgated the dichotomy between the divine and human spirits in biblical reference works with a certain inelegance and a measure of exegetical lack of necessity, as they transmitted a needless divide between the spirit of creation and the spirit of salvation. More than a half-century after the initial publication of Gunkel's book, and a quarter-century after Barth's lecture, Geoffrey Lampe partitioned the human soul from the divine spirit in his entry on the Holy Spirit in the influential *Interpreter's Dictionary of the Bible*. He divided the spirit of life given at birth from the spirit given at salvation with statements such as this: "In these last instances the thought is primarily of the 'inbreathing' by God of the life principle or 'soul' of living creatures, but although this life principle is not to be identified with the actual Spirit of God, it is represented by the Hebrew writers as an effect of its operations." See Geoffrey Lampe, "Holy Spirit," in *The Interpreter's Dictionary of the Bible*, 4 vols., ed. George Buttrick (Nashville:

Spiritus Sanctificans *and* Spiritus Vivificans

Several twentieth-century theologians have taken pneumatology in a direction that avoids this dichotomy.[13] According to Jürgen Moltmann, the ability to connect the divine and human spirits is of paramount importance:

> In both Protestant and Catholic theology and devotion, there is a tendency to view the Holy Spirit solely as *the Spirit of Redemption*. Its place is in the church, and it gives men and women the assurance of the eternal blessedness of their souls. This redemptive Spirit is cut off both from bodily life and from the life of nature. It makes people turn away from "this world" and hope for a better world beyond. They then seek and experience in the Spirit of Christ a power that is different from the divine energy of life, which according to the Old Testament ideas interpenetrates all the living.[14]

What Moltmann has to say is noteworthy in two respects. First, it establishes that the Old Testament, which has occupied much of our attention in this book, is indispensable to the construction of pneumatology. Second, it uncovers the flaw in a spirituality that divides body from soul, salvation from liberation, spirit from Spirit. As Moltmann goes on to say

---

Abingdon, 1962), 2:629. A generation later and more than a century after the publication of Gunkel's small study, Friedrich W. Horn reasserted this dichotomy in another influential reference work, the *Anchor Bible Dictionary*. He began with a discussion of the "Meaning of the Term" (i.e., *ruach*). Here one discovers *ruach* as wind, demon, and, in what Horn called "this essentially physical meaning," the spirit as breath. Then he turned to the "History of the Concept," a section that begins with a very different tenor: "References to the power of the spirit of God in the OT period occur first with the charismatic judges and ecstatic prophets." The dichotomy is clear: the meaning of the term includes the life-breath, while the history of the concept concerns the power of the Spirit. The life-breath is "essentially physical," while the Spirit of God has to do with charisma and ecstasy. This sort of division between a concept and a term, the life-breath and ecstasy, should not be superimposed on Jewish scripture. See Friedrich W. Horn, "Holy Spirit," in *Anchor Bible Dictionary*, ed. David Noel Freedman, 6 vols. (Garden City, NY: Doubleday, 1992), 3:262.

13. This section could proceed as far back as the writings of Cyril of Alexandria, particularly his commentary on the Gospel of Luke, and, more recently, Friedrich Schleiermacher. This would be fascinating, but I have limited my examples to twentieth-century and twenty-first-century theologians, from Karl Barth to Frank Macchia. I have included enough theologians, I believe, to make the point that theology and exegesis complement one another on the topic of the holiness of the spirit that people possess from birth.

14. Moltmann, *Spirit of Life*, p. 8.

slightly later, "if redemption is the resurrection of the body and the new creation of all things, then the redeeming Spirit of Christ cannot be any Spirit other than Yahweh's creative *ruach.*"[15] He puts it more urgently later still: "Faced with 'the end of nature,' the churches will either discover the cosmic significance of Christ and the Spirit, or they will share the guilt for the annihilation of God's earthly creation."[16] Moltmann has pinpointed foundational insights for the future of pneumatology that are rooted in the relationship, even the identity, between the spirit within human beings and the spirit of God. To put it in more traditional terms, the spirit of salvation is the spirit of creation, the *spiritus sanctificans* is the *spiritus vivificans.* If we sequester these from one another and pay careful attention only to the spirit of redemption, we doom our world to annihilation.

Elsewhere, Moltmann connects eschatology, trinity, and creation in a single, coherent expression of unity between the spirit of creation and the spirit of salvation:

> The experience of the eschatological reality of the Spirit leads to the conclusion that this is the same Spirit in whose power the Father, through the Son, has created the world, and preserves it against annihilating Nothingness: "When thou takest away their breath, they die and return to their dust. When thou sendest forth thy breath, they are created; and thou renewest the face of the ground" (Ps. 104:29-30). This means that the Spirit is the efficacious power of the Creator and the power that quickens created beings. It also means that this power is itself creative, not created, and that it has been "breathed forth" by the Creator, that is to say, emanated. And this, in its turn, means that in the Spirit the Creator himself is present in his creation. Through the presence of his own being, God preserves his creation against the annihilating Nothingness.[17]

For Moltmann, there can be no facile distinction between breath and spirit, or spirit and Spirit, even when Spirit is set in the context of the Christian trinity.[18] Wolfhart Pannenberg offers a comparable exploration of the trinity.

15. Moltmann, *Spirit of Life,* p. 9.

16. Moltmann, *Spirit of Life,* p. 10.

17. Jürgen Moltmann, *God in Creation: A New Theology of Creation and the Spirit of God* (San Francisco: Harper & Row, 1985), p. 96.

18. In *God in Creation,* pp. 99-101, Moltmann contends, "What believers experience in the Holy Spirit leads them into solidarity with all other created beings" (p. 101). He con-

If we are to regard creatures in their plurality as the work of the Son both as deriving from God and among one another, and if the Son, as the Logos of creation, is the principle of its order, by which all phenomena in their variety are related to one another, then, according to the biblical testimony, the Spirit of God is the life-giving principle, to which all creatures owe life, movement, and activity. This is particularly true of animals, plants, and humans, of which Ps. 104:30 says: "Thou sendest forth thy Spirit; they are created, and thou renewest the face of the ground." In keeping with this is the second creation account, which says that God "formed man of dust from the ground, and breathed into his nostrils the breath of life, and man became a living being" (Gen. 2:7; cf. Job 33:4). Conversely, all life perishes when God withdraws his Spirit (Ps. 104:29; Job 34:14f.). The souls of all living things and the breath of all people are in the hands of the Spirit (Job 12:10).[19]

Pannenberg encapsulates this succinctly elsewhere, after citing a similar catena of texts: "The human spirit is not an independent reality of its own, but a mere participation of the divine spirit, and a passing one."[20]

Spirit and Virtue

This is an important statement, but it does not reflect the whole of scripture, in which the spirit is the source of life *for all*, but the font of virtue, insight, understanding, and skill *for some*. We have garnered enough from Moltmann to know that the spirit, to his mind, is not just about breathing and existing; his is a holistic pneumatology — the German title of his

nects the holy spirit with the spirit of creation in two ways. First, he argues that our understanding of the holy spirit guides our perception of the spirit in creation: (1) the new creation of the holy spirit leads us to understand the creativity of the spirit in creation; (2) the holy spirit in community leads us to see harmony and cooperation in creation; (3) individuation leads us to see the concomitant impulses in creation toward self-transcendence and self-preservation; (4) hope engendered by the holy spirit leads us to see a world open to a common future. Moltmann uses a second strategy, rooted in Romans 8, to demonstrate that the spirit in believers is also the spirit in creation: (1) the longing of the firstfruits of the spirit (Rom. 8:23) causes the whole creation to long (Rom. 8:19ff.); (2) inexpressible human sighing corresponds to the sigh of creation.

19. Wolfhart Pannenberg, *Systematic Theology*, 3 vols. (Grand Rapids: Eerdmans, 1991), 2:76-77. See also *Systematic Theology*, 1:373.

20. Wolfhart Pannenberg, Avery Dulles, Carl E. Braaten, *Spirit, Faith, and Church* (Philadelphia: Westminster, 1970), p. 17.

book, *Eine ganzheitlich Pneumatologie,* says precisely this — that leads him to an enthusiastic and open-ended endorsement of all sorts of life-affirming initiatives. "The new approaches to an 'ecological theology,' 'cosmic Christology,' and the rediscovery of the body, start from the Hebrew understanding of the divine Spirit and presuppose that the redeeming Spirit of Christ and the creative and life-giving Spirit of God are one and the same."[21]

Because Pannenberg, too, is keen to embrace the ubiquitous presence of the spirit, he affirms with Moltmann that "the breath of Yahweh is a creative life force,"[22] which cannot be isolated within the church:

> The work of the Spirit of God in his church and in believers serves the consummating of his work in the world of creation. For the special mode of the presence of the divine Spirit in the gospel and by its proclamation, which shines out from the liturgical life of the church and fills believers . . . is a pledge of the promise that the life which derives everywhere from the creative work of the Spirit will finally triumph over death, which is the price paid for the autonomy of creatures in their exorbitant clinging to their existence, in spite of its finitude, and over against its divine origin.[23]

It is essential to note that Pannenberg does not construct what we might want to call a pneumatology of naïveté, a theology without sin. He is trenchant in his awareness of sin and death, the price paid for creaturely autonomy and "exorbitant clinging to . . . existence." There is no room for facile optimism or German Idealism in Pannenberg's pneumatology. Human flourishing is not a natural or inevitable outgrowth of divine inbreathing.

Yet Pannenberg does not allow sin and death to efface the promise of life that "derives everywhere from the creative work of the Spirit." Since each and every human being has the divine spirit — not merely life-breath — and the promise it portends, skill and understanding rise from within. Pannenberg writes: "In an extended sense the breath of life that is already given to all of us at creation (Gen. 2:7) may be seen as endowment with God's Spirit. Beyond that, special manifestations in the course of life display specific and more intensive forms of endowment by God's Spirit, as

---

21. Moltmann, *Spirit of Life,* pp. 9-10.
22. Pannenberg, *Systematic Theology,* 1:373.
23. Pannenberg, *Systematic Theology,* 3:2.

in special capacities for insight, artistic gifts, prophetic inspiration, and leadership charisma."[24] This is a critical point: *the endowment of spirit-breath occasionally intensifies insight, artistic skill, prophecy, and leadership.*

This insight takes us back to the Israelite luminaries with whom we spent so much of our time in chapter one. Joseph, for instance, is recognized by the Egyptian ruler as a person in whom is "a spirit of God" or "the spirit of God" after having lived in fidelity and labored in faith throughout his troubled life. There is no signal in the narrative that Joseph has received a charismatic endowment of the spirit. Pharaoh asks simply, "Can we find anyone else like this — one in whom is a/the spirit of God?" (Gen. 41:38).

Recall one last time Daniel, the epitome of the cultivation of a life of virtue; his first experience of revelations took place while he was avoiding lavish food, studying ancient languages and literature, and living as a young and faithful Israelite in an alien environment (Dan. 1:8-17). Daniel's virtue, his wisdom, the spirit in him, *yattira* spirit in him, spirit to the nth degree in him — these were recognizable across several generations (Daniel 4–6). These were a lifelong presence that Daniel had cultivated. The story of Daniel, therefore, offers a model of inspiration in which *the lifelong quintessence of God's spirit is evident among those who cultivate virtue.* Revelation does not arrest Daniel. Inspiration does not spring upon him.

Call to mind as well Bezalel, chief architect of the tent of meeting in the book of Exodus. Like Joseph and Daniel, Bezalel had cultivated skill. He was *already* equipped with wisdom of heart, with knowledge, with spirit. What equipped him to lead in the construction of the tent was not a fresh endowment of the spirit but a supersaturation with spirit — what Pannenberg calls "intensive forms of endowment by God's Spirit" — a filling to the brim with the spirit that Bezalel had already cultivated. Filling here is not an initial endowment but a topping up — this is what the Hebrew verb often connotes — the way a pregnancy is filled when a baby is born, the way time is full-filled when an expected event finally occurs, the way a house or a hand or a bowl or a lap are filled entirely.[25] According to this model of inspiration, Bezalel already possessed spirit and wisdom of heart, which now, in short measure, would overflow in an inspired episode of teaching.

24. Pannenberg, *Systematic Theology,* 3:9.
25. On the meaning of "fill" as topping up, see my *Filled with the Spirit* (Grand Rapids: Eerdmans, 2009), pp. 55-58.

We see in the resonance between the stories of Israelite luminaries and twentieth-century theologies that theology — or rather pneumatology — and exegesis dovetail. Moltmann and Pannenberg do not appeal directly to Joseph or Bezalel to shore up the connection between the spirit of creation and the spirit of salvation. Yet what they say about the spirit matches the thrust of these stories: the divine breath in human beings can overflow with the fruit of virtue and learning in people whose stories lie within the purview of God's story.

We can see this resonance between pneumatology and exegesis from another tack through the lens of the prolific studies of J. D. G. Dunn. In 1970, Dunn concluded a brief analysis of the figure of Apollos by driving a wedge between the human spirit and the holy spirit. Apollos is an ambiguous figure, at once "burning with the spirit" yet aware only of the baptism of John (Acts 18:24-25). Dunn determined that Apollos, because he burned "with the spirit" and "taught accurately the things concerning Jesus," must have been a Christian. "It is presumably therefore itself a description of Apollos as a Christian, and *pneuma* must be taken as (Holy) Spirit rather than (human) spirit."[26] More than forty years later, Dunn advises against driving a wedge between the human and holy spirits: "any sharp distinction between the creator Spirit and the soteriological Spirit has . . . to be rethought."[27] Dunn notes that "there is a basic flaw in a distinction between different functions of the Spirit, as between the soteriological Spirit and the charismatic Spirit or Spirit of prophecy, which neglects that each function is an expression of the life-giving Spirit. For we are not dealing with two distinct Spirits."[28] This fresh emphasis on the relationship between the human spirit and the holy spirit, between the *spiritus vivificans* and the *spiritus sanctificans,* reflects a recent and auspicious convergence of exegesis and theology.

---

26. J. D. G. Dunn, *Baptism in the Holy Spirit* (Philadelphia: Westminster, 1970), p. 88.

27. J. D. G. Dunn, " 'The Lord, the Giver of Life': The Gift of the Spirit as Both Life-giving and Empowering," in *The Spirit and Christ in the New Testament and Christian Theology,* ed. I. Howard Marshall, Volker Rabens, and Cornelis Bennema (Grand Rapids: Eerdmans, 2012), p. 5.

28. Dunn, " 'The Lord, the Giver of Life,' " p. 6.

Spirit Outside Sacred Walls

Even before Dunn had written his famed *Baptism in the Spirit,* Roman Catholic theologian Karl Rahner, who exercised enormous influence over the Second Vatican Council, connected spirit and Spirit with considerable force. In a brief but powerful essay, "On the Theology of Worship," in his *Theological Investigations,* Rahner looks at grace from two related perspectives. In the first, grace comes, as in the writings of Karl Barth, as intervention in a sinful world; the sacraments, from this perspective, "produce something not otherwise available."[29] From the second perspective, to which Rahner himself is drawn, grace permeates the creation from the start — not just from the incarnation: "Nature is, because grace has to be. From the outset, as ground of nature, grace is the innermost centre of this nature. Consequently, nature is never actually purely and simply secular; it is always nature graciously endowed with God himself."[30] Substitute the word *spirit* for *grace,* and we discover the heart and soul of Rahner's pneumatology. There is no secular world set aside from grace, no spiritual world distinct from the rest of creation. The power of sacraments, the force of liturgy, lies in its drawing from the spiritual nature of creation. "It ought to be shown (and this is of decisive importance) how this grace has its history in man's day-to-day existence with its splendours and failure and is actually experienced there."[31]

The mystery of the spirit is that "God . . . has already communicated himself in his Holy Spirit always and everywhere and to every person as the innermost center of his existence."[32] This conviction leads Rahner, of course, to see God's revelatory presence in religious traditions other than Christianity, wherever one finds what Rahner famously calls anonymous Christians.[33]

29. Karl Rahner, *Theological Investigations,* 23 vols. (New York: Crossroad, 1983), 19:142.

30. Rahner, *Theological Investigations,* 19:143.

31. Rahner, *Theological Investigations,* 19:147.

32. Karl Rahner, *Foundations of Christian Faith* (New York: Seabury, 1978), p. 139.

33. For an analysis of Rahner's pneumatology and its influence on the groundbreaking Vatican II document *Lumen gentium,* see the superb analysis of John R. Sachs, " 'Do Not Stifle the Spirit': Karl Rahner, the Legacy of Vatican II, and Its Urgency for Theology Today," *CTSA Proceedings* 51 (1996): 15-38. Pentecostal theologian Amos Yong has done pioneering work on this topic. See his " 'Not Knowing Where the Wind Blows . . .': On Envisioning a Pentecostal-Charismatic Theology of Religions," *Journal of Pentecostal Theology* 14 (1999): 81-112; *Discerning the Spirit(s): A Pentecostal-Charismatic Contribution to*

It may not be surprising that a Roman Catholic theologian, steeped in a rich theology of creation, is disinclined to divorce the spirit of creation from the spirit of salvation. It may be more startling that Pentecostal theologians, notwithstanding a keen emphasis upon baptism in the holy spirit, move as well in this direction. Frank Macchia urges Pentecostals to acknowledge that virtue emerges from the spirit God inbreathes into all people — not just from a charismatic endowment. Macchia pleads at length with fellow Pentecostals:

> As revivalists, we bathe in the glow of born again Christianity and accent even more than other Evangelicals the supernatural character of the Spirit's presence as a gift given to those who embrace Christ by faith. This accent on the supernatural and eschatological nature of the filling of the Spirit is not problematic in itself, except we tend to think that we can only highlight this by neglecting the Spirit that inspires human wisdom and virtue "from below," so to speak. We thus tend to see life outside of (or prior to) Christ as dark, lost, and devoid of the Holy Spirit. Our talk of spiritual gifts tends to highlight the extraordinary powers of the age to come that overtake us suddenly from above rather than the propensities granted from birth that the Spirit causes to flourish in our ongoing dedication to God's will. We tend to regard any celebration of the Spirit of life outside the sacred walls of the church as "liberal" and denigrating of Christ's uniqueness.[34]

To develop a robust pneumatology, Christians cannot linger over the same questions that have occupied them day in and day out. For Pentecostals, Macchia contends, this is the issue of subsequence: the spirit comes first at salvation and subsequently during the baptism in the holy spirit, typically when a person speaks in tongues. This construal of subsequence — from salvation to sanctification, from confession of faith to baptism in the spirit — leads many Christians, including the Pentecostals Macchia addresses, to miss "the uniqueness of the accent of Old Testa-

---

Christian Theology of Religions, Journal of Pentecostal Theology Supplement (Sheffield, UK: Sheffield Academic, 2000); "A P(new)matological Paradigm for Christian Mission in a Religiously Plural World," *Missiology: An International Review* 33 (2005): 175-91; and *Who Is the Spirit? A Walk with the Apostles* (Brewster, MA: Paraclete, 2011), pp. 91-94, 119-21, 181-84.

34. Macchia, "The Spirit of Life and the Spirit of Immortality," *Pneuma* 33 (2011): 71-72.

ment pneumatology on the Spirit of creation."[35] "There is in the Scriptures," he continues,

> a deeper tension in relation to the issue of "subsequence," which makes any difference between Paul [the spirit and salvation] and Luke [the spirit given subsequently for *glossolalia* and mission] seem like small potatoes. I speak of the tension between the pneumatologies of the two Testaments. The subsequence issue . . . is not between faith and post-faith experiences but rather between the human vitality granted at birth and any further endowment of the Spirit! Spirit filling in the Old Testament is not a subsequent endowment but rather the *expansion* of the Spirit of life given to all humans from the time of Adam (Gen. 2:7) and even present in some sense in all flesh or creaturely life (Gen. 6:17).[36]

Macchia may have Pentecostals in his sights, but the powerful exhortations of Moltmann, Pannenberg, and Rahner to a similar end indicate that this is a relevant issue for the church ecumenical. Many Christians of all stripes mistakenly view "the Spirit in the Old Testament . . . as a fleeting and inadequate foretaste of the supernatural Spirit given through Christ, punctuated by momentary and noteworthy endowments, but generally experienced within a situation of relative spiritual dearth while awaiting the fullness of the Spirit that came through Christ."[37]

Macchia champions one of the primary contributions of this book. *The church must develop a pneumatology that at one and the same time prizes the spirit in the church and values the presence of the spirit outside the realm of Christianity.* His plea is direct and inescapable: "we don't need to denigrate the Spirit that inspires us from below in order to highlight the same Spirit that comes to us from above or beyond!"[38]

This plea resonates with the final invitation in the entire sweep of scripture: "The spirit and the bride say, 'Come.' And let everyone who hears say, 'Come.' And let everyone who is thirsty come. Let anyone who wishes take the water of life as a gift" (Rev. 22:17). As we have come to expect, the spirit does not concoct the words of this invitation out of nothing. In fact, this one final divine invitation resurrects, one last time, the

35. Macchia, "The Spirit of Life," p. 70.
36. Macchia, "The Spirit of Life," pp. 70-71.
37. Macchia, "The Spirit of Life," p. 72.
38. Macchia, "The Spirit of Life," p. 72.

imagery of Isaiah 40–55: "Ho, everyone who thirsts, come to the waters; and you that have no money, come, buy and eat! Come, buy wine and milk without money and without price" (Isa. 55:1). The invitation picks up precisely the three main ingredients of the ancient invitation to tattered exiles: *thirsty* people; a limitless *invitation* to come; and the *gift*, a gift that can be bought "without money and without price."

The boundless qualities of this last movement of the spirit in scripture put all other experiences of the spirit in perspective. In this light, the spirit must be more than what shows up on formal occasions when the sacraments are practiced. The spirit must inspire more than speaking in tongues, as significant as that experience may be. The spirit must even be more than what fills only Christians. After all, the spirit breathes over the entirety of creation as a first action, while the closing invitation is to all who are thirsty — an invitation that goes well beyond the confines of the faithful and orthodox. Those who have the money to buy the spirit, to put it crassly, have no money at all — at least they hold the wrong currency in their hands. The right currency consists of the parched throats that make speech labored, that make it difficult to feel the freshness of the spirit-breath rise through their throats and over their tongues in ample and sustained praise. The sole requirements for responding to the final invitation of the spirit? Hear. Thirst. Receive the spirit as a gift.

(2) The Significance of a Starting-Point

Macchia's attempt to draw Pentecostals' attention to a pneumatology from below is rooted in a hermeneutical shift from the New Testament to the Old: "The possibility that we have overlooked in the Old Testament a rich understanding of spiritual fullness that is not well represented in the New Testament should give us pause to think. . . . We need to remove our New Testament glasses in order to see it. It has been my conviction that for all of our talk about the Holy Spirit we Pentecostals still lack a fully-orbed pneumatology."[39] Macchia's daring call to "remove our New Testament glasses" in order to see "in the Old Testament a rich understanding of spiritual fullness" sets the indispensable question of starting-points front and center. This book puts a premium on the question of *selecting* a starting-point because the choice of a starting-point has significant

39. Macchia, "The Spirit of Life," p. 72.

implications for the construction of pneumatology.[40] Pentecostal Roger Stronstad, for example, in a pioneering book published in 1984, chose as his hermeneutical lens the phenomenon of an "outburst of charismatic activity."[41] From this perspective, the first Israelite text he chose to include was the story of Moses and the elders in Numbers 11, which he understood to be an outburst of ecstatic prophesying.[42] Choosing the lens of an alleged charismatic activity allowed Stronstad to privilege experiences that are particularly appealing to Pentecostals.

In *Inspired: The Holy Spirit and the Mind of Faith,* I start elsewhere: with references to the spirit-breath within. I selected this starting-point in part because it characterizes several references in Torah, the first por-

40. Robby Waddell, in "The Holy Spirit of Life, Work, and Inspired Speech: Responding to John (Jack) R. Levison, *Filled with the Spirit,*" *Journal of Pentecostal Theology* 20 (2011): 207-12, finds himself intrigued by the question of diversity that *Filled with the Spirit* raises. Waddell notes (p. 210) that I expand upon "Gunkel's contribution of diversity within the New Testament by highlighting the diverse pneumatologies within the biblical canon." Waddell then compares *Filled with the Spirit* with James Dunn's *Baptism in the Holy Spirit,* when he writes (p. 210), "In a manner that is analogous to the Pentecostal critique of Dunn, which insists that the New Testament is more diverse than he is willing to admit, Levison critiques the majority of biblical pneumatologies, arguing that the biblical canon is more diverse than most Christian theologians have been willing to admit."

41. Roger Stronstad, *The Charismatic Theology of St. Luke* (Peabody, MA: Hendrickson, 1984), p. 15. As Martin William Mittelstadt (*Reading Luke-Acts in the Pentecostal Tradition* [Cleveland, TN: CPT Press, 2010], p. ix) notes, typically this starting-point is Luke-Acts: "Any Pentecostal with a reasonable amount of history in the tradition knows of the insatiable passion of Pentecostals for Luke-Acts." His introduction begins with two quotations. Donald W. Dayton (*Theological Roots of Pentecostalism* [Peabody, MA: Hendrickson, 1987], p. 23) wrote, "In contrast to magisterial Protestantism, which tends to read the New Testament through Pauline eyes, Pentecostalism reads the rest of the New Testament through Lukan eyes, especially with the lenses provided by the book of Acts." Walter J. Hollenweger (*The Pentecostals* [Peabody, MA: Hendrickson, 1972], p. 336) wrote, "When we look for the biblical roots of the baptism in the Spirit, we discover that the Pentecostals and their predecessors based their views almost exclusively on the Gospel of Luke and the Acts of the Apostles." Mittelstadt joins this chorus in the opening paragraph of the introduction to *Reading Luke-Acts in the Pentecostal Tradition* (p. 1): "I often hear concerning Pentecostalism that no tradition in the history of Christianity exemplifies more the notion of a canon within a canon. When it comes to finding a corner in Scripture, Pentecostals may be at the top of the list. Since their unassuming arrival at the beginning of the twentieth century, the Pentecostal movement enters the twenty-first century as the fastest growing movement in Christendom. Through the first century of their existence Pentecostals found their theological and practical identity by way of their reading of Luke-Acts."

42. In "Prophecy in Ancient Israel: The Case of the Ecstatic Elders," *Catholic Biblical Quarterly* 65 (2003): 503-21, I argue that this is not an outburst of charismatic activity.

tion of both the Christian and Jewish canons. My second reason for starting with the spirit-breath is that this is the first, and most widely shared, experience of every human being. I had a third reason, too: the need for virtue and learning, to which this starting-point is particularly well suited.

In other words, I decided not to begin with a cherished New Testament book — the book of Acts in Stronstad's case — or a prized text, such as Acts 2:1-13, that resonates with a contemporary experience of a slice of Christianity, such as Pentecostalism. I began with three considerations: the shape of the canon (Torah), the most pervasive of all human experiences (breathing), and a universal, pressing need (virtue and learning).[43] On these grounds, I decided that the starting-point for pneumatology should be the spirit understood as a presence in individuals by virtue of God's inbreathing (e.g., Gen. 41:38; Exod. 31:28-35). This view of God's spirit shapes belief early in the biblical canon — long before the advent of the notion of the spirit as an intermittent charismatic presence, as in the books of Judges and 1 Samuel;[44] it is universal in scope — as universal as human breath; and it may lead to a Christian church that is at once highly spirited and deeply thoughtful.

Although I am committed to, even enthusiastic about, this starting-point for the future of pneumatology, it would be a grave error to consider it to be the sole basis for pneumatology. I prefer the starting-point I have chosen to be one among several pneumatologies that emerge from differ-

43. In this respect, though I am indebted to the History of Religions approach, I am not an exclusive proponent of this approach. I chose to organize the book along canonical lines, though with a keen eye to the literature of other cultures.

44. I should perhaps respond to the critique of Max Turner ("Levison's *Filled with the Spirit*: A Brief Appreciation and Response," *Journal of Pentecostal Theology* [2011]: 195-96) that I omit texts, such as the book of Judges and 1 Samuel 10 and 19 (Saul), which do not align precisely with my thesis about the presence of a lifelong spirit-breath within people. I do not intend to be disingenuous in doing so. I omitted them because they do not communicate clearly that the spirit actually enters into these figures. The spirit comes upon or rushes upon or clothes, but it does not fill them. The same can be said of Numbers 11, where the spirit upon Moses is distributed *upon* the elders, without a clear indication that the spirit enters into them. (I also give scant attention to Numbers 11 because I had analyzed it already in "The Case of the Ecstatic Elders.") Turner is correct when he says, of these texts, that "the Spirit of God is more naturally understood as a *donum superadditum* of special empowering." The point I wish to make is that the spirit does not enter or fill these figures. This is the reason for their omission from *Filled with the Spirit*. Nonetheless, Turner's critique does indicate that more exegesis needs to be done to determine how — or where — the spirit is present and whether various prepositions (e.g., in, upon) communicate different modes of divine presence.

ent strands of scripture — and then for all of these to coalesce in a pneu-matological chorus. Let me give you a few examples of other promising starting-points for the future of pneumatology that dovetail with the one I have selected.

The Outpouring of the Spirit

During the course of several centuries, Israel's prophets promised trans-formation of an entire people. The outpouring of the spirit, Isaiah claims, marks the shift between the desolation of Jerusalem and the restoration of justice: ". . . until a spirit from on high is poured out on us, and the wilderness becomes a fruitful field . . . then justice will dwell in the wilder-ness. . . . My people will abide in peaceful habitation . . ." (Isa. 32:15-20). Isaiah's prophetic heir, at some time during the anguish of exile, offers the solace of promise, "For I will pour water on the thirsty land . . . I will pour my spirit upon your descendants, and my blessing on your offspring. They shall spring up like a green tamarisk . . ." (44:3-4; cf. 59:20-21). Another prophet, Ezekiel, transforms this outpouring into a surprising climax of his belief that Israel would be returned from exile to a purified homeland: "and I will never again hide my face from them, when I pour out my spirit upon the house of Israel, says the Lord GOD" (Ezek. 39:25-29). Returning home, safe and sound — this is where the outpouring of the spirit can take us. The latest (perhaps postexilic) and most dramatic take on this theme occurs among the prophecies of Joel (2:28-29; Hebrew 3:1-2). Though the book as a whole is preoccupied with Judah, the breadth of this promise is wider: "Then afterward I will pour out my spirit on all flesh; your sons and your daughters shall prophesy, your old men shall dream dreams, and your young men shall see visions. Even on the male and female slaves, in those days, I will pour out my spirit." Taking his cue from Moses' hope that all Israel would prophesy (Num. 11:29), Joel envisages an outpouring that will enable all people to receive revelations of God through prophe-cies, dreams, and visions. This vision, of course, materializes in the story of Pentecost (Acts 2:1-13) and the outpouring of the spirit on Gentiles (Acts 10–11).

This starting-point fits hand-in-glove with the starting-point of the spirit, virtue, and learning. Whether in times of political uncertainty or during decades of sheer anguish, Israel's prophets believed that the spirit outpoured would refresh nature (Isa. 32:15-20), turn God's people into a green tree in a vast desert (Isa. 44:3-4), bring Israel home (Ezekiel 36–39), and turn slave-girls into prophets (Joel 2:28-29; Hebrew 3:1-2). These vivid promises stir hope within that God will pour out the spirit on our ecosystems, on our churches, on our respective nations, on the oppressed of our world. All of these transformations, like the pneumatology proposed in this book, require preparation and subsequent persistence. None of them is a simple transformation. Those who grasp beforehand the prophetic vision of God's unbounded and borderless munificence will best be prepared for this transformation. Those who know the redemptive power of discipline will be ready to roll up their sleeves and to participate in the grand drama that occurs when God's spirit is outpoured.

Anointed Leadership

Another viable starting-point is the spirit's ability to inspire wise and capable leaders. The wellspring of this starting-point is Isaiah's oracle about a root, a future king, who would emerge from Jesse's stump, from all that Assyria left in the course of its marauding destruction of the Northern Kingdom. "The spirit of the LORD shall rest on him, the spirit of wisdom and understanding, the spirit of counsel and might, the spirit of knowledge and the fear of the LORD" (Isa. 11:2). Any one of these would be enough for a lifetime: wisdom or understanding or counsel or power or knowledge or fear of the LORD.[45]

More than a century later, Jerusalem fell to Babylon and exiles cried, "My way is hidden from the LORD, and my justice is disregarded by my God" (Isa. 40:27). An heir to Isaiah's prophecies answered this by presenting Israel with God's servant: "Here is my [God's] servant, whom I uphold, my chosen, in whom my soul delights; I have put my spirit upon him; he will bring forth justice to the nations" (42:1). With a dose of the spirit, this servant would restore the balance of justice, not only to Israel, but to the entire world. In what manner? With a quiet voice. "He will not cry or lift up his voice, or make it heard in the street." By what means?

45. The spirit of the LORD that rests upon the messianic ruler will grant: (1) intellectual and practical skills needed for peacetime leadership (understanding and wisdom); (2) the skills of developing military strategies and leading in battle (counsel and courage or might, although in Prov. 8:14 this pair of words is used of peacetime leadership); and (3) devotion to God, presumably through participation in worship (knowledge and fear of God). See also Isaiah 9:6-9.

With persistent teaching. "He will not grow faint or be crushed until he has established justice in the earth; and the coastlands wait for his teaching" (42:2-4). Once again, an ounce of inspired quietness, a lifetime of teaching with an eye to restoring the universal balance of justice — this is anointed leadership.

Yet even this great hope does not exhaust the presence of the spirit. Later still, a prophet claimed, "The spirit of the Lord GOD is upon me, because the LORD has anointed me . . ." (Isa. 61:1). This mission is rooted in the understanding and wisdom of the inspired messiah (Isa. 11:1-4) and the justice that lies at the core of the exilic servant's teaching (Isa. 42:1-4). Now, however, it is not the place of Judah among the nations that is preeminent but the visceral quality of liberating the poor within Judah: the inspired one preaches good news to the oppressed, release to prisoners, comfort for those who weep in Jerusalem, and perhaps the liberating year of Jubilee (Lev. 25:8-17; see also Isa. 48:16).

Even Jesus receives this influx of the spirit to accomplish his life's work. To accomplish his task — to rescue the sinners, the prostitutes, the poor — he needs to be anointed by the spirit. He cites Isaiah 61:1-2, with an added phrase, "to let the oppressed go free," from Isaiah 58:6.[46] His healing, the cures he accomplishes, these too, Matthew knows, fulfill the anointed servant's vocation.[47]

This starting-point for pneumatology, with its emphasis upon inspired leadership, has rich points in common with the starting-point of the spirit, virtue, and learning. The inspiration of the spirit in Isaiah 11 and in the texts that follow from it underscores the preeminence of wisdom and justice in visionary leaders. This vision, which champions a leader committed to those on the margins of society, also shares common ground with the transformation envisioned in the promise of the spirit outpoured — especially Joel's vision, in which the status quo will tumble when the spirit is outpoured on all flesh.

---

46. See the postbiblical development of Isaiah 61 in 4Q521, the so-called *Messianic Apocalypse.*

47. Matthew 12:15-21.

Liberation

Begin with the way the spirit rushed upon the judges, and a pneumatology will take another tack. Think back to the paradigmatic judges Othniel, in Judges 3:9-11; Gideon, in Judges 6:34; Jephthah, in Judges 11:29-33; and Samson, in Judges 14:6, 14:19, and 15:14. And then of course there's King Saul, upon whom the spirit of the LORD rushed in power, or transformed him into a different person (1 Sam. 10:6-13).[48]

In all of these cases, something spectacular happened to these people — great people, flawed people — when the spirit rushed upon them. As a result, they accomplished magnificent things for Israel by the onrush of the spirit, through which they succumbed to a surge of uncontrolled — and uncontrollable — power.

What could this conception of the spirit as a flurry of force have in common with the starting-points for pneumatology I have identified in this book? Perhaps more than we might think. The judges, and Saul to a large extent, as the first king over a minuscule state, liberated their people from oppression. If the spirit impelled violence, it was violence from the perspective of the oppressed. That is the theme of Judges: when God handed over the recalcitrant people of Israel to oppressors, the people cried out, and God sent them a liberator (Judg. 2:11-23). Michael Welker, in his provocative book *God the Spirit,* makes this point: "Whatever may be the status of other biblical traditions with regard to the glorification of the use of military violence, those texts that talk about the *intervention of God's Spirit* into the structural patterns of human life are looking at military conflicts that are not only unambiguously defensive, but explicitly unwanted and compelled only by great distress."[49] This association of inspiration with liberation has much in common with the anointed leaders of Isaiah 11 and 61, who also liberate the oppressed, though admittedly, without a whiff of violence. Liberation, then, lies at the heart of these imaginings.

This starting-point shares relatively less common ground with the starting-point I have selected. Still, the onslaught of the spirit on the

---

48. See also the dark, mirror image of this transformation in 1 Samuel 19:18-24.

49. Michael Welker, *God the Spirit* (Minneapolis: Fortress, 1994), p. 58. See pp. 50-58 on the judges. Welker typically goes further than what he says here by denying that the spirit has a role in promulgating violence; the spirit inspired, in Welker's usual view, only renewed solidarity in Israel. I am not convinced by his exegesis, but his effort to untangle the spirit from violence is exceptionally interesting and significant.

judges, as well as Saul's experiences of the spirit — what the author calls prophesying — shares space with the many ecstatic, or semi-ecstatic, experiences we have explored in this book. So too does what follows the rush of the spirit: the judges, at least, go on to accomplish great things, in some cases well-laid plans, even intricate strategies, such as Gideon's, which require considerable know-how. The stories of the judges, therefore, reflect the symbiosis of ecstasy and comprehension we have detected in various guises throughout Israelite, early Jewish, and early Christian literature.

The spirit as a gale force shares space with other starting-points, too. When Saul's star fell and David's rose, the prophet-judge Samuel, who had anointed Saul, now anointed David in the presence of his brothers, and the spirit of the LORD rushed upon David from that day forward (1 Sam. 16:13). David's experience is different from those of Saul and the judges in an important respect: David received the spirit *permanently*. In this detail we catch a glimpse of something that ties inspiration in the books of Judges and 1-2 Samuel with other images of the holy spirit, in which the spirit is a permanent presence. The messianic leader of Isaiah's prophecy receives a permanent endowment of the spirit; the outpouring of the spirit brings about a permanent transformation, and the spirit-breath within, which I have selected as my starting-point, underscores the permanent presence of the holy spirit.

An Array of Starting-Points

I have offered, by way of example, four possible starting-points, but an array of others remains. For instance, if one begins to construct a pneumatology with the book of Acts, particularly the story of Pentecost, then speaking in (other) tongues, or dreams and visions, or prophetic utterance with utter clarity, may become quintessential expressions of the spirit's effects. If, however, one begins with the story of Bezalel, then the quintessential expression of the spirit's effects is an expansion of skills that have been cultivated in a lifelong pursuit of excellence. And what of Isaiah 63:7-14 and Haggai 2:5, in which the spirit takes on the contours of the angel of the presence in the story of Israel's exodus from Egypt?[50] Or the ro-

---

50. For an analysis of these texts, see my article "The Angelic Spirit in Early Judaism," in *1995 SBL Seminar Papers*, ed. Eugene H. Lovering (Atlanta: Scholars Press, 1995), pp. 464-93.

bust pneumatology represented by the "eternal spirit" of the letter to the Hebrews?[51] Or the close connection of angels, seven spirits, and the spirit in Revelation, which would provide entrée to a variegated and vigorous pneumatology?[52] We have not even mentioned Paul's letters, with dozens of references to the spirit, which would offer several starting-points. Any of these — and many other starting-points — could be added to this list, but I have said enough to confirm that the point at which I have started is one among many viable alternatives. A thoroughgoing pneumatology would encompass all of these. That pneumatology is yet to be written.

(3) The Bible and the World That Shaped It

The joke is told about a priest, Father Murphy, and little Eileen O'Connell, a third-grader in his catechism class. Father Murphy was explaining one day that Jesus was a Jew, not a Christian. Jesus was born a Jew, lived a Jewish life, and died a Jew. The implacable, red-haired Eileen O'Connell shoved her freckled arm into the air and shook it violently. "Yes, Eileen," the unflappable priest responded, "What is it?" "Well, Jesus may have been a Jew, Father Murphy, but his mother was a Catholic!"

An onslaught of books in recent years, both scholarly and popular, has made the case that Jesus — along with his mother — was a Jew. Yet many a Christian may still shove a hand in the air, shake it violently, and protest, "Well, Jesus may have been Jewish, but the *Holy Ghost* is *Christian!*" Perhaps they forget that the holy spirit overshadowed Mary before there ever was a church to inspire, that the holy spirit came to Jesus at his baptism before he had even begun his public work, or that the holy spirit overtook the church — still just a devoted band of Jesus' friends and family — while they celebrated Pentecost, a Jewish feast.

Long-held beliefs, however, take a long time to break, and this belief — that the holy spirit is the defining force behind Christianity, *but not Judaism* — has been around a very long time. As long ago as 1888, Her-

---

51. Relatively little has been written on the pneumatology of the letter to the Hebrews. For an exception, see David M. Allen, "'The Forgotten Spirit': A Pentecostal Reading of the Letter to the Hebrews?" *Journal of Pentecostal Theology* 18 (2009): 51-66.

52. See, for example, Bogdan G. Bucur, *Angelomorphic Pneumatology: Clement of Alexandria and Other Early Christian Witnesses,* Vigiliae Christianae Supplements 95 (Leiden: Brill, 2009); Richard Bauckham, *The Climax of Prophecy: Studies on the Book of Revelation* (London/New York: T. & T. Clark, 1993), pp. 150-73.

mann Gunkel — the same young scholar who held his scholarly fist up to German Idealism and its influential proponents — made another revolutionary argument: "It is a grave error in method," he wrote, "which must result in a mass of misconceptions, to attempt to derive Paul's sphere of ideas or even his usage directly from the Old Testament and consequently to ignore the apostle's origin in Judaism. The question can only be, Is Paul dependent on Palestinian or Hellenistic Judaism or is he not?" According to Gunkel, New Testament pneumatology cannot be grasped on the basis of the Old Testament alone; early Christian beliefs in the holy spirit must be understood in their Jewish context.[53]

Despite the strength of this thesis and the force with which he argued it, Gunkel followed the German savant, Emil Schürer, in portraying Judaism in Jesus' day as a movement that had lost Israel's prophetic fervor and retained "only very few pneumatic phenomena."[54] Judaism, Gunkel claimed, set the scene for Jesus' arrival, but only in a negative way: "what a powerful impression the *pneuma* must have made when its fullness appeared to a Judaism bereft of the Spirit," wrote Gunkel. In fact, Jesus could not have been a child of his time. The era was "so spiritually impoverished . . . that a man such as Jesus [could] not come from it. He [was] not a child of his time. He must belong to Israel's antiquity, long past and mighty of spirit."[55] In short, according to Gunkel, if there are analogies to early Christianity to be unearthed, they must be found, not in the arid soil of Judaism, but in the fertile soil of Israelite religion.[56]

A century of scholars followed lockstep behind Gunkel. On the basis of a mishmash of Jewish texts, they constructed a view in which Jews themselves believed the spirit had departed from Judaism. Kittel's influential wordbook, which pastors and scholars consult still today, refers to

53. Gunkel, *Influence of the Holy Spirit*, p. 76. Gunkel wrote this incendiary statement sixty years before the discovery of the Dead Sea Scrolls, at a time when most Jewish texts were still untranslated. Gunkel himself would translate some of them in Emil Kautzsch's monumental collection of apocryphal and pseudepigraphical sources.

54. Gunkel, *Influence of the Holy Spirit*, p. 21.

55. Gunkel, *Influence of the Holy Spirit*, p. 68.

56. Despite his negative appraisal of Judaism, Gunkel left behind a substantial legacy. Slightly more than two decades after the appearance of Gunkel's *Influence of the Holy Spirit*, Paul Volz, in a pioneering study of pneumatology, adopted Gunkel's emphasis upon Judaism without inheriting his negative assessment. Volz even included Judaism in the title of his impressive but undervalued book, *Der Geist Gottes und die verwandten Erscheinungen im Alten Testament und im anschliessenden Judentum* (Tübingen: Mohr, 1910). Gunkel, we may recall, had contended that Jesus was not a child of "spiritually impoverished Judaism."

"a widespread theological conviction" about the withdrawal of the holy spirit.[57] Famed British New Testament scholar C. K. Barrett quoted G. F. Moore, a leading early twentieth-century exponent of Judaism: "The Holy Spirit is so specifically prophetic inspiration that when Haggai, Zechariah, and Malachi, the last prophets, died, the Holy Spirit departed from Israel."[58] In the *Interpreter's Dictionary of the Bible,* a staple of the pastor's study for half a century, G. W. H. Lampe concluded, "In the main, the Spirit continues to be thought of as being, pre-eminently, the Spirit of prophecy, manifested in the distant past in such great figures as Elijah (Ecclus. 48.12) or Isaiah (v. 24), but which was now no longer present in Israel."[59] Gordon Fee, an early and influential Pentecostal New Testament scholar, also fell in step when he wrote, "Noticeably missing in the intertestamental literature . . . is the sense that the Spirit speaks through any contemporary 'prophet.' This is almost certainly the result of the growth of a tradition called 'the quenched Spirit,' which begins in the later books of the Old Testament and is found variously during the Second Temple period."[60]

If it were true that Judaism was a barren wilderness of spirituality, then I could not have written this book, every chapter of which attests to the presence of the spirit in early Judaism. Whether I analyzed the relationship between the spirit and virtue (chapter one), the symbiosis of ecstasy and intellectual acuity (chapter two), or the inspired interpretation of scripture (chapter three), I had at hand a plethora of Jewish references to the spirit — so many, in fact, that in preparing each chapter I was forced

57. E. Sjöberg, *"pneuma,"* *Theological Dictionary of the New Testament,* ed. Gerhard Kittel, 10 vols. (Grand Rapids: Eerdmans, 1964-76), 6:385.

58. Charles Kingsley Barrett, *The Holy Spirit and the Gospel Tradition* (London: SCM, 1947), pp. 108-9.

59. Geoffrey Lampe, "Holy Spirit," in Buttrick, ed., *Interpreter's Dictionary of the Bible,* 2:630. See also the renowned German New Testament scholar Joachim Jeremias, who subtitled section nine of his *New Testament Theology* (New York: Charles Scribner's Sons, 1971), p. 81, "The Return of the Quenched Spirit," and summarized this view: "With the death of the last writing prophets, Haggai, Zechariah and Malachi, *the spirit was quenched* because of the sin of Israel. After that time, it was believed, God still spoke only through the 'echo of his voice' . . . a poor substitute."

60. Gordon D. Fee, *God's Empowering Presence: The Holy Spirit in the Letters of Paul* (Peabody, MA: Hendrickson, 1994), p. 914. For an analysis of this alleged dogma, including its proponents and critics, see my "Did the Spirit Withdraw from Israel? An Evaluation of the Earliest Jewish Data," *New Testament Studies* 43 (1997): 35-57. More recently, Stephen L. Cook, *On the Question of the "Cessation of Prophecy" in Ancient Judaism,* Texts and Studies in Ancient Judaism 145 (Tübingen: Mohr Siebeck, 2011).

INSPIRED

to make difficult decisions about which references to exclude. In addition to many texts from the first centuries BCE and CE, I excluded the whole of rabbinic Judaism, notwithstanding myriad texts on the holy spirit to be found in this rich corpus.[61]

Parallels and Parallelomania

Despite so many references to the spirit, many Christian scholars, students, ministers, and priests are reluctant to affirm the presence of the spirit in early Judaism. Some of this reluctance, of course, may be due to a simple unawareness that Judaism was (and is) rich in spiritual vitality.[62] Another reason may be the suspicion that correspondences between Christianity and Judaism (or other religions of the Greco-Roman world, for that matter) undermine the superiority of Christianity. One Pentecostal scholar expresses this succinctly in his response to *Filled with the Spirit*, in which I incorporated massive amounts of Greco-Roman and Jewish literature; James Shelton writes, "Dante presented Virgil as a spiritual guide, but he could take the poet only to the edge of Paradise; it was Beatrice, the figure of the Church, who escorted Dante further. Moreover, who has not gazed upon a Zen garden and not experienced profound peace, which Paul says is a fruit of the Spirit (Gal. 5:22)? But, as the writer of Hebrews says, the Christian revelation is better than and definitive of all that came before, whether from Jew or Gentile (11:1-3)."[63]

I am not convinced that there is something hazardous about setting early Christianity in its Greco-Roman and Jewish contexts. I am not sure that what we learn from these cultures might undermine what is unique in early Christianity. To argue like this is to suggest that setting W. B. Yeats's

61. Although rabbinic literature preserves traditions from the first century CE, as a literary corpus it emerged in later centuries. For an excellent overview of the spirit in rabbinic Judaism, with copious primary sources in German translation, see Philip Schäfer, *Die Vorstellung vom heiligen Geist in der rabbinischen Literatur,* Studien zum Alten und Neuen Testament 28 (Munich: Kösel, 1972), pp. 116-34, especially 121-23; H. Parzen, "The Ruaḥ Haḳodesh in Tannaitic Literature," *Jewish Quarterly Review,* new series, 20 (1929-30): 51-76; and W. D. Davies, *Paul and Rabbinic Judaism: Some Rabbinic Elements in Pauline Theology,* 4th ed. (Philadelphia: Fortress, 1980), pp. 177-226.

62. See the recent popular book by Rachel Timoner, *Breath of Life: God as Spirit in Judaism* (Brewster, MA: Paraclete, 2011).

63. James B. Shelton, "Delphi and Jerusalem: Two Spirits or Holy Spirit? A Review of John R. Levison's *Filled with the Spirit,*" *Pneuma* 33 (2011): 57.

212

poignant poetry against the foreground of Ireland's fractious relationship with England will undermine its uniqueness, that setting Upton Sinclair's powerful prose against the foreground of the horrors of exploitation during the Progressive Era will undermine its uniqueness, or that setting Bob Dylan's stirring songs against the foreground of the Vietnam War will undermine their uniqueness.[64]

The reality is that *Jewish* authors — and they were Jewish, notwithstanding little Eileen O'Connell's protests — opted to write the New Testament in Greek, the language of their *Greco-Roman* environment. The entire New Testament lies at the nexus of Jewish and Greco-Roman cultures. Consequently, many of the most illuminating texts for understanding the New Testament come from Jewish and Greco-Roman literature. This is true, for example, of the Sabbath, where the ultra-stringent prohibition of work at Qumran makes the Pharisees appear lenient rather than as Sabbath legalists; the Pharisees were more indulgent and pragmatic than the community at Qumran (CD 11.13-14). We can plot Jesus' Sabbath practices more accurately when we utilize the Dead Sea Scrolls and rabbinic (post-Pharisaic) literature in tandem to interpret the gospels.

What of Greek sources? The answer is simple: Who would argue that Paul's words in Athens, "For we too are his offspring," are somehow less compelling if we know they may be derived from the third-century BCE astronomical poem of the Stoic Aratus? The truth of the matter is this: *good scholarship and good preaching require a balanced and thorough knowledge of Jewish and Greco-Roman literature if they are to illuminate the New Testament accurately.*

This illumination is not merely a matter of identifying parallels — what Samuel Sandmel famously called parallelomania — between Judaism and early Christianity or Greco-Roman literature and the New Testament.[65] The effort to identify parallels, critics of this method correctly point out, can function in a facile way to undermine the distinctiveness of early Christianity; such a polemical effort is just as misguided as ignoring the cultural matrix of early Christianity altogether. The relationship between the Greco-Roman world, Judaism, and Christianity is more tex-

---

64. Archie T. Wright, whose primary expertise lies in early Jewish literature, engages the Jewish material with perspicacity without needing to ask whether it is appropriate to set the New Testament in its Jewish context. His critique ("The Spirit in Early Jewish Biblical Interpretation: Examining John R. Levison's *Filled with the Spirit,*" *Pneuma* 33 [2011]: 35-46) correctly assumes the value of Jewish literature.

65. Samuel Sandmel, "Parallelomania," *Journal of Biblical Literature* 81 (1962): 1-13.

tured than a simple list of parallels can communicate. Let me offer, therefore, two ways in which a nuanced approach to the relationship between Christianity and the cultures in which it grew prove indispensable to our understanding of the early church.

Filling in the Gaps

Jewish and Greco-Roman literature supplies what is simply not available in early Christian literature. Take, for example, the understanding of ecstasy with which New Testament writers flirt. Luke adopts the word *ekstasis,* but he does not define ecstasy. Nor does Paul — or any other New Testament author. Not even the author of Revelation, which identifies itself as a book of prophecy (22:18-19) and contains numerous visions, defines ecstasy. However, Philo Judaeus, a first-century Jewish cosmopolitan author who had traveled from Alexandria to Rome and who possessed knowledge of communities in Palestine, does define ecstasy, and in no small measure of detail. He actually devotes considerable attention to *ekstasis* when it appears in Genesis 15:12.[66] Philo supplies, in short, what the New Testament (or Old) lacks: a clear definition of a word adopted but unexplained in the New Testament. It would be shortsighted to ignore Philo's definitions of ecstasy.

It would be shortsighted as well to ignore the priceless writings of the Roman author Plutarch, whose life spanned practically the whole of the early church — from about 46 until the 120s CE. Recall the importance of Plutarch's writing for our analysis of ecstasy, not just because he offers a clear definition of inspiration, but also because, as a devotee of the New Academy, he laid out alternative conceptions rather than a single point of view. In this respect, his writings prove at times to be even more fruitful than Philo's because Philo tends to champion his own point of view. A dialogue such as *On the Obsolescence of Oracles* offers several mutually exclusive explanations of Delphic inspiration, while *On the Genius of Socrates* pays meticulous attention to possible explanations of Socrates' uncanny inspiration. Plutarch offers in painstaking detail an array of views on the mechanics of inspiration that are indispensable for understanding what New Testament authors adopt without explanation. In short, Plutarch supplies what we simply cannot find in the New Testament (or Old).

66. Philo Judaeus, *Who Is the Heir?* 249, 258, 263-65.

Matching Bookends, Different as Night and Day

The second reason scholars, teachers, and preachers benefit from paying careful attention to the relationship between early Christianity and cultures is this: the identification of *parallels* often fits hand-in-glove with the discovery of *differences*. This realization came home to me when I spoke on the holy spirit in Seattle's Town Hall as part of a lecture series that accompanied an exhibit of the Dead Sea Scrolls at the Pacific Science Center. I began that lecture with a video clip from *The Patty Duke Show,* a television series to which my family was glued during the sixties. The show is about "identical cousins," both played by Patty Duke. One identical cousin is an educated and urbane Briton, the other a rock 'n rolling teenager from Brooklyn — "One pair of matching bookends, / Different as night and day," as the show's theme song put it.

In many ways, the Dead Sea Scrolls and the New Testament are matching bookends, different as night and day. They look like identical cousins, a wild duet to the historian who is desperate to discover analogous texts and contexts that illuminate the complex and confounding character of the early church. Yet the value of alleged parallels often lies in the differences that cause otherwise negligible or unobtrusive features of the New Testament to emerge.

In 1 Corinthians, for example, Paul asks the Corinthians, point blank, "Do you not know that you are God's temple and that God's spirit dwells in you?" The metaphor of the spirit-filled temple occurs in a question posed, not to individuals, but to an entire community — as in the southern American expression *y'all.* This temple, this community, is also holy: "For God's temple is holy, and you are that temple" (1 Cor. 3:16-17).

The charter document of the Qumran community, the *Community Rule,* contains a similar conception of the community. The inhabitants of this desert enclave exist "in order to establish the spirit of holiness in truth eternal, in order to atone for the guilt of iniquity and for the unfaithfulness of sin . . . without the flesh of burnt offerings and without the fats of sacrifice," for they are "a holy house for Aaron, in order to form a most holy community, and a house of the Community for Israel, those who walk in perfection" (1QS 9.3-6).[67]

---

67. For a similar combination of conceptions in *4QFlorilegium,* see Bertil E. Gärtner, *The Temple and the Community in Qumran and the New Testament,* Society of New Testament Studies Monograph Series 1 (Cambridge: Cambridge University Press, 1965), pp. 30-42. The detailed description of the annual covenant renewal ceremony during Pentecost,

The similarity between the Dead Sea Scrolls and Paul's letter to the Corinthians underscores the differences between them. First, the Corinthians, in contrast to the community by the Dead Sea, are a collection of cliques whose place in the communal hierarchy is determined by the alleged worth of individual spiritual gifts.[68] Second, the inhabitants of Qumran associate the spirit with *eternal truth,* but the Corinthians, in their penchant for speaking in tongues, privilege an "unproductive mind" (1 Cor. 14:14). And third, the community at Qumran is regulated by a quotidian passion for holiness, which the spirit of holiness imparts,[69] but the Corinthians tolerate what Paul calls shameless acts of impurity, such as a man who lives with his father's wife (5:1-8) or greed and schism at the Lord's table (11:17-22) — acts that would have brought with them permanent expulsion from the community at Qumran rather than Paul's more lenient command to exclude temporarily the offending man so that he can be restored to the community.

These two communities — one the gateway of a lively Greek seaport and the other an isolated enclave near the Dead Sea — are both identical and different as night and day. The people who built their enclave by the Dead Sea and who, when the Romans threatened their peaceful existence, hid scrolls high in caves, understood that the holy spirit inspires an entire community. Their ability to understand this point, however, arose from a flaw in their foundation. Unity at Qumran arose from uniformity. All were Jews. All were disenfranchised Jews, joined in opposition to the Jerusalem priests. All, or most, were male Jews. All of these male Jews underwent a rigorous two- or three-year period of initiation. All, throughout

---

in which new members were taken into the community at Qumran, exhibits a similar communal self-consciousness (1QS 1.21-3.12, especially 3.6-9). Elsewhere, the community is "an everlasting plantation, a holy house for Israel and the foundation of the holy of holies for Aaron . . ." (1QS 8.5-6). It is a "precious cornerstone," "the most holy dwelling of Aaron . . . a house of perfection and truth in Israel" (1QS 8.7, 9).

68. See 1 Corinthians 1:10–3:23 and 12–14.

69. A believer at Qumran was "drawn near" or brought into the community by the giving of the spirit of holiness within. This "drawing near" entailed a sort of purification that was directly related to the gift of the spirit of holiness: "I have appeased your face by the spirit which you have placed [in me,] to lavish your [kind]nesses on [your] serv[ant] for [ever,] to purify me with your holy spirit, to bring me near by your will according to the extent of your kindnesses . . ." (1QH 8.19-20). For detailed analysis, see H.-W. Kuhn, *Enderwartung und gegenwärtiges Heil: Untersuchungen zu den Gemeindeliedern von Qumran,* Studien zur Umwelt des Neuen Testaments 4 (Göttingen: Vandenhoeck & Ruprecht, 1966), pp. 117-39.

their tenure as members of the community, could be severely disciplined: spitting in the assembly brought a penalty of thirty days of exclusion; unnecessary walking about naked in front of others led to six months of punishment; defaming another individual meant a full year of punishment and exclusion from the community meal, while defaming the community as a whole led to permanent exclusion. It was probably not difficult to maintain unity, to live as a holy, spirit-filled temple, when that unity was imposed through regularized uniformity and the threat of expulsion.

The Corinthian church, in contrast, was a mission church, the product of the early church's passion for constant expansion. In this community on the coast of Greece, wealthy and poor ate a community meal together. Some were soldiers who had prior commitments to the Roman Empire; some were slaves, others wealthy urbanites, perhaps even their owners. Women, too, were leaders, praying and prophesying during worship (1 Cor. 11:5). All of these disparities — and the tensions they inflamed — contributed to the kaleidoscopic social structures — and no doubt to the schisms — that plagued Corinth and prompted Paul to remind them that they were a spirit-filled temple.

Despite the flaws of the ingrown community clustered at the Dead Sea, their virtues enable the scholar or teacher or preacher who stands two millennia away in time to grasp the reality, even the disappointment of Corinth. The Corinthians were splintered, fractured by the use of what they called spiritual gifts — teaching, healing, generosity — to generate chaotic hierarchies, based upon whichever gift was thought to be best. The Corinthians lacked a hunger for holiness and, instead, allowed reprehensible moral lapses to fester before their eyes. And the Corinthians separated themselves into pockets of loyalty to different leaders. It is these faults that the metaphor of the temple — which we grasp so clearly in the Dead Sea Scrolls — pointedly addresses. The metaphor of a spirit-filled temple, of a unified community whose holiness transcends mere individuals, provides a direct critique of the Corinthian lapse into discordant cliques and moral confusion.

This cursory comparison between the Dead Sea Scrolls and the New Testament highlights the signal importance of identifying points of resonance and resistance between the New Testament and its cultural matrix — a lesson that goes well beyond the origins of pneumatology. There is little to fear in the identification of correspondences; it would be odd, even unthinkable, for a collection of documents written in Greek by Jews to share nothing with the cultures that cradled them. Yet it is essential as well to bear in mind that Greco-Roman and Jewish foregrounds to the New Testament provide elements of both continuity and discontinuity. The spirit-filled temple — a shared conception of the Community Rule and 1 Corinthians — looks very different in communities situated along the shores of the Dead Sea and the Corinthian Gulf. One is homogeneous, predominantly male, and rigorously ordered; the other is diverse, led in part by female prophets, and riding along the edge of spiritual anarchy. The faults and virtues of one community help us to identify the virtues and faults of the other.

Little Eileen O'Connell, it seems, had nothing to fear, no grounds for claiming Mary for the Catholics. Christians have no reason to fret the continuity and discontinuity that tether the early church to its Greco-Roman and Jewish environments.

The Vitality of Judaism

Jews, heirs to Israel's grand and honest heritage, laid claim to the holy spirit long before Christianity came into being. Rabbinic literature demonstrates as well that Jews laid claim to the spirit long after Christians arrived on the scene. They claimed to have it from birth, and they claimed, in other contexts, to receive the spirit in animated experiences. Israelite and early Jewish literature, therefore, cannot be read any longer as a negative foil for the vitality of Christianity. Slightly over a century ago, Paul Volz made precisely this point, but, in an unfortunate sleight of scholarship, his agenda for the origins of pneumatology went largely unheeded. Volz noted with particular acuity:

> The habit of comparing a form of Judaism that is coming to an end with a youthful form of Christianity has led regularly to a misunderstanding of the former. This is historically unsuitable and, moreover, it is far more probable that the new religion arose out of a period of religious stirring and deep feeling rather than out of a torpid and dying one.[70]

It is a pity that Volz's construal of the compatibility between Judaism and Christianity, which he framed before the onset of two world wars and the horrors linking them, went silent, while a view of Judaism as arid and legalistic, void of the spirit and empty of prophecy, held sway. This is a pity

70. Volz, *Geist Gottes,* p. 144 (translation mine).

from a historical standpoint; extant literature, including the Dead Sea Scrolls, discovered long after his death, proves Volz right. And it is a pity as well from a contemporary standpoint. So much water during the twentieth century has gone under the bridge, yet many Christians continue to divide themselves from the source of their spirituality, which reaches far back in time, beyond the inspiration of the early church, deep into the experiences of Israel and the vitality of Judaism.

(4) A Model of Inspiration and a Unified Future for the Church

In 1801, in the rolling hills of Kentucky's bucolic landscape, the holy spirit, according to bystanders, let loose and broke the peace with the roar of Niagara Falls. One of the spectators, the Reverend James B. Finley, recalled the remarkable signs of the spirit's presence:

> A vast crowd, supposed by some to have amounted to twenty-five thousand, was collected together. The noise was like the roar of Niagara. . . . Some of the people were singing, others praying, some crying for mercy in the most piteous accents, while others were shouting most vociferously. . . . My heart beat tumultuously, my knees trembled, my lip quivered, and I felt as though I must fall to the ground. . . . The scene that then presented itself to my mind was indescribable. At one time I saw at least five hundred swept down in a moment, as if a battery of a thousand guns had been opened upon them, and then immediately followed shrieks and shouts that rent the very heavens.[71]

Barton Stone, one of the organizers of the meeting, described what he called exercises: jerks, dancing, barking, laughing, running, and singing.[72] The Cane Ridge revival captures the essence of American revivalism, with its deep passion, the ignition of fervor, and extraordinary physical manifestations.

Fast-forward to a time slightly more than a century later, where similar phenomena erupted, not now in the pastoral topography of Kentucky, but in a nondescript and worn section of Los Angeles:

71. *Autobiography of Rev. James B. Finley; or, Pioneer Life in the West,* ed. William Peter Strickland (Cincinnati: Methodist Book Concern, 1853), pp. 166-67.

72. Barton Stone's vivid description can be found in Sydney E. Ahlstrom, *A Religious History of the American People* (New Haven: Yale University Press, 1972), pp. 434-35.

INSPIRED

On a foggy evening in the spring of 1906, nine days before the San Francisco earthquake, a small group of Black and white saints gathered in a house in a run down section of Los Angeles to seek the baptism in the Holy Spirit. Before the night was over a terrified child ran from the house to tell a neighbor that the people inside had fallen on the floor, shouting strange languages. Several days later the band moved to an abandoned livery stable on Azusa Street where they were discovered by a Los Angeles *Times* reporter. The "night is made hideous . . . by the howlings of the worshippers," he wrote. "The devotees of the weird doctrine practice the most fanatical rites, preach the wildest theories and work themselves into a state of mad excitement."[73]

Though there were prior rumblings and serious manifestations elsewhere throughout the world, that night at Azusa Street marks the birthday of modern Pentecostalism.

Other branches of Christianity were hardly dormant during the spring of 1906. A decade earlier, Charles M. Sheldon had published a wildly popular book, *In His Steps: What Would Jesus Do?* which encapsulated the ideals of the Social Gospel movement — and sold millions of copies as well.[74] Slightly more than a decade later, Walter Rauschenbusch published his *Theology for the Social Gospel,* in which he conveyed "a grim conception of the kingdom of Evil and a strikingly evangelical conception of the kingdom of God. While never minimizing individual sin, he stressed the evil in unredeemed social structures — inherited customs and institutions that foster self-love so that 'one generation corrupts the next.'"[75]

This unnecessary but entrenched divide, represented by Azusa Street and the Social Gospel, continues to this day in North America. In an introductory course I have occasionally taught on spiritual formation, students use both the Book of Common Prayer and *Salvation on Sand Moun-*

73. Grant Wacker, "A Profile of American Pentecostalism," in *Pastoral Problems in the Pentecostal-Charismatic Movement,* ed. Harold D. Hunter, Thirteenth Annual Conference of the Society for Pentecostal Studies (Cleveland, TN, 1983), p. 1. This volume contains a collection of papers; Wacker's paper begins with page one of his own contribution, as do all papers in the volume. See further Grant Wacker, *Heaven Below: Early Pentecostals and American Culture* (Cambridge, MA: Harvard University Press, 2001).
74. The book was originally published in 1896, but Chicago Advance did not use proper copyright, so it was published elsewhere as well.
75. Grant Wacker, "The Social Gospel," in *Christianity in America: A Handbook,* ed. Mark A. Noll (Grand Rapids: Eerdmans, 1983), p. 320.

tain, a gripping account of Appalachian snake handlers. Two quotations from these books represent the ends of the pneumatological spectrum. The Anglican Book of Common Prayer contains simple words, which locate the work of the spirit in a sacrament, water baptism.

> You are sealed by the Holy Spirit in Baptism.

The seal of the spirit, on the one hand, is simple and undeniable, whether or not a person feels the presence of the holy spirit in any tangible way. In *Salvation on Sand Mountain,* on the other hand, the work of the holy spirit is described differently. A certain Brother Cecil experiences the holy spirit in a dramatic way.

> Now there's a man who really gets anointed by the Holy Ghost. He'll get so carried away, he'll use a rattlesnake to wipe the sweat off his brow.[76]

The work of the spirit is so powerful that Cecil loses consciousness of himself and wipes his forehead with a rattlesnake.

This divide has had a severe and serious impact upon local churches. The heir — or cousin — of Pentecostalism, the charismatic movement, which took root in the 1960s, blossomed in the 70s, and continues to this day, has made deep inroads into local churches, often leading to deep fault lines within churches. One sociological analysis of a local church in the Blue Ridge Mountains, which tracks the path toward schism, begins:

> In 1990 the Hinton Memorial United Methodist Church experienced a schism. Wracked by conflict for almost three years, the congregation finally divided along the fault lines of suburban charismatic versus small town traditional Methodists. For anyone who has spent much time examining the clashes and rapprochement of Pentecostal-mainline encounters, the story may seem familiar: a slow simmer, open factionalism, and then painful division. Behind this expected sequence of local congregational events, however, lay hints of front-line skirmishes over denominational restructuring, resulting, in part, from the influence of the charismatic movement on the mainline.[77]

76. Dennis Covington, *Salvation on Sand Mountain* (New York: Penguin, 1995), p. 46.

77. Nancy L. Eiesland, "Irreconcilable Differences: Conflict, Schism, and Religious Restructuring in a United Methodist Church," in *Pentecostal Currents in American Protestantism,* ed. Edith L. Blumhofer, Russell P. Spittler, and Grant A. Wacker (Urbana and Chicago: University of Illinois Press, 1999), p. 168.

The schism at Hinton took place on a local scale. On a global scale, the impact of a burgeoning Pentecostal and charismatic form of Christianity has been appreciable. In Latin America, for instance, Pentecostalism and mainline Christianity have not always been the most comfortable of bedfellows. While liberation theologians called for the established church to abandon its alignment with the ruling elite because God has a preferential option for the poor, many of those same poor were drawn away from the mainline Protestant churches and the Roman Catholic Church to Pentecostal communities.

Whether in historic movements of the twentieth century, an ecclesial impasse in Latin America, or simple local churches in the Blue Ridge Mountains, it is difficult to avoid the impression that the church may be on a course toward two Christianities rather than one. The dividing line, at least in part, is rooted in whether Christians think the spirit appears in the spectacular or in a steady spirituality. This trajectory is worrisome because the heart of ecstasy beats hardest in so-called developing nations of the Global South, such as Nigeria, which has seen an explosive growth of Pentecostal churches. It is conceivable that the divide produced by drastically different experiences of the spirit will spawn, if exacerbated by deep geopolitical divides, two Christianities.

Scripture and the Spirit

As we look toward the future, we do so with a mandate to develop a pneumatology that can bridge this divide and bring Christians to the center, though without sacrificing the distinctives at both ends of the spectrum. A viable and vibrant pneumatology for the future must embrace the symbiosis of ecstasy and comprehension, spontaneity and study. The seedbeds of such a pneumatology lie, I suggest, in this book. Chapter three, in particular, offers a foothold for unity: the inspired interpretation of scripture.

Along this vein, the spirit inspires what appears at first to be spontaneous activity, with figures overtaken by the spirit. On closer scrutiny, it becomes clear that the alchemy of the spirit includes preparation, particularly the study of cherished literature. Recall the relatively obscure figures of Amasai and Jahaziel. The clothing and coming of the spirit on these men is dramatic, forceful — like the spirit that inspired the judges, who perform remarkable feats. When the spirit comes upon Amasai and

Jahaziel, however, they do something else; they gather together bits and pieces of Israelite literature in an inspired way. Inspiration, in other words, entails the application of what they already know to a particular concrete historical situation.

Jewish authors Ben Sira, Philo Judaeus, and Josephus hold firmly to the conviction that God inspires them when they interpret scripture. The author(s) of the Qumran hymns clings firmly to inspiration by the spirit while citing text after text of Torah and prophetic literature in new and, to his mind at least, inspired words of prayer and worship.

The combination of intense inspiration with the interpretation of scripture characterizes as well countless New Testament texts, from the story of Simeon in Luke's Gospel to the book of Revelation, a self-proclaimed prophecy that is rich with the tandem languages of the spirit and scripture, particularly the books of Daniel and Ezekiel. Simeon, though a minor figure in Luke's Gospel, is an outstanding model of the inspired interpretation of scripture. He is ready, not because he has experienced, like Elihu, the unsettling sensation of the holy spirit's presence. Simeon is ready because he is devout — a code word for someone devoted to the disciplines of Judaism. Simeon has also awaited the "consolation of Israel," a promise of salvation poignantly depicted in the concluding chapters of the prophetic book of Isaiah. Simeon is suffused with this vision, shaped by the expectation it kindled, and his own words about Jesus are traceable to the songs of the servant in Isaiah 40–55. His intimate knowledge of the book of Isaiah is so thorough that, when the time comes, the spirit can inspire him to recognize the culmination of their words in the life and death of a baby boy. Simeon is inspired because he is vigilant, because he is regular in devotion, and because he has studied the prophecies of Isaiah 40–55, which he now sees taking shape in the baby who will be a light to the nations and offer salvation to all the world's peoples.

The inspired interpretation of scripture, in fact, pervades the New Testament. The paraclete in the Fourth Gospel brings Israelite scripture to mind in order to understand the words and works of Jesus. The spirit in the letter to the Hebrews does not so much inspire the scriptures as *extend* their message in subtle ways so that it is relevant to recipients of the letter. And Paul, himself a teacher and, like the revealer of mysteries in the hymns of the Scrolls, lays claim to the holy spirit as he unlocks, applies, and modifies the text of the Old Testament in unusual and surprising ways. Recall his idiosyncratic — he might say *inspired* — interpretation of the story of Moses and the Israelites in 2 Corinthians 3, how

Paul spins the text, turning it in different directions, modifying its words, interpreting it on several levels all at once to apply the detail of the veil to Moses, synagogue readers in his own day, believers in Jesus, even the gospel itself. Paul's thought possesses a deftness, a malleability that lends it force. When I reflect on the movement of 2 Corinthians 3, I am reminded of a bantamweight boxer, who relies on speed and swiftness of foot rather than the power of severe blows. A surprising range of applications in Paul's reading of the Moses story draws our attention to *his* way of reading, as he leads the Corinthians from Moses to Christ, from the desert to the written text, which is a source of transformation, of glory, when it is read right, from back to front, from end to beginning, from Christ to Moses, from spirit to Torah.

Ecstasy and Edification

Paul's claim to the inspired interpretation of scripture reflects his more general commitment to preserving the shared space between ecstasy and edification. Notwithstanding the damaging hierarchy that *glossolalia* helped to create at Corinth, Paul never once throws the baby out with the bath. He refuses to jettison ecstasy because of the aberrations to which it may lead. Instead, he discovers ways in which the Corinthians can maintain ecstasy — an ecstasy that educates, incomprehension that, once translated, edifies the community as a whole.

The symbiosis between ecstasy and comprehension is fundamental as well to the book of Acts, where the spirit combines the best of ecstasy with profound abilities of comprehension. In the narrative of Acts we discover an uncanny coalescence of ecstasy and restraint that is both rife with the fragrance of Greco-Roman rapture and rooted in a profound knowledge of Jewish scripture. This chemistry leads beyond typical divides. From the perspective of this symbiosis, Acts is not about *xenolalia* (comprehension) versus *glossolalia* (incomprehension). Acts is not about ecstasy (incomprehension) versus restraint (comprehension). Acts is not about water baptism versus spirit baptism. Luke offers much more: a mode of inspiration that unites the quintessence of ecstasy with intellectual acuity.

Recall in this regard the narrative of Pentecost, which exhibits both the accoutrements of ecstasy — fire, filling, and apparent drunkenness — and the compulsion of comprehensibility, when Jesus' followers recite the litany of God's praiseworthy acts in comprehensible tongues. Elsewhere in Acts, inspired believers who are filled by the spirit preach and teach about Jesus in light of the Jewish scriptures. Peter, filled with the spirit, recollects Psalm 118:22. And so it goes: *filling with the spirit in the book of Acts is evident principally through the inspired interpretation of scripture.*

Recall as well how the powerful symbiosis in Acts between ecstasy and exegetical acuity is evident in a triad of speaking in tongues. In Acts 2, Jesus' followers speak in *other* tongues, reciting God's praiseworthy acts in comprehensible dialects. In Acts 10, they speak in tongues and *praise* — once again, reciting God's praiseworthy acts. In Acts 19, they speak in tongues and *prophesy* — a form of communication that is always intelligible and concrete in the book of Acts. All of these are comprehensible speech acts, though their association with speaking in tongues suggests that they are not *merely* comprehensible speech acts. Luke refuses to opt for either comprehension or ecstasy, because his understanding of inspiration combines the most respected forms of Greco-Roman ecstasy — so respected, in fact, that Jews such as Philo Judaeus adopted them to explain prophetic inspiration — with the richest interpretation of Jewish scripture to illuminate the life, death, resurrection, and ascension of Jesus.[78] Luke's portrayal of speaking in (other) tongues, then, welds ecstasy to comprehension — what Pentecostal Blaine Charette calls "controlled comprehensible ecstasy" and what Philo Judaeus might have identified as an instance of "sober intoxication."[79]

Inspiration and Investigation

I have not been the first to showcase the inspired interpretation of scripture. David Aune wrote a pioneering article on the subject.[80] David Orton, in *The Understanding Scribe: Matthew and the Apocalyptic Ideal,* identifies significant facets of the inspired interpretation of scripture in early Judaism and the Gospel of Matthew. The recent book *Spirit and Scripture:*

78. See *Filled with the Spirit,* pp. 343-44, for a fuller statement.
79. On sober intoxication in the writings of Philo Judaeus, see *Filled with the Spirit,* pp. 332-34; on controlled comprehensible ecstasy, see Blaine Charette, " 'And Now for Something Completely Different': A 'Pythonic' Reading of Pentecost?" *Pneuma* 33 (2011): 62.
80. David E. Aune, "Charismatic Exegesis in Early Judaism and Early Christianity," in *The Pseudepigrapha and Early Biblical Interpretation,* ed. James H. Charlesworth and Craig A. Evans, Journal for the Study of the Pseudepigrapha: Supplement Series 14 (Sheffield, UK: JSOT, 1993), pp. 126-50.

Examining a Pneumatic Hermeneutic offers other examples and types of inspired interpretation. In that book, Mark Boda explores, to lengths I do not, the notion of the inspired scribe and prophet in Israel.[81] Archie Wright offers an excellent appraisal of inspired interpretation during the Second Temple period, during which time Christianity emerged.[82] Ronald Herms writes on the book of Revelation — a text I decided to devote only a few lines to in this book, though it too can be considered an instance of inspired interpretation.[83]

I will not end this book with a bibliographical essay; this would be, I think, anticlimactic. Yet I do want to make clear that I have only scratched the surface. I hope to have done this deftly by exposing enough to demonstrate that this was a pivotal way of understanding inspiration in Israel, early Judaism, and early Christianity.

This point — a historical one — is not where I will conclude this book, because I am concerned for, even anxious about, the divide that is developing due to the stagnancy of many mainline denominations and the explosive growth of Pentecostalism. How does knowledge of the inspired interpretation of scripture two to three millennia ago speak to the threat of a global dichotomy in the church?

In Israelite literature, the spirit moves to transform older texts and traditions into resources for more recent eras. In Judaism, the spirit moves to illuminate the relevance of scripture for situations that are new and challenging, from the creation of a desert community on the shores of the Dead Sea to Alexandrian Egypt, where inspired allegorical interpretations resolve difficulties in Torah, such as how snakes can speak in gardens of delight. Throughout the New Testament, the holy spirit anchors an understanding of Jesus to the scriptures of Israel. Time and again, the spirit calls to mind those ancient texts that illuminate who Jesus was and what Jesus did. Simeon is not alone in experiencing that sort of inspiration. The followers of Jesus in the Gospel of John receive revelation in this way. The apostles speak to hostile crowds in this way. The author of the letter to the Hebrews instructs his people in this way. And Paul finds

81. Mark Boda, "Word and Spirit, Scribe and Prophet in Old Testament Hermeneutics," in *Spirit and Scripture: Examining a Pneumatic Hermeneutic,* ed. Kevin L. Spawn and Archie T. Wright (London: T. & T. Clark, 2012), pp. 25-45.

82. Archie T. Wright, "Second Temple Period Jewish Biblical Interpretation: An Early Pneumatic Hermeneutic," in Spawn and Wright, eds., *Spirit and Scripture,* pp. 73-98.

83. Ronald Herms, "Invoking the Spirit and Narrative Intent in John's Apocalypse," in Spawn and Wright, eds., *Spirit and Scripture,* pp. 99-114.

the deepest level of meaning in scripture in this way. Inspired all of them — yet inspired as they stoop to peer (as Philo so adroitly phrases it) into Torah, prophets, and writings.[84]

From this perspective, *the principal task of the holy spirit for Christians is to illuminate the person of Jesus by setting his words and actions in the context of Israel's poetry, stories, and prophecies.* These are the connections that prove so fruitful, so momentous, so inspired. Remember for just a moment the story of the Jerusalem Council in Acts 15, a meeting that opened the door to an inclusive church rather than an ethnic enclave. Recall how seriously those early believers took Peter's experience of the outpouring of the spirit upon Gentiles. Recall how ruthlessly they debated the evidence. And recall how James appealed naturally, finally, and wisely to a little-known text from the prophecy of Amos — a relatively unfamiliar text, an arcane oracle, an obscure saying — and the church accepted it, so that James could write in a letter to a mature church in Antioch, "For it has seemed good to the holy spirit and to us . . ."

84. Philo Judaeus, *On the Special Laws* 3.1-6.

Index of Modern Authors

Index of Subjects and Ancient Names

INDEX OF SUBJECTS AND ANCIENT NAMES

Index of Subjects and Ancient Names

Samuel, 75, 81, 144, 169, 208

Sanctuary, 27, 31n27, 144n37, 155, 159

Sarah, 171

Satan, 100

Saul, 7, 16, 75-77, 130, 133-34, 144, 169, 203n44, 207-8

Saul (Paul), 60, 98n63, 99, 100n64, 101, 107-9, 110n67, 167

Second Temple Judaism, 211, 226

Seneca, 12, 41-42, 44-45

Sex, sexuality, 20, 38, 51, 62-64, 70, 93, 119

Sextus Empiricus, 41n36

Shadrach, Meshach, and Abednego, 33

Sibyl, 85

Silas, 96, 113, 122

Simeon, 12, 99, 100, 101, 145, 146-48, 153, 179, 183-84, 223, 226

Simmias, 140n26

Sin, 20-21, 43n40, 45, 51, 57-58, 61, 158, 161, 165, 188, 195, 211n59, 215, 220

Sinai, Mount, 37, 77, 129, 180

Sirach. *See* Ben Sira

Socrates, 10, 78, 140, 214

Solomon, 131n11

Soul(s), 22n15, 39-47, 51n52, 72, 80, 85, 87, 89, 92, 94, 117, 120, 137, 141-42, 189, 191n12, 192, 198, 205

Speaking in (other) tongues, 1, 5, 16, 49, 72, 88-91, 94-97, 102, 120, 152, 201, 216, 225. *See also* Glossolalia

Spirit. *In addition to Spirit entries below, see* Anointing; Ascent of mind or soul; Charismatic endowment; Dreams; Ecstasy; Glossolalia; Inspiration; Knowledge; Laying on of hands; Paraclete; *Pneumatikoi;* Pneumatology; Prophecy; Speaking in (other) tongues; Virtue; Visions

Spirit, characterizations as:

aether, 41n36, 44n41, 45n42, 189

angelic or daemonic being, 140-41

breath (life itself), 4, 7, 17-18, 20, 23n17, 24-25, 27, 35, 48-49, 55-56, 65, 68-69, 178

communal, 3, 12, 54, 60, 75-77, 111, 113, 116, 120-23, 171, 181, 216

of creation, 7, 191n12, 193, 194n18, 197, 199

customary friend, 141, 145

fire, 92-95, 97, 128-29, 224

holy, 1-2, 4-9, 14, 16, 19-23, 33, 38-45, 47-52, 54-70, 72, 74, 82, 91-94, 96-98, 102-6, 109-23, 126-29, 138-39, 145-62, 166-67, 169, 173, 178-79, 182-84, 186-87, 189, 194n18, 197, 199, 208-12, 215-19, 221, 223-24, 226-27

life force/life principle, 191n12, 195

new, 21n13, 31, 173, 176

power, 16-17, 29, 43n38, 44n41, 50, 52n54, 61, 126, 138, 166, 187, 189, 191n10, 192-93, 207, 221

revealer, 61

seal/pledge, 221

spiritus sanctificans, 192-93

spiritus vivificans, 192-93

supernatural and divine, 189-90, 199-200

teacher, 44, 61, 151

truth, 61-62, 149-51, 216

vapor, 92-93

voice, 102, 140-41, 145, 152

water, 93, 187, 200-201, 204

Spirit, effects of:

adoption, 52

charismatic endowment in the new creation, 50, 52-53, 57-58

comprehension, 4, 5, 88-91, 94, 96-97, 102-6, 117, 126, 133, 208, 222, 224-25

discipline, 37, 43-45, 47-48, 50, 52n54, 59, 68-69, 101, 111, 117, 120-22, 137, 146-48, 189, 205, 223

enthusiasm, 83, 92, 141, 145

faith, 52-54, 57, 61, 104-6, 112, 200

faithfulness, 3, 4, 35-36, 48, 62, 137, 196

frenzy, 9-10, 75, 80, 85, 94, 139, 141, 152, 181

healing, 16-17, 126, 217

235

INDEX OF SUBJECTS AND ANCIENT NAMES

holiness/integrity, 19, 40, 51, 56, 58,
62-64, 66-67, 70, 192n13, 215-17
interpret dreams/scripture, 26,
94-101, 127-28, 135-38, 141, 143-45,
147, 152-62, 164-65, 167, 170-71, 175,
181, 184
intoxication, 92-94
justice, 72
knowledge/understanding, 3, 6, 16,
24, 28-33, 37, 46-47
learning, 2, 4, 58, 62, 65, 107-9, 112,
185, 188
life itself, 19-20, 24-25, 41n36
mental control, loss of, 82-83, 92, 97
miracles, 87, 126, 128, 152, 163, 176,
190
new creation, 4, 52, 69, 193, 194n18
perception and movement, 9, 41,
194n18
praise, 90, 96, 110-11, 201, 225
prayer, 91
preaching, 126, 158, 184
sanctification, 187
speech, edifying or inspired, 134
teaching, 12-14, 32, 116, 135-36,
141n29, 148, 168-71, 182, 184, 196,
206, 217
trances, 126
unity, 112-23
visions, 4-5, 11, 35, 74, 77, 85-87, 98-
101, 118, 137, 152, 204, 208, 214
Spirit, modes of presence:
abiding within, 42
clothing, 16, 130, 134
coming upon, 28, 96, 132, 134,
203n44, 223
endowment, 3, 19, 25, 29, 31, 32n28,
33, 49, 53, 55, 58, 62, 136n17, 137,
195-96, 200, 208
filling, 3, 6, 19, 28-32, 34n29, 36-37,
43, 50, 52n54, 53-54, 58, 63-64,
66-69, 79-80, 82, 89, 92, 94-97, 118,
121, 135-37, 139, 145, 151-53, 166-67,
179, 182-84, 186, 195-96, 199-201,
203, 215, 217-18, 224-25

guiding, 44, 58-59, 61, 146, 149,
194n18
indwelling, 41
leaping upon, 82
lifting up, 74, 171
possessing, 10, 75, 78, 80-81, 82n26,
84, 142, 145, 152
poured out upon, 4, 7, 17, 98, 101-3,
105, 114, 116, 118, 120-21, 187, 204-6,
208, 227
put/placed within, 18, 21, 28, 72, 76,
205
resting upon, 4, 76, 92, 146
rushing upon, 16, 207-8
withdrawal from Israel, 211
Spirit, and translation issues, 17, 19-20,
32n28, 33, 56, 67, 74n2, 82n25, 95, 105,
108, 127, 135, 159, 181, 210n53
without capitalization, 19-20
Stephen, 54, 60, 74, 85-87, 99
Stoicism/Stoic, 40-41, 52, 213
Strabo, 79
Synagogue(s), 12, 16, 59-60, 65, 167,
169, 177, 180, 182, 224

Tabernacle, 3, 27, 28n22, 29. See also
Tent
Teacher of Righteousness, 138-39, 180
Temple, 21, 29-30, 32, 41, 60, 78, 86, 99,
119, 121, 128, 134n13, 146, 148, 150-51,
179, 183, 215, 217-18. See also Second
Temple Judaism
Tent. See also Tabernacle
heavenly, 160
of meeting, 3, 29, 38, 76, 155, 159, 196
of presence, 22n15, 27, 33, 54, 66, 68,
159
Theology. See also Pneumatology
biblical, 99
of creation, 6, 199
dogmatic, 178, 186, 192, 195, 197-98
ecological, 195
of Hebrews, 154
liberation, 220
mystical, 10
Pauline, 3n3, 189, 190

236

Index of Ancient Sources

INDEX OF ANCIENT SOURCES